Law Commission

Consultation Paper No 215

FIDUCIARY DUTIES OF INVESTMENT INTERMEDIARIES

A Consultation Paper

ISBN: 9780108512728

Printed in the UK for The Stationery Office Limited
on behalf of the Controller of Her Majesty's Stationery Office

ID 2593573   33864   10/13

Printed on paper containing 75% recycled fibre content minimum.

THE LAW COMMISSION – HOW WE CONSULT

About the Law Commission: The Law Commission was set up by section 1 of the Law Commissions Act 1965 for the purpose of promoting the reform of the law.

The Law Commissioners are: The Rt Hon Lord Justice Lloyd Jones, *Chairman,* Professor Elizabeth Cooke, David Hertzell and Professor David Ormerod QC. The Chief Executive is Elaine Lorimer.

Frances Patterson QC, the Commissioner for Public Law, left the Law Commission at the end of September 2013, but participated in discussions relating to this Consultation Paper.

Topic of this consultation: Evaluating the law of fiduciary duties as it applies to investment intermediaries.

Geographical scope: United Kingdom.

Availability of materials: The consultation paper and summary are available at: http://lawcommission.justice.gov.uk/consultations/fiduciary_duties.htm.

Duration of the consultation: 22 October 2013 to **22 January 2014**.

Comments may be sent:

By email to   fiduciary.duties@lawcommission.gsi.gov.uk

OR

Before 4 November 2013, by post to

> Folarin Akinbami, Law Commission, Steel House, 11 Tothill Street, London SW1H 9LJ. Tel: 0203 334 0200

After 4 November 2013, by post to

> Folarin Akinbami, Law Commission, 1st Floor, Tower, 52 Queen Anne's Gate, London SW1H 9AG. Tel: 0203 334 0200

After the consultation: After analysis of the responses, we will present a final report to the Government by June 2014.

Consultation principles: The Law Commission follows the Cabinet Office Consultation Principles, which provide guidance on type and scale of consultation, duration, timing, accessibility and transparency. The Principles are available at: https://update.cabinetoffice.gov.uk/resource-library/consultation-principles-guidance.

Information provided to the Law Commission

We may publish or disclose information you provide us in response to this consultation, including personal information. For example, we may publish an extract of your response in Law Commission publications, or publish the response in its entirety. We may also be required to disclose the information, such as in accordance with the Freedom of Information Act 2000.

If you want information that you provide to be treated as confidential please contact us first, but we cannot give an assurance that confidentiality can be maintained in all circumstances. An automatic disclaimer generated by your IT system will not be regarded as binding on the Law Commission.

The Law Commission will process your personal data in accordance with the Data Protection Act 1998.

THE LAW COMMISSION

CONSULTATION PAPER NO 215

FIDUCIARY DUTIES OF INVESTMENT INTERMEDIARIES

CONTENTS

100706 4628 ⟨

PART 4: ANALYSIS

CHAPTER 9 Applying the law to the investment chain: our terms of reference

CHAPTER 10 Pension trustees' duties to invest in the "best interests" of others

CHAPTER 11 Duties on others in the investment chain: the courts' general approach

CHAPTER 12 Duties on others in the investment chain: specific examples

CHAPTER 13 Workplace defined contribution pensions: problems in practice

PART 5: CONCLUSIONS AND QUESTIONS

CHAPTER 14 Conclusions and questions

CHAPTER 15 List of questions

GLOSSARY

Active investment

An approach to investment which involves the continuous buying and selling of investments. An active investment manager will typically seek to outperform an investment benchmark.

Actuary

A professional who specialises in statistics and risk who gives advice on a pension scheme's assets and liabilities. They will predict movements in the scheme, such as deaths, retirements and withdrawals, and estimate the costs of providing the benefits due and accruing in the future.

Annuity

A fixed sum of money paid to individuals each year upon retirement. This may be for an agreed period or for the rest of the individual's life. The amount of money paid will depend on the individual's total accumulated pension savings.

Asset manager

See "investment manager".

Association of British Insurers (ABI)

A trade association representing the majority of UK insurers.

Automatic enrolment

Also known as "auto-enrolment". A new legislative requirement introduced by the Pensions Act 2008 which requires all employers (beginning with the largest) to automatically enrol their qualifying employees into a qualifying pension scheme.

Best of sector

Also known as "best of class". Companies that perform best in their industry sector against specified indicators.

Broker

An individual or organisation that acts as an intermediary between a buyer and seller, usually in return for the payment of a commission.

Bundled scheme

A pension scheme where the pension provider also administers the scheme.

COBS

Conduct of Business Sourcebook. The section of the Financial Conduct Authority's Handbook that deals with business standards.

Contract-based scheme

These may be work-based or individual. In work-based contract-based schemes, the employer appoints a pension provider, usually an insurance company, to administer their pension scheme. The employees enter into a contract directly with the pension provider, although the employer may make arrangements to collect and pay contributions. In individual contract-based scheme, an individual enters into a contract directly with a pension provider.

Contributions

The money paid by members and employers into the pension scheme.

Custodian

An institution that is responsible for the safekeeping and administration of assets belonging to another. Custodians will often handle administrative arrangements such as collecting coupons and dividends.

Default fund

The investment fund into which employees' contributions are paid if they fail to make an active choice of fund. It is usually designed for this purpose.

Defined benefit (DB) schemes

Also known as "final salary" schemes. A type of pension where the amount an employee receives on retirement is pre-determined, and is often calculated on the basis of the employee's final salary and length of service. The amount received on retirement does not depend on the performance of the pension scheme's investments.

Defined contribution (DC) schemes

Also known as "money purchase" schemes. A type of pension where the amount received by a member on retirement will be calculated by reference to the contributions the employee makes to the scheme and the investment return on those contributions.

Department for Work and Pensions (DWP)

The government department responsible for pensions policy.

Direct payment arrangements

Arrangements between the member and the employer under which contributions fall to be paid by the employer towards the scheme. Such arrangements will exist where the employer arranges to make employer contributions to a personal pension scheme and/or where the employer arranges to deduct the member's contributions from pay and to pay them across to the pension scheme for the member.

Ethical, social and governance (ESG) factors

Sometimes referred to as "responsible investing". Refers to the use of certain non-financial factors in the investment decision-making process.

Financial Conduct Authority (FCA)

The regulator of the financial services industry. Took over some of the functions of the now abolished Financial Services Authority (FSA). The FCA is responsible both for regulating the infrastructure of financial markets and standards of conduct. It regulates defined contribution (contract-based) schemes and individual personal pensions.

Financial Services Authority (FSA)

A now defunct financial services regulator. Abolished in 2013 and replaced by the Financial Conduct Authority (FCA) and the Prudential Regulation Authority (PRA).

Financial Ombudsman Service (FOS)

A body set up by the Financial Services and Markets Act 2000 to deal with complaints in relation to financial services and products.

Financial Reporting Council (FRC)

The regulator responsible for corporate governance standards and financial reporting. It publishes the UK Stewardship Code, which sets out a number of areas of good practice to which the FRC believes institutional investors should aspire.

FSMA

Financial Services and Markets Act 2000. The main piece of legislation governing UK financial markets regulation.

Fund manager

See "investment manager".

Investment consultant

An individual (or organisation) that gives strategic advice on the making of investments and/or the selection of an investment manager.

Investment manager

Also known as a "fund manager" (for example, in the pensions legislation) and an "asset manager". An individual (or organisation) to whom the responsibility for the day-to-day management of the scheme's assets is delegated. The investment manager will act on the basis of instructions given to them in the investment mandate.

Investment mandate

The agreement between an investment manager and their client outlining how the assets of the pension scheme are to be managed. The mandate may contain performance targets by reference to a benchmark, or may contain restrictions on which investments the investment manager can make.

Lifestyling

An investment strategy where the allocation of a member's investments is adjusted depending on age and length of time to retirement. For example, as a member gets older, a member's investments are likely to be moved out of equities and into less risky investments such as cash and bonds.

Mark-to-market

A valuation of assets on the basis of their current market value, rather than the potential value they are expected to achieve.

Member

An individual who contributes or has contributed to a pension scheme.

Modern portfolio theory

A theory that emphasises the risk level of the entire portfolio rather than the risk attaching to each investment taken in isolation. Assets that are particularly risk may be offset by other, safer, investments to form a balanced portfolio of investments.

National Association of Pension Funds (NAPF)

Provides representation and services for those involved in the workplace pension industry.

National Employment Savings Trust (NEST)

A government-sponsored defined contribution occupational pension scheme. It is intended to be the default scheme made available to employees as employers become subject to auto-enrolment. NEST must accept any employer who wants to use the scheme for auto-enrolment. Employers can use NEST as their only pension scheme or alongside other pension schemes. NEST is regulated by HM Revenue and Customs and the Pensions Regulator.

Negative screening

The use of ethical, social and governance (ESG) factors to exclude investment in particular companies or sectors, such as tobacco companies or pesticide manufacturers.

Passive investment

An approach to investment which typically involves tracking the investment performance of a specific market index. A passively managed fund is also known as an "index fund".

Pension Protection Fund (PPF)

A statutory fund created by the Pensions Act 2004. Its function is to provide compensation to members of eligible defined benefit pension schemes in the event that there is a qualifying insolvency event in relation to the employer, and where there are insufficient assets in the pension scheme to cover the Pension Protection Fund level of compensation.

Platform

Also known as an "investment platform". May refer both to a "platform" as a piece of technology or to an intermediary who facilitates the purchase of investments.

Portfolio-churning

The excessive buying and selling of investments in a portfolio. It is characterised by very short holding periods for stocks.

Positive screening

The use of ethical, social and governance (ESG) factors to select firms (in which to invest) engaged in what are considered to be desirable practices, such as renewable energy supply.

Proxy agent

Advise on how votes should be cast and cast votes at company meetings on behalf of others.

Shareholder engagement

An approach to investment which emphasises the importance of effective dialogue between investors and investee companies. Engagement may involve an exchange of views on issues such as strategy, performance, board membership and quality of management.

Stakeholder pension

A type of defined contribution pension plan introduced in 2001 by the Welfare Reform and Pensions Act 1999. They are designed to be a low-cost and easy-to-understand.

Statutory funding objective

A funding requirement set by law which requires defined benefit pension schemes to maintain sufficient and appropriate assets to cover the amount required, on an actuarial calculation, to make provision for the scheme's liabilities.

Stewardship

A philosophy which aims to promote the long term success of companies in such a way that protects and enhances the value that accrues to the ultimate beneficiary of an investment. It is usually discussed in the context of institutional investors. Stewardship activities include monitoring and engaging with companies on matters such as strategy, performance, risk, capital structure, and corporate governance, including culture and remuneration.

Stock lending

The temporary transfer of shares, by a lender to a borrower, with agreement by the borrower to return equivalent shares to the lender at pre-agreed time. The lender will give the borrower collateral as security and will pay lending fees. The purpose of stock lending is to usually to allow the borrower to sell short, that is sell shares that the borrower does not own. The borrower will then purchase equivalent shares in the market to return to the lender. If the market price of the shares has fallen below the price at which the borrower sold the shares, the borrower will make a profit.

The Pensions Ombudsman (TPO)

An independent officer who investigates and decides complaints and disputes about the way pension schemes are run.

The Pensions Regulator (TPR)

The statutory regulator of work-based pensions (including both trust-based and contract-based schemes). Its objectives are to protect the benefits of members of occupational pension schemes (and personal pension schemes where there is a direct payment arrangement), to promote and improve understanding of the good administration of work-based pension schemes and to maximise employer compliance with their duties under the Pensions Act 2008. TPR is also responsible for reducing the risk of situations arising that may lead to compensation being payable under the Pension Protection Fund.

Trust-based scheme

A pension scheme that is established using a trust. The trustees are responsible for managing the scheme and for reviewing and monitoring investments.

PART 1

INTRODUCTION

CHAPTER 1
INTRODUCTION

1.1 This project has been commissioned by the Department for Business, Innovation and Skills (BIS) and the Department for Work and Pensions (DWP). In broad terms, we have been asked to investigate how the law of fiduciary duties applies to investment intermediaries and to evaluate whether the law works in the interests of end investors.

1.2 We seek views on our conclusions and replies to our questions by 22 January 2014. Replies should be sent to the address on page iii.

THE KAY REVIEW

1.3 Our work arises from the Kay Review, published in July 2012.[1] Professor Kay conducted a year-long review of the UK equity market and was highly critical of the way it worked.

Criticisms of the market

1.4 Professor Kay considered that investment chains were too long, with growing numbers of intermediaries between an investor and the company in which they invest. He argued that this led to increased costs, misaligned incentives and reduced trust.

1.5 The central problem was "short-termism", in which many investment managers "traded" on the basis of short-term movements in share price rather than "investing" on the basis of the fundamental value of the company. Furthermore, shareholders did little to control bad company decisions:

> We observe a wide variety of examples of companies that have made bad long-term decisions, and consider that equity markets have evolved in ways that contribute to these errors of managerial judgment. We conclude that the quality – and not the amount – of engagement by shareholders determines whether the influence of equity markets on corporate decisions is beneficial or damaging to the long-term interests of companies. And we conclude that public equity markets currently encourage exit (the sale of shares) over voice (the exchange of views with the company) as a means of engagement, replacing the concerned investor with the anonymous trader.[2]

Observing fiduciary standards

1.6 Professor Kay set out ten principles which should guide the UK equity market. Principle 5 was that "all participants in the equity investment chain should observe fiduciary standards in their relationships with their clients and customers". He continued:

---

[1] J Kay, *The Kay Review of UK Equity Markets and Long-Term Decision Making: Final Report* (2012) Recommendation 9.

[2] Above, Executive Summary para vii.

3

Fiduciary standards require that the client's interests are put first, that conflict of interest should be avoided, and that the direct and indirect costs of services provided should be reasonable and disclosed. These standards should not require, nor even permit, the agent to depart from generally prevailing standards of decent behaviour. Contractual terms should not claim to override these standards.

1.7 He noted that fiduciary duties are a legal concept created by case law. Fiduciary duties clearly apply to pension and other trustees, but there was uncertainty and debate about how far they applied to others in the investment chain. Even among pension trustees there was uncertainty over what fiduciary duties required:

> A number of submissions – in particular, powerful argument from FairPensions – suggested that some pension fund trustees equated their fiduciary responsibilities with a narrow interpretation of the interests of their beneficiaries which focused on maximising financial returns over a short timescale and prevented the consideration of longer term factors which might impact on company performance, including questions of sustainability or environmental and social impact … . Lawyers who participated in our discussions, however, suggested that the law allowed a more robust interpretation. Several commented that pension fund trustees who insisted on a narrow view of fiduciary duty were often hiding behind risk-averse legal advice, designed to protect the adviser and client rather than to provide guidance as to the proper discharge of fiduciary duty.[3]

1.8 Therefore, Recommendation 9 said:

> The Law Commission should be asked to review the legal concept of fiduciary duty as applied to investment to address uncertainties and misunderstandings on the part of trustees and their advisers.

The Government's response

1.9 In November 2012 the Government published a response to the Kay Review which accepted the analysis and conclusions of the report. As far as fiduciary duties were concerned, the Government commented that the phrase could be used in several different ways:

> Since the Kay Report was published there has been a great deal of discussion of the meaning and scope of the word "fiduciary". Many interpret it in the strict legal sense of a relationship in which the principal is reliant or dependent on the knowledge, expertise and discretion of an agent, and to which the strictest duties of loyalty and prudence are applicable. Others however use the word fiduciary to describe a more general duty of care.[4]

---

[3] J Kay, *The Kay Review of UK Equity Markets and Long-Term Decision Making: Final Report* (2012) para 9.20.

[4] Department for Business, Innovation and Skills, *Ensuring equity markets support long-term growth: The Government Response to the Kay Review* (2012) para 2.8.

1.10 The Government therefore elected to avoid using the word "fiduciary" and instead set out the following principle for equity markets:

> All participants in the equity investment chain should act:
>
> - in good faith;
>
> - in the best long-term interests of their clients or beneficiaries;
>
> - in line with generally prevailing standards of decent behaviour.
>
> This means ensuring that the direct and indirect costs of services provided are reasonable and disclosed, and that conflicts of interest are avoided wherever possible, or else disclosed or otherwise managed to the satisfaction of the client or beneficiary.
>
> These obligations should be independent of the classification of the client.
>
> They should not be contractually overridden.[5]

OTHER REVIEWS

1.11 Other reports have reached similar conclusions about the functioning of UK equity markets and pensions.

1.12 The Cox Review, an independent review commissioned by the Labour Party, reported in February 2013. Like Kay, the Cox Review was concerned with "short-termism" within British business. It found that the pressure to deliver quick results had become an entrenched feature of the UK business environment, which often acted to the detriment of the longer-term development of a company.[6] The increase in intermediation was partly to blame:

> The ultimate shareholder, the individual saver or pension holder, is a long way removed from the company on whose growth his or her prosperity ultimately depends. The individual may well have a long-term interest, but that is not served by the cumulative behaviour of all the participants in the chain.[7]

1.13 The Review also thought that shareholders should do more to question companies:

---

[5] Department for Business, Innovation and Skills, *Ensuring equity markets support long-term growth: The Government Response to the Kay Review* (2012) para 2.8.

[6] Sir George Cox, *Overcoming short-termism within British business: The key to sustained economic growth* (2013) p 6.

[7] Above, pp 20-21.

> Enlightened long-term shareholders ought to be asking management not just what they are doing to drive down costs during a period of economic downturn, but what they are doing to preserve the capacity for long-term success.[8]

1.14 These issues have also been recognised at a European level. In March 2013 the European Commission adopted a Green Paper on long-term financing, which addressed problems of financial intermediation.[9] The Green Paper argued that several factors prevent intermediaries from participating in long-term financing, including biases created by accounting principles and misaligned incentives.[10]

1.15 Several reports have looked specifically at pensions regulation. In May 2013 the Fabian Society published a report on pensions which called for reform of pensions regulation[11] and stressed the benefits of trust-based pensions.[12] In September 2013 the Office of Fair Trading published a market study of defined contribution workplace pensions, which highlighted concerns about charges and governance.[13] We summarise the findings in Chapter 13.[14]

1.16 Finally, in relation to what issues may or must be taken into account when making investment decisions, bodies such as ShareAction,[15] the National Association of Pension Funds,[16] Freshfields,[17] the Prince's Trust Accounting for Sustainability Project[18] and Tomorrow's Company[19] have all reviewed practice and produced influential reports.

THIS PROJECT

1.17 Our terms of reference from BIS and DWP are set out in full in Appendix A. They go beyond Recommendation 9 in the Kay Review. Briefly, we have been asked to do five things:

---

[8] Sir George Cox, *Overcoming short-termism within British business: The key to sustained economic growth* (2013) p 19.

[9] European Commission, *Long-term financing of the European economy* (2013) COM(2013) 150 final.

[10] Above, p 14-16.

[11] Fabian Society, *Pensions at Work, that Work: Completing the unfinished pensions revolution* (2013) p 31.

[12] Above, p 29.

[13] Office of Fair Trading, *Defined contribution workplace pension market study* (2013).

[14] See para 13.29 and following below.

[15] See FairPensions (later known as ShareAction), *Whose duty? Ensuring effective stewardship in contract-based pensions* (2012); FairPensions (later known as ShareAction), *The Enlightened Shareholder: Clarifying investors' fiduciary duties* (2012); FairPensions (later known as ShareAction), *Protecting our Best Interests: Rediscovering Fiduciary Obligation* (2011).

[16] National Association of Pension Funds, *Responsible Investment Guide* (2013).

[17] Freshfields Bruckhaus Deringer, *A legal framework for the integration of environmental, social and governance issues into institutional investment* (2005).

[18] See The Prince's Trust Accounting for Sustainability Project, *Accounting for Sustainability Report: The Connected Reporting Framework* (2007).

[19] See Tomorrow's Company, *Tomorrow's Stewardship: why stewardship matters* (2011).

(1)   To investigate how fiduciary duties currently apply to investment intermediaries and those who provide advice and services to them.

(2)   To clarify how far those who invest on behalf of others may take account of factors such as social and environmental impact and ethical standards.

(3)   To consult relevant stakeholders.

(4)   To evaluate whether fiduciary duties (as established in law or as applied in practice) are conducive to investment strategies in the best interests of the ultimate beneficiaries. We are asked to carry out this evaluation against a list of factors, balancing different objectives, including encouraging long-term investment strategies and requiring a balance of risk and benefit.

(5)   To identify areas where changes are needed.

1.18   The project started in March 2013. Since then we have talked to 39 stakeholders and set up an Advisory Committee, with members drawn from academia and practice. We also published a short interim paper on our website and received eight written responses. We are very grateful to all those who have discussed these issues with us so far, and we draw on their comments in this paper. Our intention is to produce a final report by June 2014.

1.19   Although the research for this project has focused principally on the law of England & Wales, the equities market is a UK one, not neatly split between England & Wales and Scotland. In many (though not all) respects, the law of fiduciary duties is the same in Scotland. We have worked closely with the Scottish Law Commission to identify similarities and differences between the law in the two jurisdictions, which we note from time to time. We are very grateful for the help given to us by the Scottish Law Commission, but this is not a joint publication of the two Commissions.

THE MEANINGS OF "FIDUCIARY DUTY"

1.20   As the Government acknowledged in its response to the Kay Review, the term "fiduciary duty" is used in different ways by different people.[20]

1.21   First, the term is often used by pension trustees to emphasise their ethos, which is to act in the interests of the beneficiaries. Many trustees were aware of their status as fiduciaries, which resonates with a sense of altruism.[21] Trustees contrasted their special status as fiduciaries with the focus of others in the investment chain on making money. The association between "fiduciary duty" and altruism has given the term some rhetorical power. The rhetoric has been used to visualise an alternative approach to financial markets, which is less driven by financial gain and more attuned to the needs of investors.

---

[20]   Department for Business, Innovation and Skills, *Ensuring equity markets support long-term growth: The Government Response to the Kay Review* (2012) para 2.8.

[21]   See, for example, the statements made to Anna Tilba and Terry McNulty: A Tilba and T McNulty, "Engaged versus Disengaged Ownership: The Case of Pension Funds in the UK" (2013) 21(2) *Corporate Governance: An International Review* 165 at 172.

1.22   To lawyers, the term denotes an area of "judge-made" law, often associated with trusts and equities. Lawyers tend to think in terms of litigation, so the statement "intermediaries should owe fiduciary duties to the end investor" implies that investors should be able to sue intermediaries for breach of these duties, with the various costs and risks that entails.

1.23   Even for lawyers, the term "fiduciary duties" is used in different ways. In the past, it has been used in a broad sense to encompass all the various duties owed by a fiduciary to their principal, including duties of care and duties which arise from the exercise of a power. The courts have issued stern warnings against using the term in this broad, loose sense. In Chapter 5 we describe the case of *Bristol and West Building Society v Mothew*,[22] where Lord Justice Millett said that the core of fiduciary duty is "the obligation of loyalty", so breach "connotes disloyalty or infidelity".[23] Mere incompetence is not enough. Fiduciaries often also owe duties not to be negligent, but these are distinct from fiduciary duties.

1.24   We have not interpreted the term "fiduciary duty" in this narrow sense. To answer practical questions about legal duties in financial markets, it is often necessary to draw on three or four different types of law. For example, to understand the investment duties of pension trustees we look at pensions legislation, duties that attach to the exercise of a power and duties of care as well as "fiduciary duties" in the strict sense. This paper attempts to unpick the various strands of law applicable to financial intermediaries to bring greater clarity to the debate.

WHO INVESTS IN UK EQUITIES?

1.25   If we are to evaluate how well the law meets the needs of end investors, our first task is to establish who those end investors are. This is not an easy question to answer. In Chapter 3 we describe the current systems of holding shares through tiers of intermediaries, which make it difficult to know where the final interest lies.

1.26   The Office for National Statistics (ONS) provides data on the ownership of UK shares, which are set out in the following graph. These data have obvious limitations: most of the owners listed are not end beneficiaries but financial institutions.

---

[22]   [1998] Ch 1.

[23]   Above, at 18.

Figure 1.1: Ownership of UK quoted shares by sector of beneficial ownership, 1963-2012.

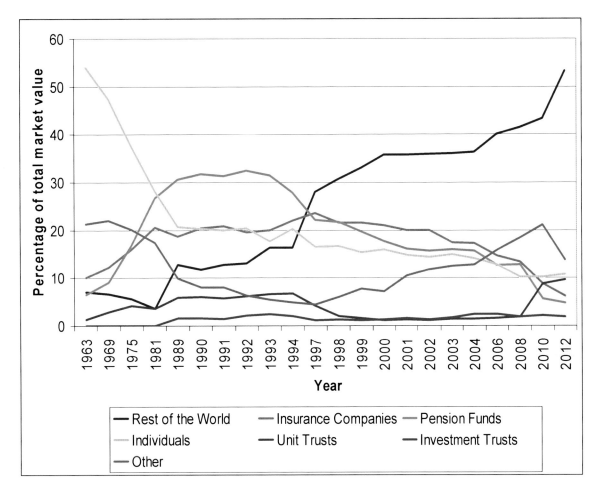

Source: Office for National Statistics, *Ownership of UK Quoted Shares, 2012* (25 September 2013).

1.27   Although the ONS data has been criticised, a picture emerges from it. Since the mid-1990s, insurance companies and pension funds have been moving out of UK equities and into overseas markets and safer asset classes, such as bonds. Meanwhile, in an increasingly globalised world, the UK market has seen a substantial increase in overseas ownership. In his evidence before the BIS Select Committee, Professor Kay commented that although the picture is more complicated than the ONS statistics suggest:

> The basic element in this is that there are more foreign beneficial holders of UK equities, and there are more foreign based asset managers in the market, than there were 20 years ago. There is also an element of sovereign wealth fund involvement in this, of which Norway and Singapore are the largest.[24]

---

[24] The Kay Review of Equity Markets and Long-Term Decision Making, Third Report of the Select Committee on Business, Innovation and Skills (2013-14) HC 603 at Ev 2.

1.28   In this paper we have not considered the needs of foreign owners, such as overseas pension funds or sovereign wealth funds. One reason is that many of the links in the chain will not be governed by UK law. For example, if a Dutch pension scheme is advised by its Dutch fiduciary manager[25] to invest in the UK, the obligations of the fiduciary manager to the pension scheme will be governed by Dutch law. Furthermore, as the Law Commission of England and Wales we did not think we had the authority or experience necessary to assess the needs of overseas investors.

THE ROLE OF PENSION FUNDS

1.29   Much of the focus of this paper is on UK pension funds. UK pension funds may no longer be the largest investors in the UK equities market but pensions are a crucial investment for many UK citizens, and an area where people are particularly vulnerable to the failures of financial markets.

1.30   Not all market participants invest in equities for the long-term, nor should they be required to. There are legitimate and diverse reasons for shorter-term trading. Pension funds, however, are designed to generate returns over a long-term period and their investment approach ought to reflect this. They are a particularly significant form of long-term investment.

1.31   To provide practical commentary, it is important to focus on specific problems and contexts. We therefore use pensions as the exemplar of long-term investment, tracing the investment chain from the prospective pensioner/saver to the registered shareholder of a UK company. The chain involves, among others, investment consultants, investment managers, collective investment schemes, brokers and custodians.

1.32   Even by limiting the investment chain in this way, the law is remarkably complex. As we discuss in Chapter 2, pensions may be trust-based or contract-based, and the law of fiduciary duties differs markedly between the two. It is clear that pension trustees are subject to fiduciary duties, as established in case law and as set out in the pensions legislation. The main area of uncertainty is how far pension trustees may take into account factors which are not concerned with immediate financial returns, such as social and environmental impact and ethical standards. We address these questions in Chapter 10.

1.33   By contrast, many stakeholders denied that contract-based pension providers were subject to fiduciary duties at all. As we explain in Chapter 12, we think that this statement may be an over-simplification. There are, however, significant uncertainties about the duties of contract-based pension providers to ensure the suitability of their products over time.

1.34   There are similar uncertainties about how far fiduciary duties apply to others in the investment chain, such as investment consultants, investment managers, brokers and custodians. It is necessary to look not only at case law but at pensions legislation and the Financial Conduct Authority Handbook. In many cases we are able to express no more than a tentative view.

---

[25]   The concept of fiduciary management is explained at paras 3.18-3.20 below.

1.35 We are aware that only a minority of pension assets are in UK equities and that only a minority of UK shareholders are pension schemes. We think, however, that a description of the chain from pension saver to registered shareholder provides a helpful lens through which to understand the duties of investment intermediaries more generally. Although we focus on the investment factors and stewardship involved in equities, many of the duties owed by those in the pension investment chain apply to all asset classes. Furthermore, many of the intermediaries involved in pension chains are the same intermediaries as those involved in other forms of savings. For example, the description of collective investment schemes, brokers and custodians apply equally to those saving through an investment ISA.[26]

OTHER TRUSTS

1.36 There are other types of trusts which invest on behalf of others. Family trusts and charities are common examples. Many of the general principles we have outlined in relation to pension trustees will apply to other forms of trusts. However, the practical consequences may differ. Family trusts will be smaller and have a more clearly defined group of beneficiaries. Meanwhile, charity trusts may invest for an income or for charitable purposes. In some cases, they may invest for mixed purposes – partly to provide an income and partly to further the purposes of the charity, as where a homelessness charity invests in low-cost housing.

1.37 The Law Commission is conducting a separate review of mixed purpose investment by charities, including charity trusts, as part of its project on Selected Issues in Charity Law. The review, which is expected to be open for consultation in summer 2014, was prompted by concerns that the legal basis for such investment is unclear. It will consider whether reform is necessary to clarify the powers and duties of charity trustees in making mixed purpose investments, in particular whether a specific statutory investment power should be introduced for this purpose.

LONG-TERM TRENDS IN EQUITY MARKETS

1.38 Given the focus of the Kay Review on the need for long-term investment, it is helpful to look briefly at long-term trends in equity markets. Figure 1.2 shows trends in the UK stock market, looking at the FTSE All-Share Index from 1972.

---

[26] ISA stands for Individual Savings Account. Investment ISAs are a way in which individuals may save tax-free in stocks and shares up to a specified limit, which in 2013/14 was £11,520.

Figure 1.2: FTSE All-Share Index, adjusted close prices (29 Dec 1972 to 1 Oct 2013).

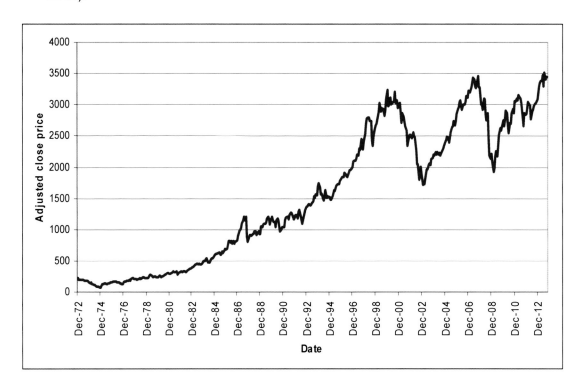

Source: FTSE International Ltd. We are grateful to them for allowing us to use these data.[27]

1.39   Essentially, the graph shows a period of growth from 1985 to 2000, followed by a period of volatility and flat growth thereafter. It is unsurprising that many pension funds have moved out of equities to escape this volatility.

1.40   Unfortunately, the FTSE index does not extend long enough to show long-term trends. To gain an idea of growth over a longer time span it is helpful to look at the US Dow Jones index, given the high correlation between the UK and US markets. Figure 1.3 shows the Dow Jones Industrial Average from 1900. The main pattern to emerge from it is exponential growth.

Figure 1.3: Dow Jones Industrial Average (linear, 1 Jan 1900 to 1 Aug 2013).

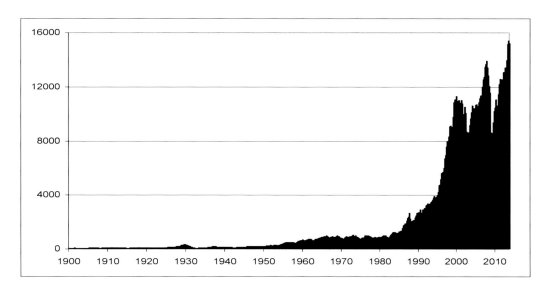

Source: S&P Dow Jones Indices. We are grateful to them for allowing us to use these data.

1.41   The problem with this graph is that, given the exponential growth, the peaks and troughs since 2000 appear to be much more dramatic than any previous periods of volatility. For example, the great stock market crash of 1929 is no more than a small blip at the bottom of the graph. In order to focus on patterns over time, it is helpful to plot the same figures on a logarithmic scale. This appears in Figure 1.4.

Figure 1.4: Dow Jones Industrial Average (logarithmic, 1 Jan 1900 to 1 Aug 2013).

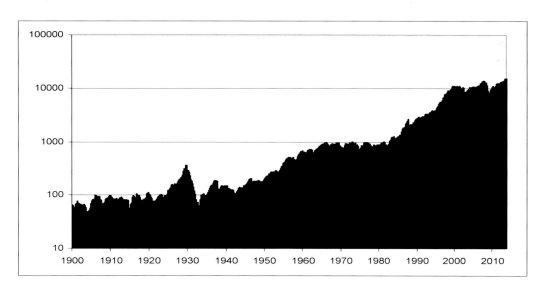

Source: S&P Dow Jones Indices. We are grateful to them for allowing us to use these data.

1.42 This logarithmic graph shows forty year cycles: twenty year periods of growth are succeeded by intervals of volatility and flat growth. In very broad terms, 1900-1920, 1940-1960 and 1980-2000 were periods of growth, interspersed with more volatile periods (from 1920 to 1940, from 1960 to 1980, and since 2000). On this basis the stock markets have not necessarily changed fundamentally from investment markets to casinos, but are experiencing another period of volatility.

1.43 People react to these data in different ways. As we see, many mature defined benefit pension funds are moving from equities to more stable investments. However, younger employees in defined contribution schemes are continuing to invest in equities – often in low-cost tracker funds. The assumption is that for a 25 year old investing for a pension in 40 years time, the equities markets will outperform other asset classes, as they enter a new period of growth. Others pointed out that a new period of growth will not simply arise spontaneously.[28] It will be the product of the many decisions made by investors and the companies in which they invest. Without good decisions which look at the underlying value of companies and which monitor company practices, this growth may not take place.

1.44 We do not attempt to predict events. The main point to emerge from these graphs is that the future is uncertain.[29] Any long-term pension investment strategy requires review over time. In Chapter 13 we summarise the evidence that pension scheme members are ill-suited to carry out these reviews themselves. People rely on others to look after their interests. It is therefore important that legal duties, industry structures and regulatory oversight combine to ensure that these reviews are conducted in the interests of future pensioners.

PREVIOUS LAW COMMISSION REPORTS

1.45 Several previous Law Commission projects are relevant to this project:

    (1) Fiduciary Duties and Regulatory Rules. This was a project, conducted in consultation with the Scottish Law Commission, which considered the extent to which the relationship between fiduciary duties and regulatory rules gave rise to problems in practice. We published a consultation paper in 1992[30] and report in 1995.[31] The report looked generally at the law of fiduciary duty but did not consider the investment duties of trustees.

---

[28] See paras 10.67-10.73 below.

[29] For an analysis of the effect of unexpected events (or "black swans") see N Taleb, *Fooled by Randomness: The Hidden Role of Chance in Life and in the Markets* (2001) and *The Black Swan* (2007)

[30] Fiduciary Duties and Regulatory Rules (1992) Law Commission Consultation Paper No 124.

[31] Fiduciary Duties and Regulatory Rules (1995) Law Com No 236.

(2)   Trustees' Powers and Duties. This was a joint report with the Scottish Law Commission. We reviewed the law governing trustees' powers to invest trust funds where there were no express powers in the will or trust instrument. We also considered a wide range of other powers, including trustees' power to delegate, to insure, to use nominees and custodians and to remunerate professional trustees. We published a consultation paper in 1997[32] and a joint report in 1999,[33] which led to the enactment of the Trustee Act 2000 for England & Wales and Part 3 of the Charities and Trustee Investment (Scotland) Act 2005.

(3)   Trustee Exemption Clauses. This considered the extent to which, in England & Wales, trustees should be permitted to exclude or restrict liability for breach of trust, either by expressly excluding liability or by modifying the trustees' powers and duties. We published a consultation paper in 2003[34] and a report in 2006.[35]

(4)   Intermediated Securities. This project considered the legal implications of the transition from paper based share certificates to electronic entries in intermediaries' accounts. From 2006 to 2008, the Law Commission analysed successive drafts of the UNIDROIT Convention on the Law of Intermediated Securities.[36] We advised the UK Government to sign and ratify the Convention to bring legal clarity to this area of law at an international level.

THE STRUCTURE OF THIS CONSULTATION PAPER

1.46   In this paper, we trace the investment chain from prospective pensioner/saver to the registered shareholder of a UK company and describe the law which applies to each stage. This paper is split into four further Parts.

Part 2: market structures

1.47   Part 2 looks at market structures. Chapter 2 is a broad overview of the pensions landscape. Chapter 3 then outlines the investment chain, describing the various roles, including that of trustee, investment consultant, investment manager, broker and custodian. We give specific examples based on interviews for this project.

---

[32]   Trustees' Powers and Duties (1997) Law Commission Consultation Paper No 146. This Consultation Paper was not a joint publication of the two Law Commissions.

[33]   Trustees' Powers and Duties (1999) Law Com No 260; Scot Law Com No 172. This Report is joint only for its Part I and II, and implementation has thus not had the same effects throughout the UK. See paras 6.47-6.52 and 7.28-7.40 below.

[34]   Trustee Exemption Clauses (2003) Law Commission Consultation Paper No 171.

[35]   Trustee Exemption Clauses (2006) Law Com No 301. The Scottish Law Commission is considering this question as part of its Trust Law project: see Breach of Trust (2003) Scottish Law Commission Discussion Paper No 123. A Report is expected to be published in 2014.

[36]   Law Commission, *The UNIDROIT Convention on Substantive Rules regarding Intermediated Securities: Further Updated Advice to HM Treasury* (2008).

Part 3: current law

1.48 Part 3 describes the current law. Following an introduction, it is divided into four further chapters. Chapter 5 considers fiduciary duties in a narrow sense. Chapter 6 looks at other "judge-made" duties, including duties arising from the exercise of a power and duties of care. Chapter 7 considers the pensions legislation and Chapter 8 looks at the Financial Conduct Authority Handbook.

Part 4: analysis

1.49 Part 4 is the core of the paper. It analyses how the law applies in practice. We introduce this part in Chapter 9.

1.50 It is clearly established in law that pension trustees are required to act in the best interests of their beneficiaries. There are, however, some difficult questions in determining how far pension trustees can take into account environment and social factors and other factors which go beyond maximising financial return. We consider these issues in Chapter 10.

1.51 Many of those involved in the investment chain are not trustees but operate under contracts. Contractual arrangements are not necessarily incompatible with fiduciary duties, but fiduciary duties are more flexible and less certain. Chapter 11 considers the courts' general approach. We explain that the courts tend to interpret fiduciary duties and duties of care as subject to contractual terms and regulatory rules.

1.52 The courts are more likely to impose fiduciary-type duties to protect unsophisticated and vulnerable individuals at the bottom of the chain. These duties play a less significant role at the top of the chain, when apparently sophisticated parties trade with each other on a professional client or eligible counterparty basis and where their relationship is governed by a contract they have bargained for.

1.53 In Chapter 12 we attempt to apply these principles to specific intermediaries in the chain. We do so highly tentatively. We start by looking at the potential liabilities of those involved in contract-based pensions, including employers, financial advisers and pension providers. Financial advisers and pension providers are required to consider the suitability of the scheme when a member first enters the scheme. A provider who fails to consider suitability may incur a liability. The problems arise in ensuring the suitability of the scheme over time. We then consider the fiduciary duties on others in the investment chain, where the law of fiduciary duties is even more uncertain.

1.54 Chapter 13 looks at problems in how the governance of workplace defined contribution pension schemes works in practice. Drawing on recent reviews, including a market study by the Office of Fair Trading, we summarise concerns about high charges and lack of independent governance. We then contrast the UK approach with pension regulation in Australia, drawing on a paper by the Australian law firm, Clayton Utz.

Part 5: conclusions and questions

1.55   Part 5 sets out our conclusions and questions. We have been asked whether fiduciary duties (as established in law or as applied in practice) are conducive to investment strategies that are in the best interests of the ultimate beneficiary. In general, we think that the law of fiduciary duties which applies to pension trustees is satisfactory. The problems arise from other factors, such as the structure of the market. We ask consultees if they agree.

1.56   By contrast, we have concerns about the way that fiduciary duties apply to contract-based pension providers. The law does not necessarily ensure that investment strategies continue to be in the best interests of members throughout the investment period. We ask whether the duties on contract-based pension providers to act in the interests of scheme members should be clarified and strengthened.

1.57   For other intermediaries in the investment chain, the law is extremely flexible but also uncertain. We do not think that it would be desirable to reform the law of fiduciary duty by statute: this would create new uncertainties and have unintended consequences. If there is a need to clarify the law, we think it would be better to enact specific duties. One possibility would be to extend the right to sue for breach of FCA rules. We have reservations about this: it would add to costs and may be disruptive. Nevertheless, we ask for views.

1.58   Finally, we reach the conclusion that many of the problems raised with us can only be addressed through FCA regulation. Our project does not attempt to review all the relevant rules. However, we ask if there is a need to review regulations of investment consultants and custodians, as stakeholders expressed particular concerns about these. We will pass views to the FCA and BIS.

1.59   The research paper we commissioned on the Australian pensions landscape and fiduciary duties law is included, in full, as an Appendix at the end of this paper.

THANKS AND ACKNOWLEDGEMENTS

1.60   We are very grateful for the help of our Advisory Committee: Professor Alastair Hudson, Vanessa Knapp OBE, Professor Hector MacQueen, Deborah Sabalot and Dr Anna Tilba. We also give particular thanks to Clayton Utz and Freshfields for all their help on the Australian research paper and to Deborah Shedden for her interviews with market participants.

1.61   We also extend our thanks to those we met with, provided responses to our short paper or provided research materials for us to draw on. A full list of participants is included in Appendix D.

PART 2

MARKET PRACTICE

CHAPTER 2
THE PENSIONS LANDSCAPE

2.1 Pensions have dominated our discussions. For most people, their pension is their most significant long-term investment in financial markets. It is the area of people's lives in which they most rely on investment intermediaries to look after their interests, and where they are most vulnerable if the system fails them. Historically, the pensions industry has also been a significant investor in the equity markets, meaning that pension decisions have implications for equity markets as a whole.

2.2 Yet the pensions landscape is changing rapidly, as the old defined benefit pension schemes close and people are increasingly entering into more individual contract-based arrangements, particularly under auto-enrolment.[1] We start with a brief description of the different types of pension arrangements which are used to supplement state benefits. We then consider some of the issues facing the pensions industry.

2.3 Our initial discussions with stakeholders suggested that many of the barriers to long-term investment approaches had little to do with the law. Rather, they arise from the way in which UK pensions are structured. We return to this issue in Chapter 14, when we evaluate the law.

TYPES OF OCCUPATIONAL PENSION SCHEME

2.4 Pensions may be arranged through an employer or by an individual privately. We start by looking at UK occupational schemes administered by or on behalf of an employer.[2]

2.5 There are two main types:

(1) "*Defined benefit*" (DB). In the private sector all DB schemes are set up under trust, though some public sector schemes are governed by statutory instruments instead.

(2) "*Defined contribution*" (DC). These may be set up under trust or may be made on a contractual basis with a private provider, typically an insurer. Within contract-based pension schemes, it is helpful to distinguish between low cost "stakeholder pensions", which are subject to specific regulations, and the less regulated "group personal pension" schemes.

---

[1] See paras 13.5-13.9 below.

[2] See Finance Act 2004, s 150 and Pension Schemes Act 1993, s 1.

DB schemes

2.6   DB schemes provide a pre-determined amount on retirement, often calculated on the basis of the employee's final salary and length of service. Crucially, the amount an employee receives does not depend on the performance of investments. Instead, the employer makes a contractual promise to pay a pre-determined amount. Typically, both the employee and the employer make contributions which are invested to hedge against the employer's promise. If the fund underperforms, the employer is required to top up the fund to ensure it is capable of meeting its liabilities.

2.7   By comparison with other pension schemes, DB contributions are generous. The Pensions Policy Institute calculates that the total level of contributions required to fund a typical final salary scheme is 21% of salary.[3] By contrast, average contributions to open DC schemes in 2010 were under 9%.[4] DB membership peaked in 1967;[5] many schemes have, therefore, been established for several decades and have built up substantial assets. In 2012 they controlled £1,031 billion of assets, compared with only £697 billion of assets in DC schemes.[6]

2.8   However, DB schemes are a dying breed. Rising life expectancy coupled with low investment returns have increased their cost significantly. As schemes have gone into deficit, many employers have been required to make additional contributions. Many DB schemes have reduced benefits and closed schemes to new members. By 2011, only 16% of private sector DB schemes were open to new members.[7]

Trust-based DB schemes

2.9   In the private sector all DB schemes are set up under trust. Subject to some limited exemptions, at least one-third of trustees must be nominated by the scheme's members.[8] We discuss the role and regulation of trustees in detail in Parts 3 and 4 of this paper.

Statutory DB schemes

2.10   The Civil Service Pension schemes are not funded, so are not discussed here. Other public sector schemes, such as the Local Government Pension Scheme (LGPS) and the National Health Service Pension Scheme, are funded. They are governed by statutory instruments and are usually unaffected by other pensions legislation, though they may be subject to European Directives.

---

[3]   Pensions Policy Institute, *The changing landscape of pension schemes in the private sector in the UK* (2012) p 3.

[4]   Above, p 20. This figure has been arrived at by adding together average employer contributions (6.2%) and average employee contributions (2.7%).

[5]   Above, p 13.

[6]   Source: National Association of Pension Funds.

[7]   Pensions Policy Institute, *The changing landscape of pension schemes in the private sector in the UK* (2012) p 17.

[8]   Pensions Act 2004, ss 241 and 243. All of the active or pensioner members (or organisations which adequately represent their respective interests) must be allowed to participate in the nomination of these trustees.

2.11 For example, the LGPS is established under section 7 of the Superannuation Act 1972 and the regulations made under it.[9] These create a single pension scheme which is divided into a number of pension funds, each managed by a designated administering authority, often the employer. The administering authority does not act as a trustee, but on the basis of their statutory powers and duties. The duties on administering authorities may be different from the duties on trustees.

DC schemes

2.12 In DC (or "money purchase") schemes, the contributions from employee and employer are specified, but the retirement benefits are uncertain. Contributions are invested and are typically assigned to a notional individual "pot". When the employee retires, assets equal to that pot of money are used to buy an annuity, which provides a fixed income for life. Thus the individual's pension will depend not only on the level of contribution, but also on the performance of investments, the fees charged and the annuity rate obtained.[10] The employee and not the employer bears the risk of poor performance.

2.13 DC schemes are "the growth story of pensions".[11] It is estimated that there are currently 7.9 million memberships in DC schemes.[12] As we see below, this is predicted to increase rapidly.

Trust-based DC schemes

2.14 DC schemes may be trust-based or contract-based. Where DC schemes are set up under trust, the trustees have a responsibility to review and monitor the investments.[13] Like DB trustees, DC trustees are under fiduciary duties and duties to act in the best interests of their beneficiaries. However, they are not subject to the same funding oversight by the regulator as DB schemes. For example, they do not need a statutory funding objective.[14] The primary concern of regulators is whether the employer failed to pay their set contribution amount or failed to pay in time.[15]

Contract-based DC schemes

2.15 Under contract-based schemes, pension providers are not subject to the same fiduciary duties. Because there are no trustees, there is less oversight of investment strategy over time and more dependence on specific regulations. Contract-based pension schemes may be regulated in two ways: as stakeholder pensions or as personal pensions. We discuss these regulations in Chapter 13.

[9] See, for example, the Local Government Pension Scheme (Management and Investment of Funds) Regulations 2009 SI 2009 No 3093.

[10] See further: Mercer, *DC Connections, Is your DC plan successful? Factors to consider when measuring success* (2012).

[11] M Harrison, "Coming of age?" (July 2013) *Pensions World* 1 at 1.

[12] Spence Johnson, *Defined Contribution Market Intelligence* (2013) p 14.

[13] D Pollard and C Magoffin, *Freshfields on Corporate Pensions Law* (1st ed 2013) para 17.1.20.

[14] Pensions Act 2004, s 221(1)(a).

[15] For example, with stakeholder or personal pension schemes the provider must monitor the payment of contributions by the employer: see Pension Schemes Act 1993, s 111A.

GROUP STAKEHOLDER PENSIONS

2.16 Stakeholder pensions were established by the Welfare Reform and Pensions Act 1999 as a new way for low earners without a pension to save for retirement.[16] They are primarily governed by the Stakeholder Pension Schemes Regulations 2000.[17]

2.17 The focus is on keeping costs low. Administration charges are capped by law at 1.5% of the fund value per year for the first 10 years and, thereafter, at 1%.[18] The regulations also require schemes to allow low contributions and penalty-free transfers.

2.18 Stakeholder schemes may offer a choice, but members must not be required to make a choice. Stakeholder schemes must offer a default investment option.[19] Where the individual member enters the default scheme, the investment strategy must be adjusted as the member gets older to move out of risky investments, like equities, towards fixed income products such as bonds. This is known as "lifestyling" and is designed to reduce the impact of market volatility as the member reaches retirement.[20] It is commonly achieved by pooling funds with other investors of the same age.

GROUP PERSONAL PENSION SCHEMES

2.19 Personal schemes were first introduced by the Social Security Act 1986 and were an option for those who were self-employed or had opted out of their employer's occupational pension scheme. However, it is becoming more common for employers to offer "group personal pension schemes".

2.20 Personal pensions are much less restricted than stakeholder pensions and may charge higher fees.[21] They often offer a broader range of investment choices. Traditionally, group schemes have not always offered the security of a default scheme. However, if the scheme is used for the purposes of auto-enrolment (see below) it must include a default option.[22] For non-stakeholder pensions, the default fund does not have to be lifestyled, though this is recommended in guidance.[23]

---

[16] For the Government's consultation document and Green Paper, see Department of Social Security, *Stakeholder Pensions: A Consultation Document* (1997); A new contract for welfare: Partnership in pensions (1998) Cm 4179.

[17] SI 2000 No 1403.

[18] Stakeholder Pension Schemes Regulations 2000 SI 2000 No 1403, reg 14.

[19] Stakeholder Pension Schemes Regulations 2000 SI 2000 No 1403, reg 3.

[20] Stakeholder Pension Schemes Regulations 2000 SI 2000 No 1403, reg 10A(2).

[21] Nabarro Pensions Team, *Pensions Law Handbook* (11th ed 2013) para 14.16.

[22] Pensions Act 2008, s 17(2).

[23] Department for Work and Pensions, *Guidance for offering a default option for defined contribution automatic enrolment pension schemes* (2011).

Automatic enrolment

2.21   Auto-enrolment is being phased in from October 2012 to October 2018. The scheme has started with large employers and will gradually be extended to medium and small employers.

2.22   Employers will be required to enrol all employees between the ages of 22 and state pension age into a pension scheme if they earn over the threshold (currently £9,440 a year). Employees have the right to opt-out, but they must make a positive decision to do so. When the scheme is fully introduced, contributions must be at least 8% of band earnings (that is, earnings between £5,668 and £41,450 in 2013/14). Of this, at least 3% must come from the employer.

2.23   Employers have a choice of pension schemes for auto-enrolment. They may use an existing scheme or set up a new scheme. However, to give every employer access to a scheme, the Government has set up the National Employment Savings Trust (NEST).[24] NEST is a low-cost trust-based DC scheme, and is part of the Government's initiative to ensure a greater number of employees have access to a pension plan. It is run on a not-for-profit basis and has low contribution and annual management charges.[25]

THE CHANGING NATURE OF OCCUPATIONAL PENSIONS

2.24   The changes from DB to DC schemes are illustrated by the following diagrams.

2.25   Figure 2.1, below, shows that 60% of active members of occupational pension schemes are still in DB schemes, and a further 15% are in trust-based DC schemes. The role of pension trustees is, therefore, still crucial to UK pensions policy.

---

[24]   The legislation establishing NEST is contained in the Pensions Act 2008, Pt 1 Ch 5 and orders and regulations issued under this Act.

[25]   Currently, the contribution charge is 1.8% and annual management charge is 0.3%. See NEST, *Charges explained*, available at http://www.nestpensions.org.uk/schemeweb/NestWeb/public/NESTforSavers/contents/charges-explained.html.

Figure 2.1: Employee membership of an occupational pension scheme, by pension type (2012).

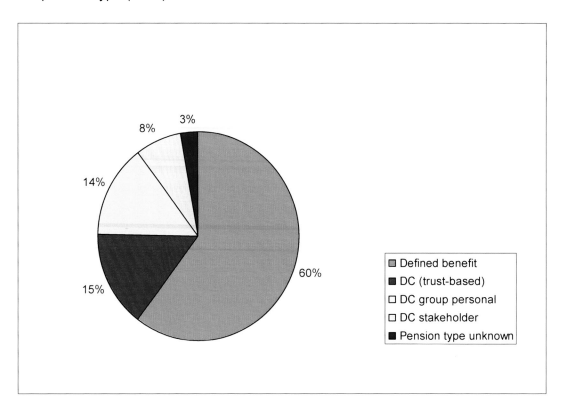

Source: Office for National Statistics, Pension Trends, Chapter 7: Private Pension Scheme Membership, 2013 Edition (16 July 2013).

2.26 However, these proportions are changing rapidly. Figure 2.2 shows the steady decline in DB membership and a rise in contract-based stakeholder and personal schemes. This trend will accelerate with the introduction of auto-enrolment. It is predicted that auto-enrolment will mean around six to nine million more individuals will join DC pension schemes by 2018.[26] Investment and Pensions Europe states that DC assets will surpass DB assets by 2022.[27]

---

[26] See Office of Fair Trading, *Defined contribution workplace pension market study* (2013) para 1.4, citing Department for Work and Pensions, *Workplace Pension Reform: digest of key analysis* (2012), available at http://www.gov.uk/government/uploads/system/uploads/attachment_data/file/223031/wpr_digest _0712.pdf.

[27] Investment & Pensions Europe, *Fiduciary management: A catalyst for growth* (1 October 2012), available at http://www.ipe.com/magazine/fiduciary-management-a-catalyst-for-growth_47675.php.

Figure 2.2: Employee membership of an occupational pension scheme, by pension type (1997 to 2012).

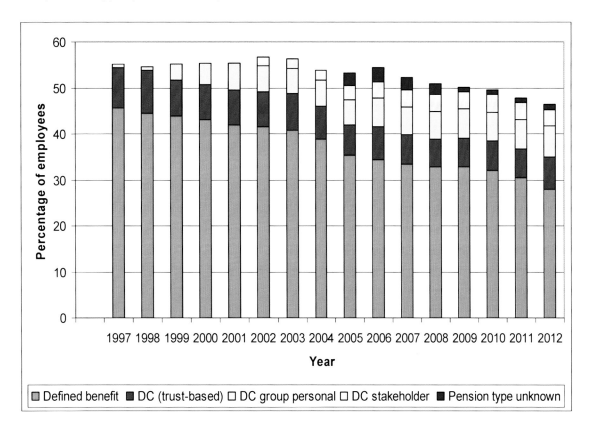

Source: Office for National Statistics, Pension Trends, Chapter 7: Private Pension Scheme Membership, 2013 Edition (16 July 2013).

2.27 The graph shows that over half of employees are not currently active members of a workplace pension scheme. Some may be making private provision, but most are not. With the introduction of auto-enrolment, membership of pension schemes will increase, but the level of contributions required by auto-enrolment is much lower than for DB schemes. Those born after 1980 are unlikely to receive anything like the final salary pensions enjoyed by the baby boomer generation.

PRIVATE PERSONAL PENSIONS

2.28 As an alternative to a workplace pension scheme, individuals may enter into private pension arrangements. Typically, they will contract individually with a personal pension scheme provider such as an insurance company. As with DC schemes, individuals pay a set amount. The scheme provider invests this, and on retirement the accumulated pot of money is used to buy an annuity. There is no reliable data on how many individuals contribute to private pension plans, either in addition to or instead of occupational schemes.

PENSION SCHEMES AND EQUITIES

2.29 Historically, pension funds have been major players in the UK equities markets. Since 2000, however, funds have held fewer direct equities. The volatile nature of the equities markets is considered unsuitable for many DB schemes, which need to invest in safer asset classes as they reach maturity. This will continue to be the case as the age profile of DB schemes increases, in the absence of new members. Further, in recent times when equity fluctuations can lead to sudden deficits within the scheme and in the employer's company accounts, equities have generally been seen as less attractive. As Figure 2.3 shows, there has been a move from equities to safer asset classes such as bonds and indirect mutual funds.

Figure 2.3: Self-administered pension fund holdings of corporate securities, by type of UK asset (1986 to 2011).

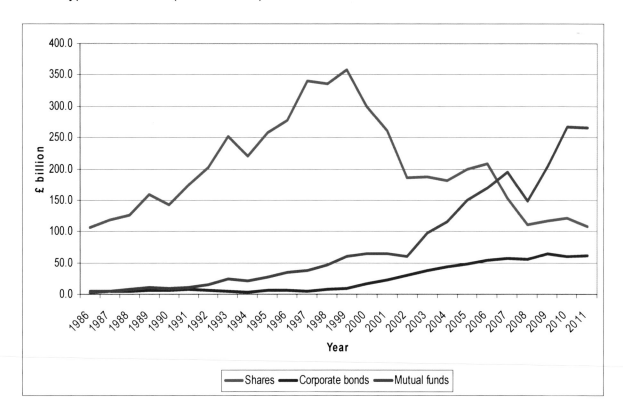

Source: Office for National Statistics, *Pension Trends, Chapter 9: Pension scheme funding and investment, 2011 Edition* (20 April 2011). Self-administered pension funds include funds managed by scheme trustees or investment managers, the LGPS and insurance-managed funds, where an insurance company acts as investment manager but does not have title to the assets.

2.30 When pension funds do hold equities, the equities are not necessarily in the UK, but may be elsewhere in the world. We have been told that for some trust-based schemes only 8% of the fund's investments are in UK equities.

2.31 DB pension schemes are increasingly using "liability driven investment" (LDI) strategies. The aim is to match returns to the time frame over which the liabilities arise (say 20 years), so as to make the fund less vulnerable to interest rate and inflation risks. Typically, LDIs use swaps and other derivatives to hedge against the risk of changes in the economic climate that might affect the value of their investments in the medium or long term. The Pensions Policy Institute reports that LDI assets under management in the UK increased from £243 billion at the end of 2010 to £312 billion at the end of 2011, a rise of almost 30%.[28] As we discuss in Chapter 3, these hedging arrangements can be highly complex and require specialist advice.

PENSION SCHEME REGULATION: A DUAL SYSTEM

2.32 Pension schemes are subject to two separate regulators: The Pensions Regulator and the Financial Conduct Authority. Here we give a brief introduction to each and mention the Pension Protection Fund and ombudsman schemes. We examine the criticisms made of this regime in Chapter 13.

The Pensions Regulator (TPR)

2.33 Trust-based schemes are mainly regulated by TPR, which replaced the previous regulator (the Occupational Pensions Regulatory Authority) in April 2005 under the Pensions Act 2004. TPR has three key statutory objectives:

(1) to protect members' benefits;

(2) to take steps to reduce the likelihood of claims being made against the Pension Protection Fund; and

(3) to promote and improve understanding of the good administration of work-based occupational, personal and stakeholder schemes.[29]

2.34 The Pensions Bill 2013-14 will add a further statutory objective of minimising any adverse impact on the sustainable growth of an employer when exercising its functions in relation to scheme funding.[30]

2.35 TPR states that its approach is to educate and enable before resorting to enforcement action.[31] It relies on trustees and others to report information to it.[32] Section 69 of the Pensions Act 2004 contains extensive whistle-blowing requirements. It requires trustees, employers and others involved in administering or advising a scheme to report suspected breaches.[33] Based on the information it receives, TPR focuses its interventions on the schemes at risk.

---

[28] Pensions Policy Institute, *The changing landscape of pension schemes in the private sector in the UK* (2012) p 46.

[29] Pensions Act 2004, s 5.

[30] Pensions Bill 2013-14, cl 42.

[31] The Pensions Regulator, *Corporate plan 2013-2016* (2013) p 23.

[32] G Thomas and A Hudson, *The Law of Trusts* (2nd ed 2010) para 45.67.

[33] There is a code of practice which provides further guidance. See The Pensions Regulator, *Regulatory Code of Practice 01: Reporting breaches of the law* (2005).

2.36 TPR has extensive powers. These include powers to collect data, to issue improvement notices and to issue contribution notices to employers who are believed to be avoiding their pension obligations.[34] TPR is also required to issue codes of practice. There are currently 12. The codes of practice are not statements of the law and there is no penalty for failing to comply with them. However, if relevant they must be taken into account by the regulator, a court or tribunal, including the Pensions Ombudsman.[35]

The Financial Conduct Authority (FCA)

2.37 We describe the FCA in Chapter 8. It has shared regulatory responsibilities with TPR for contract-based schemes, and it also authorises the investment managers used by trust-based schemes. Importantly, the FCA regulates firms that provide, promote and advise on personal pensions.

2.38 The interaction between TPR and the FCA is complex. For example, the FCA and TPR are jointly responsible for complaints and compensation in respect of stakeholder pensions.[36] And, whilst TPR registers contract-based pensions, the FCA is responsible for the authorisation and operation of the schemes.

The Pension Protection Fund (PPF)

2.39 The PPF was introduced by the Pensions Act 2004.[37] It is designed to protect members of DB schemes if their employer becomes insolvent on or after 6 April 2005. DB pension schemes pay a levy to the PPF which provides some of the funding for such protection. DC schemes are not eligible for protection.[38]

2.40 If the member has attained normal pension age at the date of insolvency, they will receive 100% of their entitlement. However, other members will only be entitled to 90%, and higher earners will receive less as compensation is subject to a cap. [39] Dependants are limited to 50% of the members' pension.

Ombudsman schemes

2.41 There are two ombudsman schemes which hear complaints about pensions. In practice, the Financial Ombudsman Service deals mainly with complaints about how pensions are sold. Meanwhile, the Pensions Ombudsman deals mainly with complaints of maladministration. We describe these two schemes in Appendix B.

---

[34] Pensions Act 2004, s 231.

[35] Pensions Act 2004, s 90; The Pensions Regulator, *Regulatory Code of Practice 07: Trustee knowledge and understanding (TKU)* (2009) para 5.

[36] *Tolley's Pensions Law* (Issue 79 2013) para A6.13.

[37] Pensions Act 2004, Pt 2.

[38] See Pensions Act 2004, s 126.

[39] For example, from April 2013, at age 65 the effective cap is £31,380.34. However, the Minister for Pensions has recently announced the government is to increase the maximum level for those receiving capped compensation by 3% for every full year of service over 20 years. See Written Ministerial Statement, *The Pension Protection Fund: Changes to the Compensation Cap* (25 June 2013), available at http://www.parliament.uk/documents/commons-vote-office/June_2013/25-June-2013/4.DWP-Pension-Protection.pdf.

PENSION CHALLENGES

2.42   The rapid changes to the pension landscape have led to many challenges, as DB schemes have gone from surplus to deficit and contract-based schemes require new forms of regulation. We look first at the issues surrounding DB schemes, followed by the new problems posed by the rapid rise of DC schemes.

2.43   The Kay Review highlights the problems caused by short-term decision-making. We were told that many of the pressures on pension funds towards short-termism are unrelated to the law of fiduciary duties. Similarly, decisions about what may or must be taken into account when making an investment decision are not primarily curbed by perceptions about the law. Here we outline some of these pressures.

FROM SURPLUS TO DEFICIT: THE PROBLEMS OF DB SCHEMES

Surpluses

2.44   During the 1980s, the growth of investments and a reduction in the workforce led to substantial surpluses in DB schemes. In retrospect, it would have been prudent to invest these surpluses to guard against future deficits. At the time, however, pension schemes were subject to competing pressures to use these surpluses in other ways. Employers suspended contributions to the pension fund and obtained repayments, employees looked to improve benefits and the Government saw pension funds as a source of tax revenue. For example, the Finance Act 1986 removed some tax advantages for exempt approved schemes.

2.45   Current legislation restricts the ability of fund trustees to pay surpluses to employers. Under sections 177 and 207 of the Finance Act 2004, a tax charge of 35% applies to payments of surpluses to employers.[40] Under section 37 of the Pensions Act 1995, trustees may only repay surpluses where trustees are satisfied that it is in the interests of the members, have a written actuarial valuation and have followed the required procedure.[41]

2.46   Where a surplus does arise, it may put pressure on the investment decisions trustees make. Those with competing interests in a scheme are likely to view the surplus differently: an employer may regard a surplus as trapped "overfunding"; members may see it as "spare" money that could be used for benefit improvements; and trustees may see it as a reserve fund providing security against future contingencies.

---

[40]   With effect from 6 April 2006: Finance Act 2004, s 284(1).

[41]   As set out in Occupational Pension Schemes (Payments to Employer) Regulations 2006 SI 2006 No 802, reg 10.

Deficits

2.47   In recent years, the challenge faced by DB schemes has been to avoid and deal with deficits. In 2012 the Pensions Policy Institute described five strategies which trustees and employers have used. These range from increasing contributions to closing schemes to new members and changing investment strategies. Schemes have also offered "enhanced transfer values" to encourage deferred members to transfer out of schemes.[42]

Statutory funding obligations

2.48   DB schemes must show they are on track to meet their liabilities.[43] Every scheme is subject to a statutory funding objective which requires it to hold "sufficient and appropriate assets" now in order to pay its accrued benefits as they fall due in the future.[44] Actuarial valuations to determine this amount must be prepared at least every three years.[45] In determining whether the scheme has "sufficient and appropriate assets", a current market rate value is given to the assets held.

2.49   Failure to meet the statutory funding objective requires the trustees to put a recovery plan in place, setting out the period over which the deficit is to be remedied. A copy must be sent to TPR.[46] TPR expects trustees to look to clear the deficit as quickly as the employer can reasonably afford.[47] The trustees are also required to ensure that the assumptions underlying the recovery plan are appropriate for the scheme.

---

[42]   Pensions Policy Institute, *The changing landscape of pension schemes in the private sector in the UK* (2012) p 35.

[43]   The detailed rules governing how employers must fund their DB schemes are in the Pensions Act 2004 and the Occupational Pension Schemes (Scheme Funding) Regulations 2005 SI 2005 No 3377, and are supported by a code of practice: see The Pensions Regulator, *Regulatory Code of Practice 03: Funding defined benefits* (2006). In part, these obligations stem from the requirements of the Institutions for Occupational Retirement Provision (IORP) Directive 2003/41/EC, Official Journal L 235 of 23.09.2003 p 10.

[44]   Pensions Act 2004, s 222.

[45]   Pensions Act 2004, s 224.

[46]   Pensions Act 2004, s 226.

[47]   The Pensions Regulator, *Regulatory Code of Practice 03: Funding defined benefits* (2006) para 101.

2.50 This has three effects. Firstly, trustees' decision-making tends to focus on the actuarial valuations and the employer's obligation to fund the scheme. Actuaries therefore play a crucial role in the investment decisions trustees make. Secondly, by generating a figure every three years (or less), investment decisions tend to be oriented to much shorter time horizons than the ultimate liabilities the scheme has to meet. Thirdly, when a valuation takes place assets are valued at current market values (known as mark-to-market valuations), which also acts as a restraint on long-term thinking. As the Church of England Ethical Investment Advisory Group stated in their response to the Kay Review:

> Current valuations of assets are irrelevant when the assets are part of a long term return-seeking strategy and there is not the slightest prospect of the assets being sold.[48]

Accounting calculations

2.51 Any pension deficit must be shown in the employer's company accounts based on accounting standards FRS17[49] or IAS19.[50] These accounting standards calculate pension fund liabilities in a different way from the approach taken by the statutory funding obligations.[51] For example, they take a different approach to calculating life expectancies. A leading pensions textbook suggests that accounts based on FRS17 may reveal a surplus even though the scheme is in deficit for statutory scheme funding purposes.[52] Like the statutory funding objective, however, the accounting standards use mark-to-market valuations, which again focuses attention on the current rather than future value of pension assets.

2.52 The amount of the deficit shown on the accounts may be crucially important to an employer, as it is used as part of the process to determine whether the employer is solvent. We are told that the need to avoid a deficit on the employer's accounts may influence pension trustees' decisions.

---

[48] Church of England Ethical Investment Advisory Group, *Church of England Ethical Investment Advisory Group and National Investing Bodies Submission to the Kay Review* (2011) p 7, available at http://www.churchofengland.org/media/1376615/eiag-nibs%20response%20to%20kay%20review%2018%20nov%202011.pdf.

[49] Financial Reporting Standard 17.

[50] International Accounting Standard 19.

[51] Under the Occupational Pension Scheme (Scheme Funding) Regulations 2005 SI 2005 No 3377, reg 5, trustees are required to choose assumptions "prudently" but the accounting standard looks for a "best estimate". It has been suggested that this may lead to a different deficit figure: see D Pollard and C Magoffin, *Freshfields on Corporate Pensions Law* (1st ed 2013) p 26.

[52] Nabarro Pensions Team, *Pensions Law Handbook* (11th ed 2013) para 11.28.

Small scale schemes

2.53   In initial discussions, stakeholders expressed concern that many UK pension schemes were too small. The 2012 Purple Book published by the Pensions Regulator shows that, of 6,316 PPF-eligible defined benefit schemes,[53] 2,260 have fewer than 100 members.[54]

2.54   Economies of scale may bring benefits in terms of lower administration and fund management charges and more control over those who make investment decisions on behalf of the fund. It also makes engagement with companies financially viable and practically possible.

2.55   Consolidation was supported by, among others, the National Association of Pension Funds (NAPF), UNISON and the Fabian Society. Stakeholders drew our attention to the study by APG, the Dutch investment manager, into the investment performance of the LGPS which suggested that "substantial improvement in investment performance could be realised by increasing the size of funds".[55] The study found that reductions in investment expenses in line with the increase in assets due to consolidation of LGPS funds could in total have led to an extra £793 million over the period 2001-2009.[56] Each member would gain £275 a year over the same period if the 101 separate LGPS funds were consolidated into 14 regional funds.[57]

2.56   The Fabian Society has commented:

> The UK workplace pension industry is organised on an inefficient basis. The industry is fragmented into thousands of schemes. These are often too small to operate at a level which will ensure that the members get the best possible deal in terms of lower costs for running the scheme, better investment strategies at lower cost ... , better communication with members, and assistance in turning the members' pensions pots into annual retirement income.[58]

---

[53]   This excludes: unfunded public sector schemes; some funded public sector schemes; schemes to which a Minister of the Crown has given a guarantee; and schemes which began to wind up, or were completely wound up, prior to 6 April 2005. This list is not exhaustive: see Pensions Act 2004, s 126 and Pension Protection Fund (Entry Rules) Regulations 2005 SI 2005 No 590, reg 2.

[54]   Pension Protection Fund and The Pensions Regulator, *The Purple Book: DB Pensions Universe Risk Profile* (2012) p 24. These figures are from the Purple Book 2012 dataset.

[55]   APG, *Performance analysis of LGPS funds*, p 2. This research was commissioned by UNISON and submitted as part of its evidence to the Independent Public Service Pension Commission. We are grateful to UNISON for sharing this research with us.

[56]   Above, p 2. See also The Smith Institute, *Local authority pension funds: investing for growth* (2012).

[57]   Above, p 3.

[58]   The Fabian Society, *Pensions at Work that Work: Completing the unfinished pensions revolution* (2013) p 21.

2.57   However, this view is not necessarily shared by all. Robin Ellison, Head of Strategic Development for Pensions at Pinsent Masons, writing in Pensions World, is sceptical of the motives behind calls for scale:

> The Regulator wants fewer schemes … because they think (probably mistakenly) that fewer, larger schemes will give them a more peaceful life. Why the NAPF says so is less clear.[59]

2.58   Where small pension schemes lack internal staff, trustees tend to be highly dependent on intermediaries, such as investment consultants and investment managers. Trustees may not have the experience or expertise to form independent opinions or challenge advice about investment decisions. In Chapter 3 we look in detail at the intermediaries which pension funds use in making investments and the effect this may have on decision-making.

WORKPLACE DC SCHEMES: DO THEY OFFER VALUE FOR MONEY?

2.59   As more individuals enter workplace DC schemes, concerns have been raised over how far these schemes provide value for money. In September 2013 a market study by the Office of Fair Trading criticised some schemes for complex charges, high charges and poor governance. We explore these issues in Chapter 13.

2.60   From a legal perspective, there are significant differences between trust-based and contract-based DC schemes. However, they fulfil a similar market function, and both types of scheme may suffer from weaknesses. Below we highlight some of the concerns.

Contract-based schemes: ensuring on-going suitability

2.61   While trustees are subject to clear legal duties to review investment strategies, the duties of contract-based providers are less clearly defined. Contract-based pension providers have only limited obligations to review the continuing suitability of investments.[60]

2.62   In contract-based schemes, members may make choices about their investments. Yet individuals are often ill-equipped to understand or review these choices.[61] The danger is that an employee will make a choice which is suitable for them when aged 30 and then fail to review it in subsequent years, so that the investment becomes unsuitable before retirement.

---

[59]   R Ellison, "Pointing the finger" (July 2013) *Pensions World* 14 at 14.

[60]   See paras 12.18-12.22 below.

[61]   For further discussion of these problems, see paras 13.38-13.41 below.

2.63   In its recent review of workplace pension schemes, the Work and Pensions Select Committee concluded:

> There are inherent weaknesses in the mechanisms for governing contract-based schemes which the Government and the regulators must address, to ensure that members of contract-based schemes are offered the same level of protection from detriment as members of trust-based schemes.[62]

2.64   In September 2013, the Association of British Insurers agreed that its members would introduce Independent Governance Committees to consider members' interests, though these committees will not have the same powers and responsibilities as trustees. We describe these committees in Chapter 13.

Problems of trust-based DC schemes

2.65   Trust-based schemes have the benefit of a board of trustees who have a fiduciary responsibility to their members. When trustees have the right skills and support they are able to look after the interests of their members by reviewing costs and investment strategies over time.

2.66   However, many schemes are small, which means that they may lack the expertise and financial clout to get the best deal for their members.[63]

2.67   Furthermore, there are some concerns about the independence of some trustees. Many new entrants to the pension market have been set up as "master trusts". Master trusts are multi-employer trust-based pension schemes, which a pension provider manages under a single account. Some, such as NEST, work on a not-for-profit basis, while others have been established by insurance companies.[64] In some schemes it may be difficult for the trustees to criticise in-house funds or make decisions to move assets elsewhere.

A COMPARISON WITH AUSTRALIA

2.68   It is interesting to compare the structure of UK pensions with the Australian system. We therefore commissioned a paper from a leading Australian law firm, Clayton Utz, which is included in full in Appendix C.

---

[62]   Improving governance and best practice in workplace pensions, Sixth Report of the Select Committee on Work and Pensions (2012-13) HC 768-I para 27.

[63]   For further discussion see paras 3.70-3.71 and 13.54 below. See also Office of Fair Trading, *Defined contribution workplace pension market study* (2013) paras 7.26-7.27; and Department for Work and Pensions, *Quality standards in workplace defined contribution pension schemes: Call for evidence* (2013) paras 57 and 59.

[64]   See Office of Fair Trading, *Defined contribution workplace pension market study* (2013) para 4.9.

2.69 Like the UK, Australian pensions have a trust structure which derives from English law. They have also moved from DB to DC schemes. However, there are some significant differences. All schemes must be trust-based under a single regulatory regime. Furthermore, the market is much more consolidated, following pressure from the Australian Government. Over half of all funds under management are now held by the largest twenty pension schemes. We summarise the paper in Chapter 13.

CONCLUSION

2.70 Pension policy faces many challenges. At present most UK occupational pension schemes are trust-based, but this is changing rapidly. Auto-enrolment will lead to a substantial increase in contract-based schemes. Concerns have been expressed about how contract-based schemes are regulated. The current system puts the emphasis on individuals to monitor their holdings over time, but people may lack the skills to do this effectively.

2.71 Meanwhile, in traditional DB schemes, as many trustees focus on reducing deficits, there is pressure to produce short-term results. We have been told that many of the factors which shape pension trustees' investment decisions do not concern the law. Other pressures are more acute, including those produced by statutory funding objectives and accounting calculations based on mark-to-market valuations. Furthermore, many trust-based pension schemes are small, which makes trustees highly reliant on others in the investment chain. We turn our attention to the various players in this chain in the next chapter.

CHAPTER 3
THE INVESTMENT CHAIN

3.1 In his review, Professor Kay argued that there were too many intermediaries between the end investor and the investee company. He thought that this increased costs and led to misaligned incentives, with too much pressure on short term returns and insufficient stewardship of company decisions.

3.2 In this chapter we describe the investment chain and the criticisms made of it. In order to give some practical substance to this discussion we start by describing the investment chain of a typical defined benefit (DB) pension scheme. We look at the different parties in the chain and at how shares are bought and owned. Whilst the start of the investment chain may begin with a pension scheme, the later levels of the investment chain are largely common to other types of end investor.

3.3 We then explain how the chain might vary in a trust-based defined contribution (DC) pension scheme and in a contract-based pension scheme. Finally we illustrate these chains with two case studies.

A DB PENSION INVESTMENT CHAIN

3.4 In the private sector, all DB schemes are trust-based. Here we focus on DB pension schemes, following the chain from trustees to shares in a UK company. We are particularly interested in the way that decisions are influenced by advisers and other professional intermediaries. A research study by Anna Tilba and Terry McNulty of 35 large pension funds looks in detail at the dynamics of the relationships between trustees and their advisers.[1] We draw on this below, together with material from our own interviews.

3.5 Figure 3.1 shows the variety of people involved in pension investments and how information flows between them. The chain starts with the trustees, who are advised by actuaries and investment consultants. The trustee then gives a mandate to the investment manager. The investment manager may invest in a variety of assets, including direct equities or collective investment schemes such as open-ended investment companies (OEICs). They do this by using platforms, brokers and custodians.

---

[1] A Tilba and T McNulty, "Engaged versus disengaged ownership: the case of pension funds in the UK" (2013) 21(2) *Corporate Governance: An International Review* 165.

Figure 3.1: Flow of information and authority in a trust-based DB scheme.

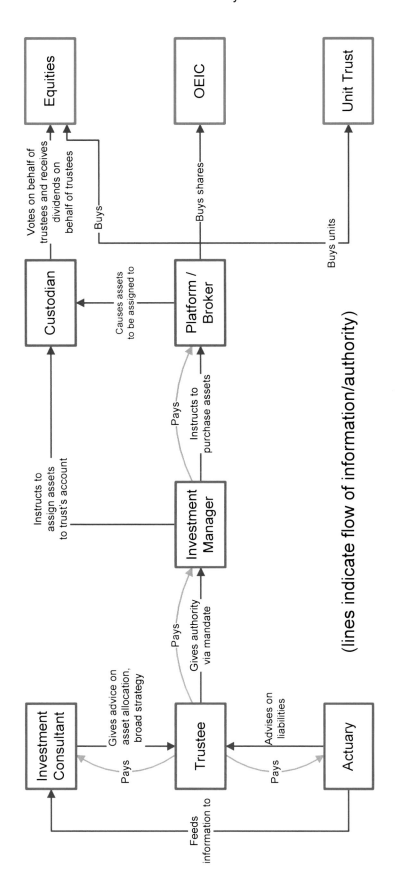

(lines indicate flow of information/authority)

Actuaries

3.6　The foundation of investment decisions is the actuarial valuation, which must be carried out at least every three years in order to comply with the statutory funding objective.[2] The actuary determines the liabilities of the scheme and calculates the returns which the scheme needs to make to meet these liabilities.

3.7　Tilba and McNulty comment on the ambiguity associated with actuarial valuation. Trustees may be presented with a choice of several assumptions, and the assumption used will set the basis of the investment strategy:

> The higher the liability, the greater demand for more funding. ... The actuary, then, plays an important role in setting the foundation for the subsequent investment choices of asset allocation and fund manager selection by trustees.[3]

3.8　We were told that in practice actuaries exercise significant influence over the way a scheme's assets are invested. It was said that actuaries see the world in mathematical terms; as a result, their approach to investment decisions may be at odds with a more holistic understanding of financial performance. Whilst actuaries do not advise between one investment and another, they may, and often do, become involved in decisions about investment policy and asset allocation. They will determine the liabilities of the scheme for the short, medium and long-term and may suggest how the various types of investment should be split to provide sufficient cash funds to provide lump sum and pension benefits for the members as they fall due.[4]

Investment consultants

3.9　The role of investment consultants is to provide strategic advice: they do not pick individual investments. Following the actuarial valuation, trustees are given precise figures (say 6.5% a year)[5] on the performance required if the fund is to meet its liabilities. The trustees form an opinion on the level of risk the employer, as the ultimate guarantor, is willing to bear. The investment consultant then produces a detailed plan of how to achieve this, focusing on how assets should be allocated between asset classes to provide appropriate levels of yield and risk. The investment consultant's advice will be used to construct one or more mandates, which are the instructions the trustees give to their chosen investment managers. The investment consultant will also organise a "beauty parade" of the different investment managers the trustees may wish to use.

3.10　Investment consultants are paid a fee for their advice. Their service is not an ongoing one, but it is likely that the trustees will return to them for continuing advice as the actuarial calculations change, typically every few years.

---

[2]　Pensions Act 2004, s 224.

[3]　A Tilba and T McNulty, "Engaged versus disengaged ownership: the case of pension funds in the UK" (2013) 21(2) *Corporate Governance: An International Review* 165 at 173.

[4]　Nabarro Pensions Team, *Pensions Law Handbook* (11th ed 2013) para 10.23.

[5]　We were told that this was the type of figure which might be required to be generated for the fund to meet its liabilities. However, it is unlikely to be achieved in current market conditions.

3.11 In Chapter 8 we discuss the regulatory position of investment consultants. The provision of "generic advice" is not regulated in the same way as advice relating to one or more specific investments.[6] Where investment consultants are advising on overall strategy, rather than specific investments, they face few regulatory requirements.

3.12 In Chapter 2 we described the increased use of "liability driven investment" (LDI) strategies. These are highly complex and require specialist advice. Few trustees possess the knowledge of financial products necessary to fully understand the way they operate. Furthermore, these strategies must be monitored over time to ensure that the arrangement continues to accurately reflect liabilities. A mandate under an LDI strategy will be more complex and will often require the continued involvement of investment consultants.

Concerns about investment consultants

3.13 We were repeatedly told that investment consultants wield significant influence over the structure of pension scheme investments, and that trustees lack the expertise or power to challenge the advice they are given. As Tilba and McNulty comment:

> While consultants perceive their role purely as advisory, the trustees for the most part regard consultant's advice to be *"telling"* or directing the trustees what investment strategy to pursue.[7]

3.14 The research study also highlighted the close relationships between investment consultants and actuaries: 45% of schemes appoint actuaries and investment consultants from the same firm.[8] Furthermore, investment consultants often recommended investment managers and developed close relationships with them.[9]

3.15 The consulting market is highly concentrated: Towers Watson, Mercer and Aon Hewitt dominate. This means the advice given to pension schemes is often broadly the same, creating "herding" patterns of investment behaviour. Consultants are criticised for focusing on short-term returns, rather than a holistic view of factors relevant to investment performance.

---

[6] D Frase, *Law and Regulation of Investment Management* (2nd ed 2011) paras 3-025 to 3-026. See also our discussion of the regulatory position of investment consultants below at paras 8.18-8.21 below.

[7] A Tilba and T McNulty, "Engaged versus disengaged ownership: the case of pension funds in the UK" (2013) 21(2) *Corporate Governance: An International Review* 165 at 173 (emphasis in original).

[8] Above, at 174.

[9] Above, at 175.

3.16   As Professor Kay said in his evidence before the BIS Select Committee:

> We have created this market for investment consultants, who are themselves the source of quite a lot of this short-termist behaviour, because they are typically making recommendations to trustees based on recent performance histories, rather than the future approach and strategy of the manager.[10]

3.17   The Myners Review raised similar issues. It found that trustees relied heavily on investment consultants in their asset allocation decisions and in their selection of investment managers, and that they lacked the experience to challenge the advice given.[11] Further, the concentration of the market led to a narrow range of advice with limited innovation.[12]

Fiduciary management

3.18   Typically, investment consultants merely advise: the trustees then appoint and monitor the investment manager or managers. Recently, some investment consultants have started to offer a more "hands-on" service, known as "fiduciary management". This term is perhaps misleading as the trustee usually retains the overall governing role and responsibility. The fiduciary manager, however, selects, appoints and monitors the investment managers and takes responsibility for functions such as portfolio constructions and risk management.

3.19   Fiduciary management originated in the Netherlands, where 75% of externally managed pension funds use this service. In the UK, we were told that only 4% of externally managed funds do, representing around £40 billion of assets.[13]

3.20   Fiduciary management may help smaller schemes to impose more control over the investment chain and the structure of their portfolios. However, several concerns were raised about it. It makes pension funds more reliant on intermediaries, who may not owe the same robust duties to the end beneficiaries. It may be difficult for pension trustees to evaluate the service or to retain control over the scheme's investments. Where a consultant advises a pension scheme to use its own fiduciary management service, this gives rise to a possible conflict of interest. Further, the service comes at a cost, which must either be met by the employer or comes out of the returns available for distribution.

The investment manager

3.21   Investment managers handle the day-to-day management of assets, acting on the basis of instructions given to them in the mandate. They may know little about the ultimate beneficiaries beyond that which is set out in the mandate.

---

[10]   The Kay Review of Equity Markets and Long-Term Decision Making, Third Report of the Select Committee on Business, Innovation and Skills (2013-14) HC 603 at Ev 4.

[11]   P Myners, *Institutional Investment in the United Kingdom: A Review* (2001) paras 3.42-3.43.

[12]   Above, para 4.44.

[13]   R Altmann, Saga, *Presentation to Time Warner Trustees: A new way forward for Europe's pension funds* (2012) p 32.

3.22 A mandate would normally specify the trustees' strategy in terms of asset allocation and acceptable risk. It would then set out the scope of the manager's discretion. The mandate might give the investment manager discretion to pick investments as they see fit in order to meet the strategic requirements. It might be more detailed and state that only certain types of investments can be picked. Alternatively, it might require that all investments are approved directly by the trustees.

3.23 Sometimes there will be only one investment manager, who has oversight of the whole investment strategy. In larger funds, different managers may be used for different parts of the strategy. In this case, the manager will only know about one slice of the portfolio and will have no understanding of the trust's entire investment structure, nor are they usually expected to.

3.24 Investment managers advise on and make specific investment decisions. They are regulated by the Financial Conduct Authority (FCA).[14] As we discuss in Chapter 7, they are also subject to specific duties under the pensions legislation. They are paid an ongoing fee, typically calculated as a percentage of funds under management.

Concerns about investment managers

3.25 Professor Kay criticised the way investment managers are monitored. He argued that asset holders monitor investment managers too frequently and on the basis of misleading benchmarks:

> Asset holders will normally receive monthly performance information from their asset managers and will typically discuss this performance on a quarterly basis.[15]

3.26 Investment managers are usually monitored and rewarded on the basis of their performance relative to an index benchmark or to the performance of other investment managers in a defined category. However:

> Past performance is not necessarily a guide to future performance: it is, in fact, virtually no guide to future performance. Savers, and asset holders, who make decisions to reallocate funds to asset managers who have recently outperformed their competitors are anchoring on noisy but copiously available quantitative information in the face of considerable uncertainty.[16]

---

[14] Financial Services and Markets Act 2000, s 19(1); Financial Services and Markets Act 2000 (Regulated Activities) Order 2001 SI 2001 No 544, reg 37. We discuss the regulatory position of investment managers in more detail at para 8.22 below.

[15] J Kay, *The Kay Review of UK Equity Markets and Long-Term Decision Making: Final Report* (2012) para 5.20.

[16] Above, para 5.21.

3.27 As Tilba and McNulty observe, the emphasis on benchmarking puts investment managers under pressure to produce short-term investment returns through "portfolio churning".[17] In the study, investment managers were not asked to take a holistic view of the value of companies, for example by looking at their environmental impact. Only one investment manager engaged with investee companies on corporate governance issues. Another said that he would keep investing in a company with a poor governance record so long as it did not affect the performance of the fund. When it did, he would simply sell the shares.

Who is responsible for considering long-term factors?

3.28 We were told that investment managers only carried out their mandates. If trustees wish them to look at environmental or governance matters or to engage with companies, this should be specifically stated in the mandate.

3.29 Some stakeholders argued that trustees should give investment managers more specific mandates, requiring consideration of wider investment factors. Tomorrow's Company comments that:

> as a trustee you can and should encourage advisors and investment managers to make decisions that reflect your values and those of your beneficiaries, by having a strong and focused investment mandate.[18]

3.30 In 2001 the Myners Review had also criticised the shape of many mandates. Lord Myners told the BIS Select Committee that this continues to be a problem:

> He who pays the piper calls the tune. The problem has been that the person who pays the piper has been somnolent, and has expressed no particular preferences for any type of tune, or even the quality of playing. He who pays the piper is the trustee of the pension scheme.[19]

3.31 In our meetings with stakeholders we were consistently told of an "accountability gap". In a 2009 study, trustees commented:

> It's not our place to dictate to a manager ... If these companies are at risk of not being sustainable as businesses, that's for them to factor into their fundamental analysis.[20]

---

[17] This refers, generally, to the excessive buying and selling of investments in a portfolio. See A Tilba and T McNulty, "Engaged versus disengaged ownership: the case of pension funds in the UK" (2013) 21(2) *Corporate Governance: An International Review* 165 at 176.

[18] Tomorrow's Company, *Tomorrow's Value, Achieving sustainable financial returns: A guide for pension trustees* (forthcoming) p 29.

[19] The Kay Review of Equity Markets and Long-Term Decision Making, Third Report of the Select Committee on Business, Innovation and Skills (2013-14) HC 603 at Ev 26.

[20] FairPensions (later known as ShareAction), *Protecting our Best Interests: Rediscovering Fiduciary Obligation* (2011) pp 65-66, citing J Solomon, *Pension Fund Trustees and Climate Change* (2009) p 24.

3.32 On the other hand, investment managers often assume that trustees should explicitly instruct them to take wider factors into account if that is what the trustees want.[21] Similarly, investment consultants are also unclear about whether they ought to consider such factors without explicit direction.[22] ShareAction told us that "this lack of clarity potentially creates an impasse whereby nobody in the investment chain is taking responsibility for managing potentially material risks".[23]

The investment platform

3.33 The term "investment platform" is used loosely to refer to both a "platform" as a piece of technology and as an intermediary who may facilitate the purchase of investments. Essentially, an investment platform is a facilitator of investments. Not all investment chains are structured around an investment platform, but many are. Platforms have two main functions. The first basic function is that of technology provider. The platform allows the investment manager to review holdings and to issue instructions to buy or sell assets, or move money into funds.

3.34 The second function of the platform is to allow efficient access to markets which the investor might have too little capital to access directly. In this case, the platform will receive instructions from the investment manager, which it may well aggregate with instructions received from other clients, before going into the market through brokers (possibly in-house) to execute the necessary trades.

3.35 The platform may also provide access to a variety of managed funds which the pension trust may not otherwise have access to, either because it is too small or because the necessary money laundering checks make it too administratively difficult to join.

3.36 The platform will be paid a fee, which may be wrapped up in the investment manager's fee. It may be set out separately on the investment manager's paperwork.

Collective investment schemes

3.37 As we saw in Chapter 2, increasingly pension funds do not invest directly in shares or bonds but in other funds. There are two main types: open-ended investment companies (OEICs) and unit trusts.

---

[21] FairPensions (later known as ShareAction), *Protecting our Best Interests: Rediscovering Fiduciary Obligation* (2011) p 65.

[22] UNEP Finance Initiative, *Fiduciary responsibility, Legal and practical aspects of integrating environmental, social and governance issues into institutional investment* (2009) p 36; Eurosif, *Investment Consultants & Responsible Investment Study* (2009) p 13.

[23] ShareAction, Response to "Fiduciary Duties of Investment Intermediaries: Initial Questions" (July 2013).

3.38 An OEIC is a company set up under the Open-Ended Investment Companies Regulations 2001[24] and is regulated by the FCA.[25] In an OEIC, investors purchase shares, which gives them contractual rights against the company. These rights are typically rights to have the shares repurchased by the company at a price determined by the performance of the underlying assets in the fund run by the company. The beneficiaries do not gain any rights against the assets which the OEIC purchases: these are owned by the OEIC itself.[26] The shares themselves may be transferable and therefore have some characteristics of property, particularly where they are highly liquid and have an easily determinable value. However, they remain merely contractual rights against a corporate entity, and do not give property rights over any securities. The open-ended nature of an OEIC means that it can increase and decrease its share capital, and issue and redeem its shares at will, so that the value of its shares matches the value of the underlying assets they represent.[27] Because an OEIC is a company, elements of general company law are potentially applicable.[28]

3.39 Unit trusts have a longer history. In a unit trust the investors, as beneficiaries under the trust, do gain collective proprietary interests as beneficial owners of the trust assets, held legally by the scheme trustees.[29] The manager of the unit trust, which may be a corporate entity, sits outside the trust and does not own any of the assets, in contrast to an OEIC. The way in which the manager is paid and the rest of the trust is funded will depend on various contractual arrangements and the terms of the trust instrument setting up the unit trust. The terms of the trust instrument are also likely to spell out some of the principles and objectives according to which the unit trust will invest, which may have important implications where the manager makes an investment not permitted by the trust instrument.[30]

3.40 The increasing emphasis on investment through funds allows wide diversification throughout the world. However, these lengthening chains also add costs to the system and mean that the interests of the ultimate beneficiary can be several steps removed from the investment decisions made.

The custodian

3.41 Where investors invest directly in shares electronically, the legal title to the shares will normally be held by a custodian. Collective investment vehicles will also use custodians to hold the title to their shares. Below we describe the system of intermediated share holdings, through which investors often hold assets through a chain of entries in different computer systems.

---

[24] SI 2001 No 1228.

[25] See FCA Handbook COLL.

[26] D Frase, *Law and Regulation of Investment Management* (2nd ed 2011) para 15-020.

[27] Above, para 15-020.

[28] Above, para 15-022. See para 12.53 below.

[29] In Scots law, where ownership is a unitary concept, the trustees of the unit trust own the investment and the beneficiaries have personal rights against the trustee.

[30] See the discussion of *Pitt v Holt* at paras 6.8-6.13 below.

3.42 There are a small number of very large custodians in existence, who between them hold the legal title to many trillion pounds worth of assets. The job of a custodian is simple: to hold the asset safely and to account for its ownership correctly. The world's financial markets depend on custodians carrying out this function honestly and efficiently.

3.43 The main criticism made of custodians is that they supplement the fee they are given for their administrative duties by lending stock to others. In stock lending, the custodian transfers the title of the investor's shares to the borrower, while the borrower promises to transfer them back, often providing collateral against this promise. Professor Kay recommended that "all income from stock lending should be disclosed and rebated to investors".[31] He expressed concern that custodians received fees for lending stock when the risk that the borrower would default was borne by the investor. He thought that this was inconsistent with fiduciary principles.[32] We return to this issue in Chapter 12.

3.44 As we discuss below, in practice securities are often owned through chains of intermediaries, each of which may lend stock.

BUYING AND OWNING SHARES: HOW THE PROCESS WORKS

3.45 Having introduced the main participants in the chain, we provide a brief overview of how the pension scheme might become the "owner" of a company share. These processes are more complex than most people would intuitively assume and the law does not always mesh clearly with market practice.

3.46 For illustrative purposes, we assume that the pension scheme, through its investment manager, decides to invest £x in BigOil plc, which is listed on the London Stock Exchange.

Agreeing a sale

3.47 The trade may be concluded in a variety of ways.

Through a platform

3.48 Firstly, the investment manager may buy the shares through a trading platform, acting as an agent on behalf of its client. Again, there are several possibilities. One possible method is that the investment bank or broker sitting behind the platform matches the trust's purchase order directly with another investor seeking to sell shares in BigOil plc. The bank or broker will then execute the subsequent trade as a book entry in its own customer securities accounts. Alternatively, the bank may sell the trust shares from those held on its own account or purchased shortly after from the open market. The bank in these circumstances will make a profit on the difference between the open market price and the price paid by the trust via the investment manager.

---

[31] J Kay, *The Kay Review of UK Equity Markets and Long-Term Decision Making: Final Report* (2012) Recommendation 10.

[32] Above, para 9.25.

Through the London Stock Exchange

3.49   Secondly, if the order is big enough to justify the costs involved, the investment manager may seek to make the trade in the market directly. To do this, the person making the trade must be a member of the London Stock Exchange. The investment manager may itself be a member through their in-house broking services. Alternatively, they may approach an external broker to carry out the trade for them. In either case, the process will be similar: the broker (in-house or external) will go into the market and seek a seller of the shares at the best possible price. There are mechanisms in most exchanges for matching buyers to sellers such that prices remain reasonably constant.

Through the investment manager

3.50   Thirdly, it is possible for the investment manager to contract with the trust as counterparty. In other words, the investment manager will sell shares that it owns to its client. When this occurs, the investment manager faces obvious conflicts of interest. It must ensure that it offers the asset to the client at as least as good a price as could have been obtained with reasonable efforts in the market. In the case of BigOil plc, the shares are sufficiently liquid that the investment manager can look to quoted prices. With less frequently traded assets, however, an investment manager may have to do more work to ensure that the price is the best that could be achieved if it went into the market.[33]

3.51   Finally, the investment manager may act as a "risk-free principal". Here the manager goes into the market and buys the shares as requested by the client, but buys them in its own name, as principal. At the same time the investment manager executes a contract with the client selling the shares for the same price as they were purchased. The price the investment manager pays is linked directly to the price received from the client, so there is no price risk borne by the investment manager.[34]

"Best execution"

3.52   These various methods of buying stock involve risks that a broker or investment manager will not necessarily act in the best interests of the investor. As we discuss in Chapter 8, regulations require that "a firm must take all reasonable steps to obtain, when executing orders, the best possible result for its clients".[35] However, these duties will not apply where the investor is treated as an "eligible counterparty" under the FCA Handbook. In the absence of regulation, the common law may also require "best execution" through common law duties of care, contractual duties and fiduciary duties.

---

[33]   D Frase, *Law and Regulation of Investment Management* (2nd ed 2011) para 10-006.

[34]   Above, para 10-006.

[35]   FCA Handbook COBS 11.2.1R, discussed at para 8.69 below.

Ownership

3.53 Once a trade is agreed, the process of transferring the shares can begin. In past times, this would have involved the transfer of paper share certificates. For most share owners, physical share certificates have now been replaced by electronic book entries, typically leading to a process of "dematerialisation" and "intermediation".[36]

3.54 Today securities are predominantly held electronically and indirectly. For example, where the security is traded internationally, the entity issuing securities may issue a single "global" security to a single custodian or depository. The "global" depository may then hold accounts for other national central securities depositories and bank-custodians. These in turn may hold accounts for dealer-brokers, for investment managers and sometimes for end investors directly (who are rich enough to justify it). These multiple tiers of securities holdings mean that a company may not know the identity of its ultimate shareholders. Instead, it is necessary to trace "ownership" from the top-tier global custodian though various tiers to the end investor.[37]

3.55 There has in the past been some debate over the legal relationship that governs this ownership structure. It can be viewed as either a back-to-back chain of creditor debtor relationships, or as a series of trusts, where each tier holds an interest for the benefit of those in the tier below.[38] It now seems settled that the arrangement is trust-based, which protects the investor's interest if one party in the chain becomes insolvent. However, some areas of uncertainty remain.[39]

3.56 The issue has been examined by UNIDROIT (the International Institute for the Unification of Private Law). In October 2009, UNIDROIT produced a convention setting out that the relationship worked as a series of trusts.[40] From 2006 to 2008, the Law Commission analysed successive drafts of the Convention to advise the UK Government on the issues involved. We advised the UK to sign and ratify the Convention to bring legal clarity to this important area at an international level.[41] Despite this work, however, little has been done. As of July 2013, the Convention has been signed by only one country (Bangladesh) and has not been ratified.

---

[36] See R McCormick, *Legal Risk in the Financial Markets* (1st ed 2006) paras 7.04-7.07; M Yates and G Montagu, *The Law of Global Custody* (4th ed 2013) paras 1.13-1.14, 2.10-2.12.

[37] D Frase, *Law and Regulation of Investment Management* (2nd ed 2011) at para 11-006; see also the Office for National Statistics' latest survey of UK equity holdings, in which it is noted that further investigation is required to discover the true beneficial owner of a share: Office for National Statistics, *Ownership of UK Quoted Shares, 2012* (2013) pp 5-6, available at http://www.ons.gov.uk/ons/dcp171778_327674.pdf.

[38] See R McCormick, *Legal Risk in the Financial Markets* (1st ed 2006) at paras 7.17-7.40; M Yates and G Montagu, *The Law of Global Custody* (4th ed 2013) at paras 5.62-5.67.

[39] For the Law Commission's analysis of the law in this area, see Law Commission, *The UNIDROIT Convention on Substantive Rules regarding Intermediated Securities: Further Updated Advice to HM Treasury* (2008).

[40] See UNIDROIT Convention on Substantive Rules for Intermediated Securities 2009.

[41] Law Commission, *The UNIDROIT Convention on Substantive Rules regarding Intermediated Securities: Further Updated Advice to HM Treasury* (2008).

3.57 The European Commission has also been looking at the issue. It published two consultations on possible new Securities Law Legislation (in 2009 and 2010).[42] The press release accompanying the second paper explained that it was concerned with "the harmonisation of the legal framework for securities holding and transactions" and that "the Commission will come forward with a legislative proposal before summer 2011".[43] However, no legislative proposals have yet been published. In Chapter 14 we ask whether further work is needed to ensure that the law on intermediated securities is fit for purpose.

3.58 We think that, under current English law, intermediated securities should be seen as a series of trusts: investors collectively own the beneficial interest held for them by the custodian one tier above. Thus, to "own" the shares that it has bought in BigOil plc, the trust needs only to have its name entered onto the computer system of one intermediary in the chain. Typically this might be the investment platform. The platform in turn will own a beneficial interest in part of the shares held by the custodian.[44]

3.59 This system of share transfer and ownership brings obvious practical benefits in terms of speed and clarity. It does, however, introduce risks. If any party in the intermediated tier is fraudulent and then becomes insolvent, the end investor will lose their holdings. Where all the scheme's assets are held by a single platform, the pension scheme risks losing it all.

Voting

3.60 These complex arrangements can lead to some lack of clarity over voting rights. We were told that in a typical pension scheme, voting rights vest with the custodian but are administered by the investment manager. Where stock is lent, the votes go to the borrower but can be recalled if either the investment manager or the trustees wish to cast their vote. This is very rare.

Proxy agents

3.61 An investment group may appoint a proxy agent to advise it on how votes should be cast and to vote at company meetings on its behalf. The aim is that, where a single investment house has many managers holding the same stock, all the votes are cast the same way so that managers do not inadvertently neutralise each others' votes. It also means that the work of scrutinising company votes is not duplicated.

---

[42] European Commission, *Legislation on Legal Certainty of Securities Holding and Dispositions: Consultation Document* (2009) and *Legislation on Legal Certainty of Securities Holding and Dispositions: Consultation Document* (2010).

[43] European Commission, *Midday Express* (5 November 2010).

[44] While in Scots law beneficial interests are personal rights, that does not prevent this sort of multi-tier set-up from being legally effective.

3.62   Some concerns were expressed about the role of proxy agents. First, the number of proxy advisers is limited, meaning that broadly similar advice was given to many investors, causing "herding". As the Securities and Markets Stakeholder Group of the European Securities and Markets Authority (ESMA) recently advised:

> Where several shareholders with substantial holdings in a company rely on the same [proxy agent], they may receive identical advice which will have a coordinating effect on the voting pattern of the company.[45]

3.63   Further, the duties of the proxy adviser may not be clear. For example, what should they know about the company or about the interests of the end investor? They are an example of the increasingly long chain of intermediation between investor and company, which raises the possibility for new conflicts of interest.

3.64   ESMA has recently conducted a study into the proxy advisory industry in Europe. It concluded that there was no clear evidence of market failure in relation to how proxy advisers act. However, there was a need for greater transparency and disclosure about what proxy advisers were offering as a service.[46] To this end, ESMA drafted a set of principles which it hoped would lead to a code of conduct.

A TRUST-BASED DC INVESTMENT CHAIN

3.65   In many ways, the investment chain for defined contribution (DC) pension schemes is similar. However, there are two main differences. First, DC schemes are free from the strictures of periodic actuarial valuation to calculate a statutory funding objective. Trustees do not need to match assets to liabilities, as the employee takes the risk that investments will not meet expectations.

3.66   Secondly, in DC schemes the assets do not have to be pooled for a common purpose. It is possible to notionally allocate assets to individual employees. This allows employees some choice over how their pension is invested. This choice may be limited, such as choosing between three investment plans with different growth/risk objectives, or it may be very broad, allowing beneficiaries to build a portfolio between different classes of assets. For example, an employee might decide to split their pension between UK bonds, European equities and Far East equities.

3.67   The trust-based DC scheme could achieve this offering in two ways. The easiest way is for the trustees to invest in a variety of external funds, each of which offers exposure to the asset classes which have been chosen. On this basis, the pension scheme effectively becomes a "fund of funds".

---

[45]   ESMA, *Final Report: Feedback statement on the consultation regarding the role of the proxy advisory industry* (2013) p 32.

[46]   Above, p 3.

3.68 Alternatively, if the scheme is very large, it could acquire equities directly, appointing different investment managers to manage the different choices offered. The process would be the same as the one outlined for the DB scheme. The trust would typically give a mandate to its investment manager to instruct it to either acquire equities according to a particular growth target and risk profile (actively managed) or to acquire equities in a pattern designed to track a particular index (passively managed).

The role of trustees in DC schemes

3.69 We asked trustees about their role in DC pension schemes. We were told that their main focus is on the design of the default fund, as this is the one most commonly chosen, typically by 80% or more of members. An experienced trustee mentioned the difficulties posed by "lifestyling" towards less risky investments as employees grow older, commenting that an automated system towards bonds may result in very low yields.

3.70 Secondly, trustees can use their financial power to negotiate lower fund costs. They can also monitor the cost of funds on an on-going basis. One trustee emphasised that costs arise throughout the system, not simply in the annual management charge. She thought that trustees should monitor stock lending to ensure that proceeds go to the fund directly, and that lending activity is safely set up with adequate collateral to cover risks. It was also suggested that trustees might employ an outside agency to monitor bid-offer spreads or currency transactions incidental to investment, to ensure that trades are being done at the best price.

3.71 As discussed in Chapter 13, the Office of Fair Trading market study found that large single employer trust-based schemes are able to exert pressure on service providers in this way. However, in small and medium sized single employer trusts, trustees may lack the necessary expertise.[47]

A CONTRACT-BASED DC INVESTMENT CHAIN

3.72 In a contract-based pension scheme, there are no trustees. Instead, the employer selects one or more insurance companies to offer pensions to its employees.

Setting up a scheme

3.73 To set up a new pension scheme, the employer is likely to use a financial adviser. Many different organisations now provide this advice, ranging from the large investment consultant firms to small independent advisers.[48] Typically, the financial adviser organises a "beauty parade" of insurance companies which offer contract-based pensions. With the advice of the financial adviser, the employer will select a provider based on a range of factors, including fund range, cost and service quality.

---

[47] See para 13.54 below.

[48] See Spence Johnson, *Defined Contribution Market Intelligence* (2013) p 24.

3.74 The employer may also ask the financial adviser to offer guidance to the workforce. This may range from an hour's talk to a large group of employees to individual consultation with executives or board members. The investment adviser may also take the opportunity of offering ongoing individual advice to employees whose pension pot is large enough to make this financially viable. In other words, lower status, lower paid employees may be given the least guidance in choosing a pension.

3.75 Unlike trust-based schemes, in contract-based schemes the financial adviser's relationship with both the company and the employee may be limited to the specific transaction of setting up the scheme and managing the transfer of money effectively. There is less ongoing monitoring of investments. Some employers may set up governance committees, but these tend to be limited to large employers.[49]

The relationship with the fund

3.76 Many elements of the chain are similar. The insurance company will use an investment manager to select investments according to a mandate. The manager then uses brokers and custodians in the way that we have described.

3.77 However, there is a difference in ownership. The contract between the provider and the member is essentially a promise by the provider to pay benefits in the future. The value of those benefits will be calculated using a formula, contained in or referred to by the contract, which will take account of the amount of contributions made, and the nominal performance of the asset classes to which the member has assigned their pot.

3.78 The key phrase here is "nominal performance". As soon as the member or their employer makes a contribution payment, the money is no longer theirs. It becomes the property of the insurance company, which may do what it will with it. This is in contrast to the position of a trustee in a DC scheme, who receives the money for the beneficiary and must use it on the beneficiary's behalf.

Stewardship

3.79 Insurance companies are more involved in stewardship than pension trustees. It is rare for pension trustees to conduct stewardship activities. Tilba and McNulty found that only 2 out of 35 schemes exhibited "engaged ownership behaviour", such as company research, voting and face-to-face meetings with senior management.[50] This chimes with what we were told by stakeholders. Only the very largest pension funds were able to monitor what companies were doing, and even then they did so in a limited way. Trustees felt that they lacked both the resources to oversee managerial decisions and the clout to influence what companies did.

---

[49] Office of Fair Trading, *Defined contribution workplace pension market study* (2013) para 5.25.

[50] A Tilba and T McNulty, "Engaged versus disengaged ownership: the case of pension funds in the UK" (2013) 21(2) *Corporate Governance: An International Review* 165 at 171.

3.80 More stewardship activity is carried out by large investment managers, particularly the investment management arms of the largest insurance companies. For example, both Aviva and Legal & General employ corporate governance teams. Legal & General is responsible for managing approximately 4% of shares in all companies in the FTSE 350, which gives it some clout in dealing with companies. It told us that in 2012 it took part in 9,475 votes arising in 591 AGMs and 132 EGMs in the UK. More significantly, it held 490 meetings with individual boards. We were told that where there is a particular problem that the company fails to address, the team will go back: for example they met one firm on 15 occasions.

CASE STUDY EXAMPLES

3.81 The following examples provide some illustrations of how pension schemes work. They are based on real life examples and interviews, but some details have been changed to preserve anonymity.

Case study 1: A small trust-based defined benefit pension scheme

3.82 This fund is small, with less than £10 million in assets to provide for between 30 and 60 scheme members. The pension scheme has been closed for some time and it has an aging member profile, with most members due to start receiving benefits in the next 10 years. For this reason it is more heavily invested in cash and fixed income assets than in equities.

3.83 The three trustees are paid a small sum to recognise their work, but are essentially volunteers. They are present or former employees of the employer and one is a beneficiary under the scheme. The scheme is too small to employ any dedicated staff, though it makes significant use of professional advice from an investment consultant and an investment manager.

3.84 Overall the fund is in a state of minor deficit. The actuaries have quantified the level of performance which the fund needs to meet its liabilities, and on the basis of this figure, the investment consultant advised on the appropriate split between asset classes. The investment manager deals with all the investments and has a large degree of discretion over which to pick. The investments are actually made through an investment platform, and any direct investments are held through a custodian. The trustees meet periodically to consider the advice they receive and direct any necessary changes to allocations of fund assets.

Case study 2: A large hybrid trust-based pension scheme

Size and structure

3.85 This is a much larger scheme, with assets of £20 billion in total. The scheme was founded as a DB trust. The DB scheme closed to new entrants in 1996 and a trust-based DC scheme was created to run alongside it. At present the DB scheme is still in deficit, though this has been substantially reduced.

3.86 In 2012 the DB element had 13,500 active members, 72,500 deferred members and 30,000 pensioners. The DC element has more active members: 37,000 in all, but fewer deferred members (23,000) and only around 1,000 pensioners. At June 2013, the assets of the DC scheme were £1.5 billion.

3.87 In 2015 the DB scheme will be closed completely and become a legacy trust, managing money only for deferred members and pensioners. At present, all members are either DB or DC members. When the DB scheme closes, many long-standing employees will have retained rights in the DB scheme but will then build up future provision within the DC scheme.

Staffing

3.88 The pension fund has a Corporate Trustee which directly employs a Chief Investment Officer (CIO) and a team of two to manage all investment aspects of the fund. The CIO is responsible for the fund's investment and overall management strategy. He reports to a board of 13 directors who are the fund's trustees.

3.89 The scheme also draws on the skills of a range of external advisers including an investment consultant, investment managers, custodians, legal advisers, accountants and the scheme actuary.

The DC "offering"

3.90 The scheme used an independent financial adviser to design its DC offering. This is based on 12 funds, three of which are "funds of funds". The trust has given mandates to each of these 12 funds which specify, for example, the asset classes, the acceptable risk tolerances from benchmark, and whether the fund may use derivatives or hold cash. In practice, these replicate the design of the chosen underlying fund, but it means that the underlying fund cannot alter its structure without the agreement of the trust.

3.91 The default "lifestyle" fund is the most important element, accounting for 85% of members. It is invested in four sub-funds: "global equities", "fixed income bonds", "diversified assets" and "cash". Until the member reaches 20 years from retirement, the fund is all in equity. From that point, the pot is moved to the "diversified assets" and "fixed income" classes, with the "cash" introduced in the last few years to protect any cash lump sum the employee might want to take.

3.92 Alternatively, the "flexicycle" option offers members a choice of all 12 funds, including an ethical and a Shariah option. Meanwhile, the "freechoice" option allows members the opportunity to build their own portfolio.

3.93 The trustee does not pick stock directly, nor do they engage with the underlying investee companies or influence voting. However, the selection of a large financial services company to manage some of these funds included an assessment of the way they used environmental, social and governance factors in making decisions.

CONCLUSION

3.94 Pension funds have relatively few in-house staff. Instead they rely on long lines of intermediaries, including consultants, investment managers, platforms and custodians to invest their assets. Furthermore, the chains appear to be growing, with some new participants finding a niche, including "fiduciary managers" and proxy agents.

3.95 These many intermediaries introduce costs into the system, and tend to guide pension schemes towards traditional investment decisions based on quantified data. It is usually these pressures, rather than the law, which discourage schemes from looking at wider investment factors such as environmental and governance issues.

3.96 In Chapter 12 we look at how far everyone in the chain can be said to be subject to fiduciary duties. Most intermediaries in the chain work on the basis of written mandates or contracts, and it is these documents which determine their legal duties. Each intermediary works within their own parameters and it is difficult to require them to take a wider view, when much of the relevant information is outside their purview.

PART 3

CURRENT LAW

CHAPTER 4
THE CURRENT LAW: INTRODUCTION

FOUR SOURCES OF LAW

4.1 Investment markets are subject to a great deal of law. The rules we outline in this Part come from four separate sources:

(1) Agreements between the parties, as set out in contracts and trust deeds.

(2) The Financial Conduct Authority (FCA) Handbook, which applies throughout the United Kingdom.

(3) Pensions legislation and its accompanying regulations, which govern the way pension trustees make investment decisions, and which likewise apply throughout the United Kingdom.

(4) "Judge-made" law, including fiduciary duties, duties of care and the duties which attach to the exercise of a power. The content of these duties is broadly similar between England & Wales and Scotland, although we will mention some differences at appropriate points in what follows.

Agreements by the parties

4.2 The starting point for understanding the obligations on financial market participants is often the contract agreed by the parties. Freedom of contract is a fundamental value of English and Scots law. Where market participants are considered to be sophisticated commercial parties, the courts will be reluctant to interfere with their commercial arrangements. Similarly, when organisations are set up as trusts, the powers and constraints on trustees are often set out in the trust deed.

FCA Handbook

4.3 For many of the stakeholders we spoke to, the regulatory regime is their overriding concern. The FCA Handbook reflects both domestic and European Union policy decisions. It is now too large to fit in a hand. In fact it is no longer a printed book, but a complex database, which may appear daunting to outsiders, with its many acronyms, classifications and exceptions. Some of the definitions are particularly difficult to follow.[1] It is, however, central to the way UK financial markets work.

---

[1] For example, the Glossary to the FCA Handbook defines a "firm" as an authorised person, but not a professional firm unless it is an authorised professional firm. Each of these terms is, in turn, the subject of a separate definition. For example, an "authorised person" is defined as including a person who has a Part 4A permission to carry on one or more regulated activities, an incoming EEA firm, an incoming Treaty firm, a UCITS qualifier, an ICVC, and the Society of Lloyd's. Once again, each of these categories is the subject of a separate definition in the Glossary.

Pensions legislation

4.4 The investment decisions of pension trustees are governed by the Pensions Acts 1995 and 2004, together with the regulations made under these Acts. For example, regulations require that the investment of assets is "in the best interests of the beneficiaries" and in a manner "calculated to ensure the security, quality, liquidity and profitability of the portfolio as a whole".[2] The 1995 Act also obliges trustees to prepare and maintain a "statement of investment principles".[3]

4.5 There are sometimes difficult overlaps between pension law, FCA rules and other legal duties. As Freshfields comment, the result can be "messy and almost nonsensical" in some areas.[4]

"Judge-made" law

4.6 The final sources of duties and obligations can be found in case law, as developed by judges over the centuries. Lawyers think in terms of different branches of law, distinguishing (for example) between the law of trusts, tort and contract. In the following chapters we discuss three separate types of "judge-made law". These include fiduciary duties, duties of care and duties that attach to the exercise of a power.

The inter-relationship between these sources

4.7 These various legal regimes are often complex in themselves, and even more complex in their inter-relationships. They have been developed by different entities, with different objectives, so it is unsurprising that there are often tensions between them. For example, the regulatory regime may be more pragmatic in dealing with conflicts of interest or undisclosed commissions than legal principles would suggest, leading Professor Kay to accuse regulators of "watering down" common law fiduciary duties.[5] Meanwhile, commercial parties often seek to escape liabilities through contract terms.

4.8 Nevertheless, to answer practical questions about legal duties in financial markets, it is often necessary to draw on three or four different types of law. For example, to understand the investment duties of pension trustees it is necessary to start with the pensions legislation and the trust deed, before considering fiduciary duties, duties that attach to the exercise of a power and duties of care.

4.9 Similar complexities arise when considering the duties of other parties in the investment chain to act in the interest of their customers or end investors. Take a case in which it is argued that a bank should have given advice about whether an investment is suitable. Again, the court will have regard to multiple factors: it will start by looking at the contract documents and FCA rules, before considering possible duties of care and fiduciary obligations.

---

[2] Occupational Pension Scheme (Investment) Regulations 2005 SI 2005 No 3378, reg 4.

[3] Pensions Act 1995, s 35.

[4] D Pollard and C Magoffin, *Freshfields on Corporate Pensions Law* (1st ed 2013) para 17.1.2.

[5] J Kay, *The Kay Review of UK Equity Markets and Long-Term Decision Making: Final Report* (2012) para 9.13.

4.10 This means that we cannot answer the questions in our terms of reference by looking narrowly at fiduciary duties. We need to draw on multiple sources of law. In the next four chapters we provide an introduction to the main legal regimes which affect the questions we have been asked to address.

THE STRUCTURE OF THIS PART

4.11 As the focus of our project is on fiduciary duties, we start with a brief explanation of fiduciary duties in their narrow, legal sense. We then set fiduciary duties within the matrix of surrounding law:

(1) Chapter 5 introduces fiduciary duties.

(2) Chapter 6 outlines the duties attaching to the exercise of a power and duties of care.

(3) Chapter 7 explains the main statutory obligations on pension trustees when they make investment decisions.

(4) Chapter 8 highlights relevant FCA rules.

FIDUCIARY AND OTHER DUTIES[6]

4.12 Fiduciary duties are said to arise from a combination of "discretion, power to act and vulnerability".[7] They are designed to protect the vulnerable when others have discretionary powers to act on their behalf. When one person is given power to act on behalf of others, fiduciary duties require loyalty. Fiduciaries should not make a secret profit: where they do, the courts will require that profit to be paid to the principal. Nor may fiduciaries allow a conflict between their principal's interests and their own interests, or those of others. The principal may consent to conflicts of interest but the consent must be fully informed.

4.13 These principles are highly flexible, but also uncertain. The application and extent of such duties are hotly contested. Primarily, this is because the content of the duties is fact-specific: they are "a flexible set of principles" to guide decision making.[8] For Kay this was part of their appeal. It is also because of the sometimes clunky adaptation of rules which developed historically, based on specific relationships such as trustee-beneficiary, to the current financial environment and to a wider class of persons.[9]

---

[6] On fiduciary duties, see *Snell's Equity* (32nd ed 2010) ch 7; *Lewin on Trusts* (18th ed 2012) ch 20.

[7] Fiduciary Duties and Regulatory Rules (1992) Law Commission Consultation Paper No 124 para 2.4.6. See para 5.7 below.

[8] J Hawley, K Johnson and E Waitzer, "Reclaiming Fiduciary Duty Balance" (2011) 4(2) *Rotman International Journal of Pension Management* 4 at 7.

[9] Fiduciary Duties and Regulatory Rules (1992) Law Commission Consultation Paper No 124 para 2.4.2.

4.14 Fiduciary duties sit in the background of other more explicit duties, such as the duty to act with reasonable care and skill. Recent cases have been at pains to distinguish careless or minor mistakes from true breaches of fiduciary duty. The courts have differentiated between "true" fiduciary duties and other duties on fiduciaries, such as those associated with the exercise of a power or duties of care. In Chapter 6 we discuss the other duties which constrain the use of fiduciary power. We then introduce the pensions legislation and the FCA rules.

COMPANY DIRECTORS' DUTIES

4.15 Company directors have consistently been held to owe fiduciary duties to the company.[10] Under the Companies Act 2006, these were replaced by a statutory code, which takes effect in place of the common law and equitable rules.[11] The codification was recommended by the Law Commission in 1999.[12]

4.16 In this paper we confine ourselves to the duties of investment intermediaries and we do not consider the duties of company directors. However, some stakeholders referred to the recent codification as an example of how reform might be conducted.

4.17 In particular, section 172 of the Companies Act 2006 states that:

> A director of a company must act in the way he considers, in good faith, would be most likely to promote the success of the company for the benefit of its members as a whole, and in doing so have regard (amongst other matters) to
>
> (a) the likely consequences of any decision in the long term,
>
> (b) the interests of the company's employees,
>
> (c) the need to foster the company's business relationships with suppliers, customers and others,
>
> (d) the impact of the company's operations on the community and the environment,
>
> (e) the desirability of the company maintaining a reputation for high standards of business conduct, and
>
> (f) the need to act fairly as between members of the company.

---

[10] See, for example, *Aberdeen Railway Co v Blaikie Bros* (1854) 1 Macq 461 (149 RR 32); *Imperial Mercantile Credit Assoc v Coleman* (1873) LR 6 HL 189; *Parker v McKenna* (1874) LR 10 Ch App 96; *Regal (Hastings) Ltd v Gulliver* [1967] 2 AC 134; *Guinness plc v Saunders* [1990] 2 AC 663; *Nant-y-glo & Blaina Ironworks Co v Grave* (1878) 12 Ch D 738; *Eden v Ridsdales Railway Lamp & Lighting Co Ltd* (1889) 23 QBD 368.

[11] Companies Act 2006, ss 170-177. Cases concerning fiduciary duties will remain of importance for the interpretation of duties under the Companies Act 2006 and the civil consequences of directors acting in breach of these duties: see Companies Act 2006, ss 170(4) and 178(1).

4.18 It enshrines what has been termed "enlightened shareholder value",[13] requiring directors to have regard to factors which have a long-term impact on the success of the company.

4.19 There are also restrictions on directors contracting out of liability. Under section 232 of the Companies Act 2006, "any provision that purports to exempt a director of a company (to any extent) from any liability that would otherwise attach to him in connection with any negligence, default, breach of duty or breach of trust in relation to the company is void".[14] However, this does not prevent the company from authorising acts which would otherwise be breaches of duty.[15]

AVENUES OF REDRESS

4.20 Participants in financial markets often think of "law" as a constraint on their behaviour. An aggrieved client, however, will think in terms of possible redress. There are three main avenues available: the Financial Ombudsman Service; the Pensions Ombudsman; and the civil courts.

The Financial Ombudsman Service (FOS)

4.21 We describe the FOS in Appendix B. It exists to provide quick and informal redress for consumers and micro-businesses, up to a limit of £150,000. The FOS is huge: in 2012/13, it dealt with over half a million complaints across all financial sectors. Of these, almost 20,000 were complaints about investments and pensions. Importantly, the FOS has jurisdiction to decide a case "by reference to what is, in the opinion of the ombudsman, fair and reasonable in all the circumstances of the case".[16] Although it will take into account law and regulation, it may decide a case by reference to what is "fair and reasonable in all the circumstances".[17] Ombudsman discretion and good practice may be as important as the strict law.

---

[12] Company Directors: Regulating Conflicts of Interest and Formulating a Statement of Duties (1999) Law Com No 261 Part 4. The Company Law Review Steering Group published a Draft Code shortly thereafter: see The Company Law Review Steering Group, *Modern Company Law for a Competitive Economy: Final Report* (2001) Vol 1 Annex C.

[13] See Companies Act 2006, Explanatory Note [325].

[14] However, s 232(4) states that nothing in that section "prevents a company's articles from making such provision as has previously been lawful for dealing with conflicts of interest".

[15] For example, s 239 of the Companies Act 2006 provides that a company may, by resolution of its members, ratify conduct by a director amounting to negligence, default, breach of duty or breach of trust in relation to the company. See also Companies Act 2006, s 180(4).

[16] Financial Services and Markets Act 2000, s 228.

[17] Financial Services and Markets Act 2000 s 228(2); see para B.6 in Appendix B below.

The Pensions Ombudsman (TPO)

4.22 TPO deals predominantly with matters concerning the administration and/or management of personal and occupational pensions. Again, more details are provided in Appendix B.[18] By contrast, FOS deals primarily with matters concerning the advice and marketing of individual pension arrangements.

4.23 A Memorandum of Understanding exists between the FOS and TPO.[19] Where a complaint or dispute is received by one of these bodies which appears better suited to the other, the receiving ombudsman will seek the consent of the complainant before transferring it to the other body.

The courts

4.24 Thirdly, aggrieved litigants may use the civil courts. Indeed, for medium to large businesses, or for those looking for binding awards over £150,000, this is the only option. In some cases, the courts have given a ruling in advance of a decision being made by the fiduciaries, as when the courts have been asked to resolve a disagreement between trustees.[20] Usually, however, the court ruling is after the event – sometimes long after the event. For example, in *JP Morgan Bank v Springwell*,[21] the loss occurred in 1998 and the Court of Appeal ruling was in 2010.

4.25 To state the obvious: litigation can be slow and expensive. Any increase in litigation will introduce further legal and friction costs and add to risk. We bear these points in mind in reaching our conclusions in Chapter 14.

---

[18] Pension Schemes Act 1993, s 146. For further details, see paras B.12-B.17 in Appendix B below.

[19] Memorandum of Understanding between the Pensions Ombudsman and the Financial Ombudsman Service (2013), available at: http://www.financial-ombudsman.org.uk/publications/pdf/memorandum-of-understanding.pdf.

[20] *Cowan v Scargill* [1985] Ch 270; *Harries v Church Commissioners* [1992] 1 WLR 1241.

[21] [2010] EWCA Civ 1221. The case is discussed at para 11.78 and following below.

CHAPTER 5
FIDUCIARY DUTIES

5.1 In this chapter we introduce the concept of fiduciary duty in its narrow, legal sense. We start by looking at who is subject to fiduciary duties and then look at what the duties entail. We explain that those entering financial markets may consent to breaches of certain duties, allowing conflicts of interest and profits, but it must be informed consent.

5.2 Finally, we touch briefly on remedies. In England & Wales a breach of fiduciary duty in the strict sense allows the court to provide a broad range of equitable remedies, which are often more generous than the compensation available for mere negligence. This has led the courts to emphasise the distinction between fiduciary duties and duties of care. As one judge put it, "not every breach of duty by a fiduciary is a breach of fiduciary duty".[1] Fiduciary duties in the strict sense sit alongside duties attached to a power and duties of care, which we describe in Chapter 6. While Scots law recognises the distinction between fiduciary duties, duties of care and duties attached to a power, the remedies available for breach of the first do not generally extend as far as in English law.

WHO IS SUBJECT TO EQUITABLE FIDUCIARY DUTIES?

5.3 This is a "notoriously intractable" question.[2] Fiduciary relationships are said to arise in two circumstances:

(1) *Status-based* – where a relationship falls under a previously recognised category, such as a solicitor and client; and

(2) *Fact-based* – where the particular facts and circumstances of a relationship clothe it in a fiduciary character.[3]

---

[1] *Bristol and West Building Society v Mothew* [1998] Ch 1 at 16, by Millett LJ.

[2] E Weinrib, "The Fiduciary Obligation" (1975) 25(1) *University of Toronto Law Journal* 1 at 5.

[3] See *Boardman v Phipps* [1967] 2 AC 46.

Status-based

5.4 It is well established that many identifiable relationships are subject to fiduciary duties. The recognised relationships include: trustee and beneficiary;[4] principal and agent;[5] mortgagee and mortgagor;[6] solicitor and client;[7] company directors and the company;[8] partners and co-partners;[9] and civil servants and the Crown.[10]

5.5 For the purposes of this paper the most important categories are trustees and agents. It is well established that where a firm or individual acts as trustee they will be subject to fiduciary duties. In initial discussions, pension trustees were conscious of their special status as fiduciaries.

5.6 A fiduciary duty may also arise where one party acts as another's agent. For example, in *Hancock v Smith*, delivering share certificates to a broker with instructions to sell was held to give rise to a fiduciary relationship.[11] In imposing fiduciary duties on agents, however, the courts will look particularly carefully at the factual circumstances, and are likely to read the duties as subject to the terms of the contract which creates the agency relationship. This issue is explored in more detail in Chapter 11.

---

[4] *Keech v Sandford* (1726) Sel Cas Ch 61; *Price v Blakemore* (1843) 6 Beav 507. For Scots law see *Gloag & Henderson, The Law of Scotland* (13th ed 2012) para 41.15.

[5] *De Busshe v Alt* (1878) 8 Ch D 286; *Kirkham v Peel* (1880) 43 LT 171; *Lamb v Evans* [1893] 1 Ch 218; *New Zealand Netherlands Society Oranje Inc v Kuys* [1973] 1 WLR 1126; *English v Dedham Vale Properties Ltd* [1978] 1 WLR 93; *Korkontzilas v Soulos* (1997) 146 DLR (4th) 214. For Scots law see *Gloag & Henderson, The Law of Scotland* (13th ed 2012) para 18.04; L Macgregor, *The Law of Agency in Scotland* (1st ed 2013) ch 6.

[6] *Farrars v Farrars Ltd* (1888) 40 Ch D 395. Scots law has not characterised the relationship between a debtor and a secured creditor as fiduciary but at common law there are obligations upon the creditor which have a fiduciary look to them: see *Gloag & Henderson, The Law of Scotland* (13th ed 2012) para 36.04(7). Note also that the proceeds of a sale under a standard security are held by the creditor on trust: Conveyancing and Feudal Reform (Scotland) Act 1970, s 27.

[7] *Re Hallet's Estate* (1880) 13 Ch D 696; *McMaster v Bryne* [1952] 1 All ER 1362; *Brown v IRC* [1965] AC 244; *Oswald Hickson Collier & Co v Carter-Ruck* [1984] AC 720; *Swindle v Harrison* [1997] 4 All ER 705; *Logstaff v Birtles* [2001] EWCA Civ 1219; *Conway v Ratiu* [2005] EWCA Civ 1302. For Scots law see L Macgregor, *The Law of Agency in Scotland* (1st ed 2013) paras 6.26-6.28.

[8] *Sinclair v Brougham* [1914] AC 398; *Regal (Hastings) v Gulliver* [1967] 2 AC 134; *Selangor United Rubber Estates Ltd v Craddock* (No 3) [1968] 1 WLR 1555; *Industrial Development Consultants Ltd v Cooley* [1972] 1 WLR 443; *Cowan de Groot Properties Ltd v Eagle Trust plc* [1992] 4 All ER 700; *Item Software (UK) Ltd v Fassihi* [2004] EWCA 1244. For Scots law see *Gloag & Henderson, The Law of Scotland* (13th ed 2012) para 46.33.

[9] *Bentley v Craven* (1853) 18 Beav 75; *Aas v Benham* [1891] 2 Ch 244; *Thompson's Trustee in Bankruptcy v Heaton* [1974] 1 WLR 605. For Scots law see *Gloag & Henderson, The Law of Scotland* (13th ed 2012) para 45.18.

[10] *Reading v AG* [1951] AC 507; *AG v Guardian Newspapers Ltd (No 2)* [1990] 1 AC 109; *AG for Hong Kong v Reid* [1994] 1 All ER 1; *AG v Blake* [1998] 1 All ER 833

[11] (1889) 41 Ch D 456.

Fact-based

5.7 These categories are not closed. It is open to the courts to extend fiduciary duties to relationships where there is an inherent element of trust and confidence between the parties.[12] In 1992, we said that the test is based on "discretion, power to act and vulnerability".[13]

General principles

5.8 In *Reading v Attorney General* an army sergeant received bribes for escorting smugglers' lorries through police checks with the aid of his military uniform.[14] The Court of Appeal held that there was a fiduciary duty between Reading and the Crown, and that the Crown was entitled to retain the money. Lord Justice Asquith explained that a fiduciary relationship exists:

> (a) whenever the plaintiff entrusts to the defendant property … and relies on the defendant to deal with such property for the benefit of the plaintiff or for purposes authorized by him, and not otherwise … and (b) whenever the plaintiff entrusts to the defendant a job to be performed … and relies on the defendant to procure for the plaintiff the best terms available.[15]

5.9 The Canadian case of *Smith v Frame* emphasised the importance of "vulnerability".[16] Where a fiduciary could use discretionary power to unilaterally affect the principal's practical or legal interests, the issue was whether the principal was peculiarly vulnerable to the fiduciary or at its mercy. Madam Justice Bertha Wilson suggested that the vulnerability arises because the principal is not able to stop an "injurious exercise of the power of discretion" and because of "the grave inadequacy or absence of other legal or practical remedies" to deal with the abuse of position.[17]

5.10 More generally, the cases suggest that the presence of the following factors may give rise to a fiduciary relationship:

(1) an undertaking to act on behalf of or for another person;

(2) a discretion or power to act which affects the interest of that other person; and

(3) the peculiar vulnerability of that other person, shown by:

(a) dependence on information and advice;

(b) a relationship of confidence; or

---

[12] See, for example, *Conway v Ratiu* [2005] EWCA Civ 1302 at [71], by Auld LJ.

[13] Fiduciary Duties and Regulatory Rules (1992) Law Commission Consultation Paper No 124 para 2.4.6.

[14] [1951] AC 507.

[15] [1949] 2 KB 232 at 236 (this was not affected by the later appeal to the House of Lords [1951] AC 507).

[16] [1987] 2 SCR 99 at 136.

[17] Above, at 137.

(c)   the significance of a particular transaction.

5.11   However, there is no universally accepted definition.[18] Furthermore, the courts may hold a relationship to be fiduciary for some purposes but not for others, showing the flexibility of equity-based rules.

Providing advice

5.12   Providing advice does not automatically mean that fiduciary duties apply.[19] However, fiduciary duties may arise where a client is particularly dependent on that advice.[20] Where the principal exercises independent judgment and represents their own interests, advice may be no more than providing information, so that fiduciary duties do not arise.[21]

5.13   One commentator illustrates the distinction as follows:

> Where advice is provided by a broker as a specialist skilled personal service to a client with the expectation that the client will rely on that advice, there will normally be a fiduciary relationship. Where the broker simply comments on factual matters relating to the current state of the market, although this too can be described as advice, it would normally be described in a regulatory context as information, since there is little or no potential for influencing the actions of the client.[22]

5.14   In Chapter 11 we discuss recent cases which illustrate this distinction.

---

[18]   See M Conaglen, "The Nature and Function of Fiduciary Loyalty" (2005) *Law Quarterly Review* 452 at 455.

[19]   *Burns v Kelly Peters & Associates Ltd* [1987] 16 BCLR (2d).

[20]   *Tate v Williamson* (1866) 2 Ch App 55; D Frase, "Conflicts of interest" (2012) 97(Jun) *Compliance Officer Bulletin* 1 at 5.

[21]   *James v Australia and New Zealand Banking Group Ltd* (1986) 64 ALR 347 at 366-368.

[22]   D Frase, "Conflicts of interest" (2012) 97(Jun) *Compliance Officer Bulletin* 1 at 5.

WHAT ARE THE EQUITABLE FIDUCIARY DUTIES?

An uncertain concept

5.15 It is said that "there are few legal concepts more frequently invoked but less conceptually certain than that of the fiduciary relationship".[23] In our 1992 Consultation Paper we described fiduciary obligations as "highly complex, poorly delimited and in a state of flux".[24] We quoted Lord Fletcher-Moulton in *Re Coomber*:

> There is no class of case in which one ought more carefully to bear in mind the facts of the case, when one reads the judgment of the Court on those facts, than cases which relate to fiduciary and confidential relations and the action of the court with regard to them.[25]

5.16 To call someone a "fiduciary" is perhaps misleading because there are no set rules which then apply to them: each relationship must be considered on its facts. As Lord Browne-Wilkinson pointed out in *Henderson v Merrett Syndicates Ltd*:

> The phrase "fiduciary duties" is a dangerous one, giving rise to a mistaken assumption that all fiduciaries owe the same duties in all circumstances. That is not the case.[26]

5.17 For both status-based and fact-based fiduciaries, it is necessary to consider the scope of the relationship to determine whether and what fiduciary duties apply. In *Boardman v Phipps*, Lord Upjohn described the process as follows:

> The facts and circumstances must be carefully examined to see whether in fact a purported agent... is in a fiduciary relationship .... [The] relationship must [then] be examined to see what duties are thereby imposed on the agent, to see what is the scope and ambit of the duties.[27]

The duty of loyalty

5.18 The irreducible core of fiduciary duty is the duty of loyalty.[28] The detail of how to act to promote the beneficiaries' interests is not regulated by fiduciary duties. Instead, fiduciary duties "define the points at which a court will be prepared to say that, whatever else the fiduciary might have tried to do, he has *not* acted in the beneficiaries' interests".[29]

---

[23] *LAC Minerals Ltd v International Corona Resources Ltd* (1989) 61 DLR 14 at 26, by La Forest J.

[24] Fiduciary Duties and Regulatory Rules (1992) Law Commission Consultation Paper No 124 para 2.4.1.

[25] [1911] 1 Ch 723 at 729.

[26] [1995] 2 AC 145 at 206.

[27] [1967] 2 AC 46 at 127, by Lord Upjohn.

[28] *Bristol and West Building Society v Mothew* [1998] Ch 1.

[29] P Finn, *Fiduciary Obligations* (1st ed 1977) para 30.

5.19 In our 1992 Consultation Paper we divided the duty of loyalty into four categories:[30]

    (1)   the "no conflict rule" – a fiduciary must not place themselves in a position where their own interest conflicts with the principal;

    (2)   the "no profit rule" – a fiduciary must not profit from their position at the expense of the principal;

    (3)   the "undivided loyalty rule" – a fiduciary owes undivided loyalty to their principal, and therefore must not place themselves in a position where their duty towards one principal conflicts with a duty they owe to another principal; and

    (4)   the "duty of confidentiality" – a fiduciary must not use information obtained in confidence from a principal for their own advantage or for the benefit of another.

However, a fiduciary will not be liable for breach of their duties not to make a profit and to avoid conflicts if its principal gives consent after a full and proper disclosure has been made.

5.20 These categories are not set in stone but are a helpful way to think about the duties a fiduciary might owe. In the later case of *Bristol and West Building Society v Mothew*,[31] Lord Justice Millett said that a principal is entitled to the single-minded loyalty of his fiduciary. He went on:

> This core liability has several facets. A fiduciary must act in good faith; he must not make a profit out of his trust; he must not place himself in a position where his duty and his interest may conflict; he may not act for his own benefit or the benefit a third person without the informed consent of his principal. This is not intended to be an exhaustive list, but it is sufficient to indicate the nature of fiduciary obligations.[32]

5.21 Below we describe the "no conflict", "no profit" and "undivided loyalty" rules in more detail.

---

[30] Fiduciary Duties and Regulatory Rules (1992) Law Commission Consultation Paper No 124 para 2.4.9.

[31] [1998] Ch 1.

[32] Above, at 18.

The "no conflict rule"

5.22   The "no conflict rule" requires that a fiduciary must not put themselves in a position or enter into a transaction where their personal interests conflict with those of their principal.[33] By having a personal interest in a transaction which conflicts with the interests of their principal, the fiduciary "puts himself in such a position that he has a temptation not faithfully to perform his duty to his employer".[34] Fiduciary duties guard against this temptation.

5.23   The duty is strict. It can be breached even where the conflict benefits the principal in some way,[35] where there is just a risk of conflict (as opposed to an established conflict),[36] or where the fiduciary has acted in good faith.[37] There must be a "real sensible possibility of conflict",[38] but there does not have to be an actual conflict.[39]

The "undivided loyalty rule"

5.24   Fiduciaries should not put themselves in a position where their duty to one client may conflict with their duty to another.[40] For example, in *Bampton v Rust*[41] an accountant persuaded some of his clients to lend to another client. The second client was financially unsound and defaulted. The accountant was found to be in breach of his fiduciary duty.

5.25   In *Marks and Spencer Plc v Freshfields Bruckhaus Deringer*,[42] Freshfields were undertaking general contractual work for Marks and Spencer. Mr Justice Collins held that if Freshfields then acted for a consortium in a proposed takeover of Marks and Spencer it would be in breach of its fiduciary duty. This was because it would be putting its name to documents, or at the least approving them, which were in direct conflict with its duty to act in the best interests of Marks and Spencer. Given the number of people involved in the contractual work, it was not possible to manage the conflict by means of a Chinese wall and Marks and Spencer were not prepared to consent to the conflict.

---

[33]   See *Bray v Ford* [1896] AC 44 at 51; *Aberdeen Railway Co v Blaikie Bros* (1854) 1 Macq 461 at 471.

[34]   *Boston Deep Sea Fishing & Ice Co v Ansell* (1888) 39 ChD 339 at 357, by Cotton LJ; *Harrods Ltd v Lemon* [1931] 2 KB 157 at 162 (affirmed on appeal [1931] 2 KB 157 at 168); *Eden v Ridsdales Railway Lamp & Lighting Co Ltd* (1889) 23 QBD 368 at 371.

[35]   For example, see *Aberdeen Railway Co v Blaikie Bros* (1854) 1 Macq 461 at 472; *Regal (Hastings) Ltd v Gulliver* [1967] 2 AC 134 at 153; *Boardman v Phipps* [1967] 2 AC 46 at 129.

[36]   *Hamilton v Wright* (1842) 8 ER 357 at 362.

[37]   *Bray v Ford* [1896] AC 44 at 48.

[38]   *Boardman v Phipps* [1967] 2 AC 46 at 124, by Lord Upjohn.

[39]   *Hamilton v Wright* (1842) 8 ER 357 at 362.

[40]   *Bristol & West Building Society v Mothew* [1998] Ch 1 at 18-19.

[41]   [2008] EWHC 3662.

[42]   [2004] EWHC 1337.

5.26 A leading textbook suggests that the undivided loyalty rule is "the main concern for asset managers".[43] The issue may typically arise in relation to "the allocation of investment opportunities, block trade executions between clients with similar investment objectives, and arranging transactions between clients (crossing)".[44] However, there are day-to-day difficulties in dealing with these conflicts. It has been said that:

> The concept is less easy to apply to services such as portfolio management and broker-dealing; services of a continuous or ongoing nature where a series of repetitive and often quite minor "conflicts" regularly occur.[45]

5.27 The current regulatory rules manage such conflicts by requiring a fiduciary faced with a potential conflict to disclose the conflict before providing the service. Should it face an actual conflict, it must obtain the principal's informed consent. We discuss the regulatory position in Chapter 8.

The "no profit rule"

5.28 The "no profit rule" is sometimes referred to as the duty to avoid a secret profit. It may apply even where there is no other conflict between fiduciary and principal.[46] The fiduciary must account to the principal for any profit made in breach of fiduciary duty.[47]

5.29 This duty arises even where there is no possible disadvantage to the principal. For example, in *Regal (Hastings) Ltd v Gulliver*[48] the directors of a company subscribed for shares in their own company to help it carry out a profitable expansion. A subsequent purchaser of the company brought a successful action against the directors for the recovery of the profit they had made. As Lord Russell stated:

> The rule of equity which insists on those, who by use of a fiduciary position make a profit, being liable to account for that profit, in no way depends on fraud, or absence of bona fides; or upon such questions or considerations as whether the profit would or should otherwise have gone to the plaintiff, or whether the profiteer was under a duty to obtain the source of the profit for the plaintiff, or whether he took a risk or acted as he did for the benefit of the plaintiff, or whether the plaintiff has in fact been damaged or benefited by his action. The liability arises from the mere fact of a profit having, in the stated

---

[43] D Frase, *Law and Regulation of Investment Management* (2nd ed 2011) para 8-011.

[44] Above, para 8-011.

[45] Above, para 8-017.

[46] See *Boardman v Phipps* [1966] 3 All ER 721; *Regal (Hastings) Ltd v Gulliver* [1967] 2 AC 134.

[47] *Imperial Mercantile Credit Association v Coleman* (1873) LR 6 189 at 198; *Parker v McKenna* (1874) LR 10 Ch App 96 at 124; *Regal (Hastings) Ltd v Gulliver* [1967] 2 AC 134 at 144, 149, 153, 154 and 158; *Brown v IRC* [1965] AC 244 at 256 and 265; *Boardman v Phipps* [1967] 2 AC 46 at 103, 105 and 115; *Don King Productions Inc v Warren* [2000] Ch 291 at [40] and [43]; *Cobbetts LLP v Hodge* [2009] EWHC 786 (Ch) at [101].

[48] [1967] 2 AC 134.

circumstances, been made. The profiteer, however honest and well-intentioned, cannot escape the risk of being called upon to account.[49]

5.30 The rule captures circumstances where the fiduciary obtains a personal benefit due to their position as a fiduciary. For example, it has been held to apply where a stockbroker trustee used his firm to value trust securities,[50] where a fiduciary obtains a "corporate opportunity" as a result of their position, such as a contract with a third party,[51] and to require a solicitor to account for the interest earned on client money despite the difficulties in crediting individual clients.[52]

Procuring a breach of fiduciary duty

5.31 In *Barnes v Addy*[53] the Court of Appeal stated that a third party can be directly liable to beneficiaries of a trust where "they assist with knowledge in a dishonest and fraudulent design on the part of the trustees".[54] The third party does not need to have personally benefited or have received trust property to be liable.[55] The authority of *Barnes v Addy* in Scots law is controversial.[56]

5.32 As we illustrate below, in *Wilson v Hurstanger Ltd*,[57] a mortgage lender was held responsible for procuring a breach of fiduciary duty by paying a commission.

MODIFYING FIDUCIARY DUTIES THROUGH CONSENT

5.33 A fiduciary will not be liable for breach of the fiduciary duties not to make a profit and to avoid conflicts if the principal gives consent after a full and proper disclosure has been made to them.[58] This is often termed "fully informed consent".

The principles

5.34 There "is no precise formula" for what amounts to fully informed consent; it is a question of fact in the circumstances of each case.[59]

---

[49] Above, at 144-145.

[50] *Williams v Barton* [1927] 2 Ch 9.

[51] *Industrial Development Consultants Ltd v Cooley* [1972] 1 WLR 443.

[52] *Brown v IRC* [1965] AC 244.

[53] (1874) LR 9 Ch App 244.

[54] Above, at 252, by Lord Selborne.

[55] *Ultraframe (UK) Ltd v Fielding* [2005] EWHC 1638 (Ch).

[56] It is followed in *Commonwealth Oil & Gas Co Ltd v Baxter* [2009] CSIH 75, 2010 SC 156; but see the criticism of N Whitty, "The 'no profit from another's fraud' rule and the 'knowing receipt' muddle" (2013) 17 *Edinburgh Law Review* 37.

[57] [2007] EWCA Civ 299.

[58] *Boardman v Phipps* [1964] 1 WLR 993, affirmed [1967] 2 AC 46; *New Zealand Netherlands Society "Oranje" Inc v Kuys* [1973] 2 All ER 1222 at 1227. For Scots law see Gloag & Henderson, *The Law of Scotland* (13th ed 2012) para 3.03.

[59] *Maguire v Makaronis* (1997) 188 CLR 449 at 466; *Farah Constructions Pty Ltd v Say-Dee Pty Ltd* (2007) 230 CLR 89.

5.35   In general, consent must be positively shown and the fiduciary bears the burden of proving full and proper disclosure.[60] It is not sufficient merely to disclose that the fiduciary has an interest[61] or to make statements that would put the principal on inquiry.[62] Further, it is no defence for the fiduciary to assert that if they had asked for permission it would have been given.[63]

An illustration: Wilson v Hurstanger Ltd

5.36   The case of *Wilson v Hurstanger Ltd*[64] illustrates these principles. Mr Wilson and Ms Burton entered into a loan with Hurstanger for £8,000 to pay off their mortgage arrears. They applied for the loan through a broker, Mr Dunk, who was to receive an arrangement fee of £1,000 out of the £8,000 loan. The contract between the borrowers and Hurstanger stated that "In certain circumstances this company does pay commission to brokers/agents". Hurstanger paid the broker a commission of £240, in addition to the arrangement fee of £1,000, Evidence at trial was that "it had become necessary for small companies like [Hurstanger] to pay commission to brokers to attract their business".[65]

5.37   On appeal Lord Justice Tuckey stated that the relationship between the borrowers and broker "was obviously a fiduciary one".[66] By being paid a commission Mr Dunk "obviously put himself in a position where he had a conflict of interest": the borrowers wanted him to find the best deal but he had an incentive to look for the biggest commission.[67] The court found that the broker could only act in this way if the borrowers had consented with their full knowledge of the material circumstances and the nature and extent of the broker's interest.[68] The burden of proving full disclosure lay on the broker.

---

[60]   *Dunne v English* (1874) LR 18 Eq 524; *Hurstanger v Wilson* [2007] EWCA Civ 299 at [35]; *JD Wetherspoon Plc v Van De Berg & Co Ltd* [2009] EWHC 639 (Ch) at [68]; *Cobbetts LLP v Hodge* [2009] EWHC 786 (Ch) at [108].

[61]   *Imperial Mercantile Credit Association Co v Coleman* (1873) LR 6 189; *Alexander v Automatic Telephone Co* [1900] 2 Ch 56; *Gluckstein v Barnes* [1900] AC 240; *Gray v New Augarita Porcupine Mines* [1952] 3 DLR 1; *Cobbetts LLP v Hodge* [2009] EWHC 786 (Ch) at [110]; *FHR European Ventures LLP v Mankarious* [2011] EWHC 2308 (Ch) at [78] (this aspect of the decision was not affected by the later appeal [2013] EWCA Civ 17).

[62]   *Dunne v English* (1874) LR 18 Eq 524 at 535; *Novoship (UK) Ltd v Mikhaylyuk* [2012] EWHC 3586 (Comm) at [83]; see also *Swale v Ipswich Tannery Co Ltd* (1906) 11 Com Cas 88 at 86-97.

[63]   *Murad v al-Saraj* [2005] EWCA Civ 959; *Gidman v Barron* [2003] EWHC 153 (Ch) at [126]; *FHR European Ventures LLP v Mankarious* [2011] EWHC 2308 (Ch) at [79] (this aspect of the decision was not affected by the later appeal [2013] EWCA Civ 17).

[64]   [2007] EWCA Civ 299.

[65]   Above, at [31].

[66]   Above, at [34].

[67]   Above, at [34].

[68]   Above, at [35].

5.38 No disclosure at all would have been "a blatant breach of his fiduciary duty".[69] But on the facts the court felt that the broker ought to have gone further; because the borrowers were "vulnerable and unsophisticated",[70] the broker should have disclosed the precise amount. This was because it was "necessary to bring home to such borrowers the potential conflict of interest".[71] Accordingly, informed consent was not obtained.[72] Interestingly, the court found that the borrowers had a claim against Hurstanger as it procured the broker's breach of fiduciary duty.[73]

Commission payments between sophisticated participants

5.39 Where the parties are sophisticated the issue is usually dealt with through a contract term. For example, a leading textbook suggests in a portfolio management agreement, such a clause might read:

> Unless otherwise required by the laws or regulations of any jurisdiction to which the client is subject, neither the firm nor any of its affiliates shall be liable to account to the client for any profit, commission or remuneration made or received from or by reason of transactions effected for the account of the client or any connected transactions (provided that the persons effecting such transactions shall do so on the best terms reasonably obtainable having regard to the interest of the client).[74]

5.40 As we explore in Chapter 11, where contracts are made between sophisticated parties the courts will generally uphold such contract terms and subject fiduciary duties to the explicit terms of the contract.

---

[69] [2007] EWCA Civ 299 at [39].

[70] Above, at [37].

[71] Above, at [37].

[72] Above, at [45].

[73] Above, at [49].

[74] D Frase, *Law and Regulation of Investment Management* (2nd ed 2011) para 8-020.

Consent in a trust context

5.41 The principle of consent also applies in a trust context. As a leading textbook describes it for English law:

> A trustee can safely depart from the provisions of the trust instrument or take an administrative step not authorised by the instrument or the general law if all the beneficiaries affected are of full age and capacity and agree to this being done.[75]

5.42 This will normally require the consent of all the beneficiaries affected by the decision. A fiduciary may not act on the wishes of one beneficiary against the others.[76] Further, although obtaining consent will protect a fiduciary against an action for breach of their duties, the beneficiaries cannot compel the fiduciary to act or deprive them of a discretion.[77]

5.43 In addition, where a fiduciary is a trustee, the trust instrument may expressly authorise what would otherwise amount to a breach of fiduciary duty, for example to allow trustees to charge fees.[78]

REMEDIES FOR BREACH OF FIDUCIARY DUTY

5.44 Breach of fiduciary duty may give rise to a wide range of remedies. These include:

(1) rescission (or in Scotland reduction), where the transaction is unwound and the parties are restored to where they were previously;[79]

(2) account of profits (or in Scotland a claim for unjustified enrichment), where the wrongdoer must pay the claimant the profit they have obtained by the wrongdoing;[80]

---

[75] *Lewin on Trusts* (18th ed 2012) para 45-03. In Scots law the beneficiaries may authorise acts of the trustee otherwise in breach of the latter's fiduciary duty; but departure from the trust deed generally requires authorisation by the court: see Gloag & Henderson, *The Law of Scotland* (13th ed 2012) paras 41.09, 41.15. The Trusts (Scotland) Act 1921, s 4 (as amended) confers a wide range of powers that trustees may exercise so long as the acts are not at variance with the trust terms or purposes. But a third party dealing with trustees apparently exercising section 4 powers need not inquire into the actual trust terms or purposes to make the transaction effective (Trusts (Scotland) Act 1961, s 2(1)). This will not however affect liability to beneficiaries or co-trustees if the transaction was beyond these actual powers.

[76] *Langston v Ollivant* (1807) G Coop 33; *Pell v De Winton* (1857) 2 De G & J 13; *Whitney v Smith* (1869) 4 Ch App 513; *Bromley v Kelly* (1870) 39 LJ Ch 274, cited in *Seton on Judgments* (7th ed) 1930.

[77] *Lewin on Trusts* (18th ed 2012) para 45-04; *Re Brockbank* [1948] Ch 206; *Stephenson v Barclays Bank Trust Co Ltd* [1975] 1 WLR 882 at 889.

[78] *Space Investments Ltd v Canadian Imperial Bank of Commerce Trust Co (Bahamas) Ltd* [1986] 1 WLR 1072 at 1075; Gloag & Henderson, *The Law of Scotland* (13th ed 2012), para 41.15.

[79] *Guinness plc v Saunders* [1990] 2 AC 663 at 697; Gloag & Henderson, *The Law of Scotland* (13th ed 2012) para 41.15.

[80] *Regal (Hastings) Ltd v Gulliver* [1967] 2 AC 134 at 158; D Cabrelli, "Scotland" in D Busch and D DeMott (eds), *Liability of Asset Managers* (1st ed 2012) para 15.21.

(3) in England & Wales, proprietary remedies, so that the principal is protected should their fiduciary become insolvent;[81] and

(4) equitable compensation in England & Wales. Although the claimant would need to show that they have been caused loss, compensation is provided on a generous basis. Unlike damages for breach of contract, it appears that the claimant does not need to show that the loss was foreseeable.[82]

5.45 The first three remedies "are primarily restitutionary and restorative rather than compensatory".[83] They focus on undoing the wrong rather than on compensating the claimant for their loss. Importantly, they operate without the claimant being required to show loss.

Cases which restrict the use of "fiduciary remedies"

5.46 These equitable remedies may prove extremely generous to claimants. They are particularly valuable in a declining market. They have led claimants to argue that, where an investment should not have been made, the whole of the sum should be returned.[84] As we see in Chapter 6, equitable remedies may also be sought by trustees wishing to "undo" their own mistakes, particularly for failed tax avoidance schemes.[85]

5.47 The courts have expressed concern about these remedies. Since the 1990s, they have attempted to restrict claims for breach of fiduciary duties and the equitable remedies that go with them. As we illustrate below, they have distinguished between fiduciary duties in a strict sense and other duties to which a fiduciary is subject, including duties of care and duties arising from the exercise of a power.

---

[81] In *Sinclair Investments (UK) Ltd v Versailles Trade Finance Ltd* [2011] EWCA Civ 347 the Court of Appeal stressed that there were limits on this remedy. It would only apply where the money had been the principal's property or had been acquired by taking advantage of the principal's rights. Money could be recovered from those who had been given it, but not from good faith purchasers who had given value for it. This issue was the subject of further discussion in the decision of the Court of Appeal in *FHR European Ventures LLP v Mankarious* [2013] EWCA Civ 17. The position in Scotland is unclear and so controversial: for a survey see L Macgregor, *The Law of Agency in Scotland* (1st ed 2013) paras 6.38-6.47.

[82] *Target Holdings v Redfern* [1996] AC 421 at 434.

[83] *Bristol and West Building Society v Mothew* [1998] Ch 1 at 18, by Millett LJ.

[84] See, for example, the argument in *Target Holdings v Redfern* [1996] AC 421.

[85] See discussion of *Pitt v Holt* [2013] UKSC 26 at paras 6.8-6.13 below.

Bristol and West Building Society v Mothew

5.48 The background to *Bristol and West Building Society v Mothew*[86] was the collapse in property prices in the early 1990s. When mortgage lenders suffered heavy losses, many attempted to recover those losses from negligent valuers and solicitors. As Lord Justice Millett explained:

> Believing that the common law rules of causation and remoteness of damage might not enable them to recover the whole amount of their loss they have turned to equity and alleged breach of trust or fiduciary duty.[87]

5.49 The claimant building society brought a claim against a solicitor. The solicitor had acted both for a couple buying a house for £73,000 and for the building society, in connection with a mortgage of £59,000. The building society instructed the solicitor to report any proposal that the buyers might create a second mortgage. The solicitor said there was no such intention. In fact, this was a careless misrepresentation. The solicitor had been told that the buyers intended to secure an existing loan of £3,350 against the house. When the buyers later defaulted, the building society enforced their mortgage and the house was sold at a loss.

5.50 Lord Justice Millett explained the different measures of loss which would apply to negligence compared to breach of fiduciary duties. Where at common law a party had given inaccurate information to enable another to make a decision:

> The measure of damages is not necessarily the full amount of the loss which the plaintiff has suffered by having entered into the transaction but only that part if any of such loss as is properly attributable to the inaccuracy of the information. If the plaintiff would have suffered the same loss even if the facts had actually been as represented the defendant is not liable.[88]

5.51 In this case, the effect of the second mortgage may have been negligible: it was for a small amount; it was for an existing debt; and it may not have contributed to the buyers' default. The building society's damages for negligence were likely to be low. However, if they could show a breach of fiduciary duty leading to an equitable remedy they would be entitled to £59,000, less the amount received for the sale of the property.

---

[86] [1998] Ch 1.

[87] Above, at 6.

[88] Above, at 12.

5.52 The Court of Appeal did not believe that it was appropriate to impose such generous damages in cases where a fiduciary had not acted dishonestly or intentionally, but only due to an oversight. Lord Justice Millett therefore delivered a stern warning against the over-use of the term "fiduciary duty".

> The expression "fiduciary duty" is properly confined to those duties which are peculiar to fiduciaries and the breach of which attracts legal consequences differing from those consequent upon the breach of other duties. Unless the expression is so limited it is lacking in practical utility. In this sense it is obvious that not every breach of duty by a fiduciary is a breach of fiduciary duty.[89]

5.53 He said that this was not just a question of semantics: "it goes to the very heart of the concept of breach of fiduciary duty and the availability of equitable remedies".[90] The core of fiduciary duty is "the obligation of loyalty", so breach "connotes disloyalty or infidelity".[91] Mere incompetence is not enough.

5.54 Following this warning, we have been careful to distinguish between the duty of loyalty and the many other duties owed by trustees and others when they act on another's behalf. These other duties are discussed in Chapter 6.

CONCLUSION

5.55 Fiduciary duties are designed to protect those who are "vulnerable" when others have discretionary powers to act on their behalf. When a person acts in a fiduciary capacity, the law requires them to be loyal. They should not make a secret profit: where they do, the courts will require that profit to be paid to the principal. Nor should a fiduciary allow a conflict between their principal's interests and their own interests, or those of others. Principals may consent to conflicts of interest and retention of profit but the consent must be fully informed.

5.56 These principles are highly flexible, but also uncertain. They tend to sit in the background of other more explicit duties, such as the duty to act with reasonable care and skill. Recent cases have been at pains to distinguish careless or minor mistakes from breaches of fiduciary duty. In doing so they have drawn a sharp distinction between fiduciary duties and other duties on fiduciaries, such as those associated with the exercise of a power or duties of care. In the next chapter we discuss the other duties which constrain the use of fiduciary power.

---

[89] [1998] Ch 1 at 16.

[90] Above, at 17.

[91] Above, at 18.

CHAPTER 6
DUTIES ON THE EXERCISE OF A POWER AND DUTIES OF CARE

6.1 As we have seen, fiduciary duties (in the strict legal sense) sit alongside other duties which constrain the way fiduciaries and others exercise their powers. Here we look first at duties connected to the exercise of a power and then at duties of care. Finally we consider how far trustees may exclude their liability to others.

DUTIES CONNECTED TO THE EXERCISE OF A POWER

What is a "power"?

6.2 The word "power" attracts various legal meanings. Broadly it means any ability to alter legal relations between parties.[1] However, powers are more commonly discussed in the context of equitable relationships and trusts. Where a person has authority to deal with or dispose of property owned beneficially by another, they are said to have a "power" in relation to that property.[2] Powers are not necessarily confined to trustees,[3] though trusts are the clearest and most obvious example. A typical example is the power of appointment, where a trustee is empowered to select, from a class of individuals, who should take the benefit of the property held under the trust.

6.3 Pension trustees are often given significant powers, including the power to amend the rules of the scheme; to increase (or "augment") members' benefits; or to deal with a funding surplus. In the present context, however, the most important power is the power of investment, provided by section 34(1) of the Pensions Act 1995 or under a trust deed. This entitles trustees and investment managers[4] to deal with the property of others to create binding contractual relationships. This power is subject to the Pensions Acts, discussed in Chapter 7. It is also subject to the trust deed and to trust law more generally. However, judges have also developed specific duties which attach to the exercise of a power.

---

[1] W Hohfeld, *Fundamental Legal Conceptions As Applied in Judicial Reasoning* (1st ed 1919) p 50-51.

[2] *Freme v Clement* (1881) 18 Ch D 499 at 504, by Jessel MR, defining a power of appointment. See G Thomas and A Hudson, *The Law of Trusts* (2nd ed 2010) para 13.01; *Thomas on Powers* (2nd ed 2012) para 1.01.

[3] See G Thomas and A Hudson, *The Law of Trusts* (2nd ed 2010) para 11.01; *Thomas on Powers* (2nd ed 2012) para 1.40.

[4] The Pensions Act 1995 uses the language of "fund manager", but the terminology of "investment manager" has been preferred throughout.

6.4 These duties are not necessarily confined to those classified as fiduciaries.[5] However, while non-fiduciaries are free to decide whether to exercise their powers, fiduciaries must consider actively whether to exercise them.[6] A fiduciary is "prohibited from sleeping on those powers given to him by virtue of his office".[7]

6.5 Below we describe the law in England and Wales. As we explain at paragraphs 6.31 to 6.32, the law in Scotland is similar, but the grounds of challenge appear more comprehensive.

What duties attach to the exercise of a power?

6.6 Here we outline six duties, drawn from the case law:[8]

(1) the duty to exercise the power for the purpose it was intended;

(2) the duty not to exercise a power fraudulently;

(3) the duty not to act under the dictation of another;

(4) the duty not to fetter discretion;[9]

(5) the duty not to act capriciously; and

(6) the duty of adequate deliberation.

6.7 The most important duty is the first: a power must be exercised for the purpose for which it was given. This deals with substance. The others are procedural, and describe how the power should be used. The various duties are not necessarily distinct; instead, they are overlapping ways of characterising the main aspects of this area of law.

Pitt v Holt

6.8 The law in this area has recently been considered by the Supreme Court in *Pitt v Holt*.[10] The case illustrates that the courts will allow trustees discretion in exercising their powers, and will act cautiously when asked to reverse decisions that trustees have made.

---

[5] For examples of these principles being applied to non-fiduciaries, see *Re Joicey* [1915] 2 Ch 115; *Re Cooke* [1922] 1 Ch 292; and *Downsview Nominees Ltd v First City Corp Ltd* [1993] AC 295 at 317.

[6] *Re Gulbenkian's Settlement* [1968] Ch 126; *Wishaw v Stephens* [1970] AC 508.

[7] P Finn, *Fiduciary Obligations* (1st ed 1977) para 74.

[8] In Scots law the duties attached to powers have been most explored in relation to trusts: *Gloag & Henderson: The Law of Scotland* (13th ed 2012) paras 41.09-41.10, 41.13-41.14.

[9] See *Re Cooke* [1922] 1 Ch 292, where the power was not a fiduciary one.

[10] *Pitt v Holt* [2013] UKSC 26. In this case the Supreme Court joined the appeals in *Pitt v Holt* and *Futter v Futter*. Both cases were the subject of separate decisions in the High Court. The Court of Appeal also heard both appeals together: see [2011] EWCA Civ 197.

6.9   In the two joined cases, trustees had relied on apparently competent advisers to guide them on how best to deal with money subject to the trusts. The advisers had overlooked tax implications and recommended arrangements which subjected the money to significant capital gains or inheritance tax liabilities which could have been avoided. The claimants brought actions to set aside the arrangements and start again. They argued that the settlements were ineffective because the trustees failed to take into account a material consideration.

6.10   The court accepted that where trustees make voluntary dispositions which they have no power to make, that disposition is void and the money may be reclaimed. However, Lord Walker expressed concern about how that rule had been used. He noted three cases since 2000 in which trustees had attempted to use the rule where tax-planning and other arrangements had gone wrong. He quoted Mr Justice Park:

> There must surely be some limits. It cannot be right that whenever trustees do something which they later regret and think that they ought not to have done, they can say that they never did it in the first place.[11]

6.11   The Supreme Court set out to provide those limits, distinguishing between three types of breach of trust:

(1)   cases where trustees went beyond the scope of their power, and did something which they had no right to do (referred to as "excessive execution");

(2)   cases where a power was used for an improper purpose (labelled "equitable fraud"); and

(3)   cases where the trustees failed to give proper consideration to relevant matters (labelled "inadequate deliberation").

6.12   In the first two cases, the transaction was void. In the third case, it was "voidable", which meant that the court had a high degree of flexibility in the range of possible responses.

6.13   The court found that in these two cases the trustees had not breached any of the three duties. In particular, the trustees had not failed to consider relevant matters. Although tax implications are clearly a relevant matter, the trustees had relied on professional advice. Trustees were not in breach of duty if that advice turned out to be wrong. The case illustrates the courts' caution in intervening with trustees' decisions, and we draw on some statements to this effect in the following discussion.

---

[11]   *Pitt v Holt* [2013] UKSC 26 at [35], quoting *Breadner v Granville-Grossman* [2001] Ch 523 at 543.

Duty to act for the purpose for which the power was given

6.14 For the purposes of our project, this is the key duty. As the House of Lords said in 1864:

> A party having a power like this must fairly and honestly execute it without having any ulterior object to be accomplished.[12]

6.15 Going beyond the permitted bounds of a power is known as "excessive execution".[13] It is "an attempt to go beyond that which is authorized by the express or implied terms of the particular power or by law".[14] In the context of a trust, this issue typically arises where a trustee distributes trust funds to individuals who are not proper objects of the power or improperly delegates their power to another.[15] Where a power is exercised for the wrong purpose, the act is void and the courts may reverse it.

6.16 The scope of the power is an objective test. In *Pitt v Holt* Lord Justice Lloyd stated:

> The test has to be objective, by reference to whether that which was done, with all its defects and consequent limitations, is capable of being regarded as beneficial to the intended object, or not. If it is so capable, then it satisfies the requirement of the power that it should be for that person's benefit. Otherwise it does not satisfy that requirement. In the latter case it would follow that it is outside the scope of the power, it is not an exercise of the power at all, and it cannot take effect under that power.[16]

Fraudulent execution

6.17 This is also known as the duty not to commit a fraud upon a power. The use of the word "fraud" in this context is not used to mean deceit, but is used in a broad sense to indicate an act which is not right.[17] It prevents a donee from exercising a power with the wrong intention.

---

[12] *The Duke of Portland v Lady Topham* (1864) 11 HL Cas 32 at [55], by Lord St Leonards.

[13] See *Pitt v Holt* [2013] UKSC 26 at [60].

[14] G Thomas and A Hudson, *The Law of Trusts* (2nd ed 2010) para 18.01.

[15] For an example of both, see *Re Boulton's Settlement Trust* [1928] Ch 703.

[16] *Pitt v Holt* [2011] EWCA Civ 197 at [66].

[17] *Re Dick* [1953] Ch 343 at 360.

6.18 Clearly, this duty is closely linked to the first. However, while the first duty focuses on the question whether, objectively, the act can be said to benefit the intended beneficiary, this duty focuses on motive. If a power is exercised in good faith in a way which goes beyond the scope of the power it will constitute excessive execution. However, where the purpose or intention is to go beyond the scope of the power it will constitute a fraud on the power.[18] In *Pitt v Holt*, Lord Walker thought it may need its own category:

> A fraudulent appointment (that is, one shown to have been made for a positively improper purpose) may need a separate pigeon-hole somewhere between the categories of excessive execution and inadequate deliberation.[19]

6.19 This duty was explained by Lord Parker in *Vatcher v Paull*:

> It merely means that the power has been exercised for a purpose, or with an intention, beyond the scope of or not justified by the instrument creating the power. Perhaps the most common instance of this is where the exercise is due to some bargain between the appointor and appointee, whereby the appointor, or some other person not an object of the power, is to derive a benefit. But such a bargain is not essential. It is enough that the appointor's purpose and intention is to secure a benefit for himself, or some other person not an object of the power.[20]

6.20 In *Dalriada Trustees v Faulds*[21] the court considered whether loans made between six pension schemes to enable their members to have access to their pension capital prior to retirement were a valid exercise of the pension trustees' investment powers. The court primarily decided the case on the basis that the loans were unauthorised payments under the Finance Act 2004. However, the court found that the payments would have been void as a fraud on the power of investment in any event. The loans were beyond the scope of the power and made for an ulterior purpose: the schemes were set up for the purpose of providing benefits on retirement, death or similar circumstances and not to set up a scheme to allow loans to members.[22]

---

[18] *Thomas on Powers* (2nd ed 2012) para 9.02; see also *Howard Smith v Ampol Petroleum* [1974] AC 821.

[19] *Pitt v Holt* [2013] UKSC 26 at [62].

[20] [1915] AC 372 at 378.

[21] [2011] EWHC 3391 (Ch).

[22] Above, at [66]-[72].

Duty not to act under the dictation of another

6.21 A power is given to an individual personally. Any exercise of that power must be a personal and conscious act of that individual and not dictated by another: the "law does not permit him to be another's puppet".[23] However, donees are permitted to take advice so long as the ultimate decision is made by the donee of the power.[24] Further, the default rule may be modified by, for example, an express provision in a trust instrument or statute.[25]

6.22 Trustees should not act at the dictation of their beneficiaries,[26] though they may consult their beneficiaries.[27] There is conflicting authority on whether beneficiaries can compel trustees to vote in a particular way in relation to shares held on their behalf. In *Butt v Kelson*[28] the Court of Appeal held that the beneficiaries were entitled to be treated as if they were the registered shareholders and could compel the trustee-directors to vote. However, this appears to conflict with other authority, such as *Re Brockbank*,[29] which was not cited in *Butt*. A leading textbook suggests that *Butt* should be treated as an exceptional case and confined to its particular facts.[30]

Duty not to fetter the discretion

6.23 Donees must not agree to exercise their powers in a pre-determined way. They must honestly and appropriately consider the facts and circumstances that are relevant at the time they act which they knew of or ought to have known.[31] This is because the circumstances may have changed by the time the discretion is exercised, with the result that the fetter could have an entirely different and unintended effect.[32]

---

[23] P Finn, *Fiduciary Obligations* (1st ed 1977) para 42.

[24] *Re Poole* (1882) 21 Ch D 397 at 404; *Re Smith ex parte Brown* (1886) 17 QBD 488; *Wilson v Turner* (1883) 22 Ch D 521; *Re Pauling's Settlement Trusts* [1964] Ch 303; *Turner v Turner* [1984] Ch 100.

[25] For example, trustees by virtue of s 25 of the Trustee Act 1925 and Part IV of the Trustee Act 2000.

[26] See for example *Selby v Bowie* (1863) 8 LT 372 (instruction to accept a particular offer to purchase trust property) and *Re Brockbank* [1948] Ch 206 (instruction to appoint a particular person as trustee).

[27] See for example *Re Agricultural Industries* [1952] 1 All ER 1188 at 1190.

[28] [1952] Ch 197.

[29] [1948] Ch 206. See *Re Whichelow* [1954] 2 WLR 5 at 8, where Upjohn J pointed out that the decision was difficult to reconcile.

[30] G Thomas and A Hudson, *The Law of Trusts* (2nd ed 2010) para 11.38.

[31] *Re Hurst* (1892) 67 LT 96 at 99, by Lindley LJ. See also *Cowan v Scargill* [1985] Ch 270; *Martin v Edinburgh City Council* [1989] Pens LR 9, 1988 SLT 329; and *Nestle v National Westminster Bank plc* [1993] 1 WLR 1260.

[32] For example, *Stannard v Fisons Pension Trust Ltd* [1992] IRLR 27.

Duty not to act capriciously

6.24 This rule ensures that a power is not exercised in an irrational way. It provides a default level of protection allowing the court "to say that, whatever the fiduciary might himself believe, he has manifestly not acted in the beneficiaries' interests even though he has not positively acted for another's benefit or discriminated between them".[33] It captures decisions which "go well beyond mere error of judgment"[34] and which might be labelled "arbitrary", "capricious", "wanton",[35] "utterly unreasonable and absurd",[36] "vexatious, oppressive or wholly unjustifiable"[37] or "mischievous or ruinous".[38] For example, in *Re Peters*, Sir George Jessel MR stated that:

> The Court will not interfere unless the trustee is doing that which is so utterly unreasonable and absurd that no reasonable man would so act.[39]

Duty of adequate deliberation

6.25 This duty is concerned with individuals who exercise a power without having given proper consideration to relevant matters.[40] An individual's decision is voidable if it is within the scope of a power but fails to take into account a relevant consideration which would or might[41] have led to a different decision.

---

[33] P Finn, *Fiduciary Obligations* (1st ed 1977) para 155.

[34] See G Thomas and A Hudson, *The Law of Trusts* (2nd ed 2010) para 11.80.

[35] These three labels are taken from *Re Bell Brothers ex parte Hodgson* (1891) 65 LT 245.

[36] *Re Peters ex parte Lloyd* (1882) 47 LT 64 at 65, by Jessel MR.

[37] *Freeman v Parker* [1895-99] All ER Rep 1013 at 1015, by Lindley LJ.

[38] *Re Brittlebank* (1881) 30 WR 99 at 100, by Kay J.

[39] (1882) 47 LT 64 at 65.

[40] *Pitt v Holt* [2013] UKSC 26 at [2].

[41] The Supreme Court in *Pitt v Holt* declined to reach a definitive ruling on this, instead leaving it for courts to reach "the best practical solution" on the facts of each case. See [2013] UKSC 26 at [92].

6.26 In determining what is relevant, it is necessary to consider the purpose for which the discretion was conferred.[42] Further, it must have been a consideration which existed at the time the discretion was exercised, which was known or knowable and which would or did have an appreciable impact on the decision made.[43] There are no "hard and fast rules" as to what might be relevant.[44] However, it is fairly well settled that the tax consequences of a decision will be relevant.[45] As Mr Justice Patten stated in *Abacus Trust Co (Isle of Man) v NSPCC*:

> The financial consequences for the beneficiaries of any intended exercise of a fiduciary power cannot be assessed without reference to their fiscal implications. The two seem to me inseparable.[46]

6.27 The court has stressed that there are limits to what is relevant. In *Breadner v Granville Grossman*[47] the court declined to apply the rule to a missed time limit for the exercise of a power of appointment, stating that "there must surely be some limits".[48]

6.28 *Pitt v Holt* sets out some important principles for assessing whether a trustee has considered relevant circumstances. First, trustees are allowed a wide margin:

> It is not enough to show that the trustees' deliberations have fallen short of the highest possible standards, or that the court would, on a surrender of discretion by the trustees, have acted in a different way.[49]

6.29 There must be a serious breach for a court to intervene. In the trust context, Lord Walker said that, apart from exceptional circumstances (such as an impasse reached by honest and reasonable trustees) only conduct sufficiently serious to amount to a breach of fiduciary duty would justify judicial intervention.[50]

---

[42] See *Harris v Lord Shuttleworth* [1994] ICR 989.

[43] G Thomas and A Hudson, *The Law of Trusts* (2nd ed 2010) paras 11.65-11.67; see also *Wild v Smith* [1996] Pens LR 275.

[44] G Thomas and A Hudson, *The Law of Trusts* (2nd ed 2010) para 11.59.

[45] *Karger v Paul* [1984] VR 161; *Abacus Trust Co (Isle of Man) Ltd v NSPCC* [2001] STC 1344 at [16]-[17]; *Pitt v Holt* [2013] UKSC 26 at [65].

[46] [2001] STC 1344 at [16].

[47] [2001] Ch 523.

[48] Above, at [61], by Park J.

[49] [2013] UKSC 26 at [73].

[50] Above, at [39] and [73].

6.30 Further, there is no breach if the trustee was badly advised. In other words, a trustee will not breach this duty if having identified the relevant considerations and used all proper care and diligence in obtaining the relevant information and advice, it turns out that the information was partial or incorrect.[51] The court stated:

> If in exercising a fiduciary power trustees have been given, and have acted on, information or advice from an apparently trustworthy source, and what the trustees purport to do is within the scope of their power, the only direct remedy available (either to the trustees themselves, or to a disadvantaged beneficiary) must be based on mistake (there may be an indirect remedy in the form of a claim against one or more advisers for damages for breach of professional duties of care).[52]

The law in Scotland

6.31 These cases are not binding in Scotland, although they are of persuasive value. Under Scots law, a challenge to the exercise of fiduciary power by trustees appears possible under the common law on the following grounds: consideration by the trustees of the wrong question, a failure of the trustees to apply their minds to the right question, the trustees' perversely shutting their eyes to the facts, or trustees' failure to act honestly or in good faith.[53] These grounds are influenced by the law concerning judicial review of administrative action, and are somewhat more comprehensive than those recognised in England. The Scottish Law Commission has consulted on a suggestion that a statutory right to challenge the exercise of fiduciary powers is granted,[54] based on the common law grounds, and will be reporting in 2014.

6.32 Furthermore, in Scotland a court may relieve a trustee from personal liability for breach of trust, where the trustee is considered to have acted honestly and reasonably and ought fairly to be excused.[55] This will not aid a negligent trustee but may provide relief for one in breach of a fiduciary duty or acting beyond powers.[56]

---

[51] [2013] UKSC 26 at [40]-[41].

[52] Above, at [41]. Later in the judgment, at [90], the court commented that the possibility of a claim for damages would have no effect on the operation of this rule.

[53] *Dundee General Hospitals v Bell's Trustees* 1952 SC (HL) 78 at 92; 1952 SLT 270 at 275.

[54] Scottish Law Commission, Consultation Paper on Defects in the Exercise of Fiduciary Powers (2011).

[55] Trusts (Scotland) Act 1921, s 32.

[56] The rule is discussed in Scottish Law Commission Discussion Paper No 123 on Breach of Trust (2003) Part 6.

DUTIES OF CARE: GENERAL PRINCIPLES

6.33 Where a person breaches a duty of care, the courts will require them to compensate the victim for losses caused by their negligence. Fiduciaries are subject to both fiduciary duties and duties of care, but the two are not the same. In Chapter 5 we drew attention to Lord Justice Millett's warning in *Bristol and West Building Society v Mothew* that "not every breach of duty by a fiduciary is a breach of fiduciary duty".[57] Similar warnings occur in other cases; in *Girardet v Crease & Co,* Madam Justice Mary Southin commented that:

> The word "fiduciary" is flung around now as if it applied to all breaches of duty by solicitors, directors of companies and so forth... to say that simple carelessness in giving advice is such a breach is a perversion of words.[58]

6.34 Fiduciary duties consider the motive or the purpose of a decision, while duties of care guard against carelessness and incompetence.

6.35 Duties of care arise in the law of trusts, tort[59] and contract. They apply to a greater or lesser extent to all participants in the investment chain and are not confined to those with fiduciary responsibility. Here we briefly describe, in general terms, when duties of care might arise in contract and tort. We then look in more detail at trustees' duties of care.

Professional negligence

6.36 It is well established that a person who contracts with another to provide a service must provide the service with reasonable care and skill.[60] Where someone purports to offer a professional service, they will be held to the standards of a competent professional. As was said in *Bolam v Friern Hospital Management Committee*:

> The test is the standard of the ordinary skilled man exercising and professing to have that special skill. A man need not possess the highest expert skill; it is well established law that it is sufficient he exercises the ordinary skill of an ordinary competent man exercising that particular art.[61]

---

[57] [1998] Ch 1 at 16.

[58] (1987) 11 BCLR (2d) 361 at 362.

[59] Or delict in Scotland.

[60] Where the supplier is acting in the course of a business, this is now in statutory form for England & Wales: see Supply of Goods and Services Act 1982, s 13. For Scotland see W McBryde, *The Law of Contract in Scotland* (3rd ed 2007) para 9.37.

[61] [1957] 1 WLR 582 at 586, by McNair J. For Scots law see *Hunter v Hanley* 1955 SC 200.

6.37   Where there is a contractual relationship between the parties, duties in tort[62] tend to mirror contractual duties.[63] In particular, duties in tort[64] may be modified by the terms of the contract.[65] In Chapter 11 we discuss the importance the courts attach to contract terms.

Duties of care in the absence of a contract

6.38   There are also situations where a contract is not in place, but where one party has wronged another through negligence. Historically, the law of tort[66] protected against damage to the person and tangible property, but liability has been expanded. In some circumstances the courts have held that a party should be held responsible for intangible financial losses caused by their negligence.

6.39   An example is "negligent misstatement". This tort was first recognised by the House of Lords in *Hedley Byrne v Heller*.[67] An advertising company sought references from their client's bankers to establish their client's creditworthiness. The bankers negligently indicated that the client was creditworthy, but included on their paperwork an explicit disclaimer of responsibility for the advice. The information supplied was incorrect and the company lost money.

6.40   The House of Lords held that to create a duty of care the defendant would have had to have undertaken or assumed some responsibility towards the claimant.[68] On the facts, the bank's disclaimer was sufficient to prevent the necessary relationship between the bank and advertising company arising such that the bank did not owe a duty of care.

6.41   In *Caparo Industries v Dickman*,[69] the House of Lords provided further guidance as to when a duty of care would be recognised. Here the claimant relied on an auditor's report when making an investment in a company. The auditor's report proved to be inaccurate and the claimants suffered loss. The court held that no duty of care was owed by the auditor to future investors. The preparation of accounts was not aimed at enabling investors to make investment decisions. Instead, an auditor's duty was to the shareholders of the company.

---

[62]   Or delict in Scotland.

[63]   See *Midland Bank Trust Co Ltd v Hett, Stubbs and Kemp* [1979] Ch 384; *Henderson v Merrett Syndicates Ltd* [1995] 2 AC 145. For Scots law see M Hogg, *Obligations* (2nd ed 2006) ch 3.

[64]   Or delict in Scotland.

[65]   *Henderson v Merrett Syndicates* [1995] 2 AC 145 at 193-194; *Esso Petroleum Ltd v Mardon* [1976] QB 801. For Scots law see M Hogg, *Obligations* (2nd ed 2006) paras 3.204-3.219.

[66]   Or delict in Scotland.

[67]   [1964] AC 465.

[68]   Above, at 483, 494 and 529.

[69]   [1990] 2 AC 605.

6.42 The court emphasised the importance of imposing strict limits on when duties of care arise in respect of pure economic loss. Three factors were relevant:

(1) It must be foreseeable that damage would occur if the defendants did not properly carry out their work.

(2) There must be "proximity" between the claimant and the defendant. The defendant must know that the information will be given to the claimant for a specific purpose and that the claimant would be very likely to rely on it. By contrast, there would be no duty where "a statement is put into more or less general circulation and may foreseeably be relied on by strangers to the maker of the statement for any one of a variety of different purposes".[70]

(3) It must be "fair, just and reasonable" to impose a duty. This allows the court to consider questions of public policy as well as all the circumstances of a case.

6.43 In subsequent cases, the courts have focused on whether the defendant assumed responsibility for their statement. For example, the House of Lords found that an employer owed a duty of care to a former employee when giving a reference.[71] However, a bank did not owe a duty to the tax authority to take care when it had been served with an order to freeze a customer's accounts.[72] The court found that the bank had not assumed responsibility for the accuracy of the information to the claimant. A duty of care normally rested on "something which the defendant has decided to *do*",[73] and here the bank had no choice.

6.44 These cases show that the courts can be flexible. It is possible that they may create new duties to take care not to cause economic loss to another, even if the parties are not in a contractual relationship. However, the courts will do so cautiously. They will not only expect a close relationship between claimant and defendant, but will look explicitly at issues of public policy. Furthermore, they will attach weight to any explicit disclaimer of responsibility. We return to this issue in Chapter 11 when we consider how far the courts will recognise obligations by market participants to ultimate beneficiaries in the absence of a direct relationship.

Should prices be reasonable?

6.45 As we saw in Chapter 1, part of the principle for the functioning of equity markets set out in the Government's response to the Kay Review is that "the direct and indirect costs of services provided should be reasonable and disclosed".

---

[70] [1990] 2 AC 605 at 621.

[71] *Spring v Guardian Assurance* [1995] 2 AC 296.

[72] *Customs and Excise Commissioners v Barclays Bank plc* [2006] UKHL 28.

[73] Above, at [38], by Lord Hoffmann.

6.46 The price of a service is not an area where the courts will generally intervene. There is no common law duty on providers to keep prices reasonable. Instead, the courts consider that this is an issue best left to the market. There is a limited power for the courts to assess the fairness of non-transparent price terms in consumer contracts which we discuss in Chapter 11.[74]

TRUSTEES' DUTIES OF CARE

Trustee Act 2000, section 1

6.47 The common law has long recognised a duty on trustees to act with care in both England & Wales and Scotland.[75] In 2000, this duty was put in statutory form in England & Wales. The Trustee Act 2000 implemented, with minor changes, the recommendations of the Law Commission and Scottish Law Commission in their 1999 Report on Trustees' Powers and Duties.[76]

6.48 Section 1 of the 2000 Act applies to the wide range of powers listed in schedule 1, including the power to invest, alongside arrangements with agents, nominees and custodians.[77] It states:

> Whenever the duty under this subsection applies to a trustee, he must exercise such care and skill as is reasonable in the circumstances, having regard in particular
>
> (a) to any special knowledge or experience that he has or holds himself out as having, and
>
> (b) if he acts as trustee in the course of a business or profession, to any special knowledge or experience that it is reasonable to expect of a person acting in the course of that kind of business or profession.

---

[74] See para 11.50 and following below.

[75] *Speight v Gaunt* (1883) 9 App Cas 1; *Re Whiteley* (1886) 33 Ch D 347 at 355, by Lindley LJ. For Scots law see *Raes v Meek* 1889 16 R (HL) 31.

[76] Trustees' Powers and Duties (1999) Law Com No 260; Scot Law Com No 172. In Scotland the Charities and Trustee Investments (Scotland) Act 2005 Part 4 implemented the Report's recommendations on powers. The Scottish Law Commission has however considered the matter of duties further in Breach of Trust (2003) Scottish Law Commission Discussion Paper No 123 Part 3; and in Supplementary and Miscellaneous Issues in the Law of Trusts (2011) Scottish Law Commission Discussion Paper No 148 ch 6. A final Report is anticipated in 2014.

[77] Section 2 states that schedule 1 "makes provision about when the duty of care applies". Schedule 1 lists powers, the exercise of which engages the duty, under the headings investment, acquisition of land, agents, nominees and custodians, compounding of liabilities, insurance and reversionary interests.

6.49   Section 1 does not apply to trustees of an occupational pension scheme in relation to these duties.[78] In broad terms, however, section 1 is merely a statement of long-standing principles as developed by the courts. In looking at what a duty of care requires, one must look not only at the words of the statute, but also at the case law on which it is based. Importantly, the case law applies with appropriate modification to all trustees, including pension trustees.

6.50   There has been a change in terminology in England & Wales. While the case law refers to the care exercised by the "ordinary prudent man",[79] section 1 talks about "reasonable" care. A leading textbook comments that replacing "prudent" with "reasonable" is to "liberate trustees from the overriding objective to be prudent in their investment advice above all else".[80] This liberation, however, is tempered by the standard investment criteria and the duty to take advice, discussed in Chapter 7. It is also clear that "prudent" does not mean avoiding all risk.

6.51   In Scotland, trustees remain "bound to exercise that degree of diligence which a person of ordinary prudence would exercise in the management of his or her own private affairs", and "it is not clear whether the standard of care required of a professional trustee is higher than that for a gratuitous trustee."[81] The Scottish Law Commission has suggested that there should be a higher standard of care only for a professional trustee who is remunerated for providing the trust with professional services.[82]

6.52   The duty requires more than mere honesty, good faith and sincerity.[83] Those subject to a duty of care are expected to apply a level of proficiency and competence. This concept is "organic and malleable".[84] It evolves to take account of prevailing social norms. For example, last century it was held to preclude local authorities from applying a standard minimum wage for adult men and women,[85] but it is highly unlikely that it would do so today.

---

[78]   Trustee Act 2000, s 36.

[79]   *Re Whiteley* (1886) 33 Ch D 347 at 355, by Lindley LJ.

[80]   G Thomas and A Hudson, *The Law of Trusts* (2nd ed 2010) para 54.15.

[81]   *Gloag & Henderson: The Law of Scotland* (12th ed 2012) para 41.16.

[82]   Supplementary and Miscellaneous Issues in the Law of Trusts (2011) Scottish Law Commission Discussion Paper No 148 ch 6.

[83]   *Cowan v Scargill* [1985] Ch 270 at 289; see also Trustees' Powers and Duties (1999) Law Com No 260; Scot Law Com No 172 para 2.15.

[84]   P Watchman, J Anstee-Wedderburn and L Shipway "Fiduciary duties in the 21st century: a UK perspective" (2005) *Trust Law International* 127 at 133.

[85]   *Roberts v Hopwood* [1925] AC 578; see also *Prescott v Birmingham Corporation* [1955] Ch 210 and *Bromley London Borough Council v Greater London Council* [1983] 1 AC 768.

The case law

Management of risk

6.53 The classic statement of a trustee's duty to invest dates from 1886. The case of *Re Whiteley* states that in exercising a power to invest, a trustee should:

> Take such care as an ordinary prudent man would take if he were minded to make an investment for the benefit of other people for whom he felt morally bound to provide.[86]

6.54 When exercising the standard of care of an "ordinary prudent man", an individual is not required to avoid all risk. In *Re Godfrey* the court stated:

> The words in which the rule is expressed must not be strained beyond their meaning. Prudent business men in their dealings incur risk. That may and must happen in almost all human affairs.[87]

Similarly, in the more recent case of *Bartlett v Barclays Trust Co* the court held that "the distinction is between a prudent degree of risk on the one hand, and hazard on the other".[88]

6.55 The courts have recognised that the concept of risk must adapt to current economic conditions and contemporary understanding of markets and investment. Those subject to duties of care are now required to manage risk by diversification and considering the suitability of investments.[89] Accordingly, trustees are:

> To be judged by the standards of current portfolio theory, which emphasises the risk level of the entire portfolio rather than the risk attaching to each investment taken in isolation.[90]

6.56 Assets which may individually be hazardous may be offset by safer investments to form a balanced portfolio. The theory is that:

> The risk of a portfolio is wholly distinct from the risk of a particular investment contained in the portfolio. The risk of a portfolio is a function of the interrelation of its component investments. Thus, a trustee can use securities and instruments that are highly risky viewed in isolation to assemble a portfolio that is safe.[91]

---

[86] *Re Whiteley* (1886) 33 Ch D 347 at 355, by Lindley LJ.

[87] *Re Godfrey* (1883) 23 Ch D 483 at 493, by Bacon VC.

[88] *Bartlett v Barclays Trust Co (No 1)* [1980] Ch 515 at 531, by Brightman J.

[89] *Nestle v National Westminster Bank plc* [1993] 1 WLR 1260 at 1282.

[90] *Nestle v National Westminster Bank plc* (1996) 10(4) Trust Law International 112 at 115, by Hoffmann J.

[91] J Gordon, "The Puzzling Persistence of the Constrained Prudent Man Rule" (1987) 62 *New York University Law Review* 52 at 67.

6.57   In *Harries v Church Commissioners*[92] the court held that the amount of diversification required was a question of degree. It may be acceptable to exclude a few companies, as it was:

> not easy to think of an instance where in practice the exclusion ... of one or more companies or sectors from the whole range of investments open to trustees would be likely to leave them without an adequately wide range of investments from which to choose a properly diversified portfolio.[93]

On the other hand, larger exclusions may make the portfolio less balanced and diversified.[94]

6.58   We return to this case and the issue of portfolio management in Chapter 10. It is important to note that diversification guards against firm-specific risk, rather than systemic risk. At times of economic stress, shares tend to fall together, leading to losses in the whole portfolio.[95]

Stewardship

6.59   A duty of care may require an element of stewardship in investments made on behalf of another.

6.60   In *Bartlett v Barclays Bank*[96] a trust held 99.8 percent of the shares in a private company which made a disastrous property speculation. The court had to consider the extent of the trustee's duty to observe and control the investment.

6.61   In this case, the trustee was a bank, which held itself out as having the skill and expertise to carry on the business of trust management. The trustee placed confidence in the company's board and did not seek information beyond that given at annual general meetings nor interfere with the running of the company.[97] The company decided to invest in large speculative property developments. Planning permission for the developments was refused and the trustee was informed that the development might have to wait for 10 years. However, the trustee still took no action. Despite problems with planning permission, the company continued to purchase properties with a view to development on one site. This caused significant losses to the company, the share price fell and dividends were reduced.

---

[92]   [1992] 1 WLR 1241.

[93]   Above, at 1246, by Sir Donald Nicholls VC.

[94]   Above, at 1251.

[95]   For further discussion, see R Thornton, "Ethical Investment: a case of disjointed thinking" (2008) 67(2) *Cambridge Law Journal* 396 at 399-401; and E Ford, "Trustee Investment and Modern Portfolio Theory" (1996) 10(4) *Trust Law International* 102 at 102.

[96]   [1980] Ch 515.

[97]   Above, at 529.

6.62 The court held that, in discharging its duty of care, a professional trustee managing a controlling interest in a private company should take an interest in what the company is doing:

> The prudent man of business will act in such manner as is necessary to safeguard his investment ... If facts come to his knowledge which tell him that the company's affairs are not being conducted as they should be, or which put him on inquiry, he will take appropriate action. Appropriate action will no doubt consist in the first instance of inquiry of and consultation with the directors, and in the last but most unlikely resort, the convening of a general meeting to replace one or more directors. What the prudent man of business will *not* do is to content himself with the receipt of such information on the affairs of the company as a shareholder ordinarily receives at annual general meetings. Since he has the power to do so, he will go further and see that he has sufficient information to enable him to make a responsible decision from time to time either to let matters proceed as they are proceeding, or to intervene if he is dissatisfied.[98]

6.63 The actions an individual ought to take and the information they should seek will depend on the facts of a particular case. The purpose is not to monitor every move of the directors but to ensure "an adequate flow of information in time to enable the trustees to make use of their controlling interest".[99] On the facts, the trustees failed to ensure they had sufficient information about the company. If they had received it, it should have caused them to "step in and stop" the property development project.[100]

6.64 This case concerned a controlling interest in a small private company. The same activities would not be required where a trust fund holds a few shares in a major public company and the trustees have little ability to control what the company does.[101]

Obtaining advice

6.65 Trustees are required to obtain and consider advice where a decision requires special knowledge which they do not have.[102] For example, in the Court of Appeal's decision in *Pitt v Holt*, Lord Justice Lloyd said "where tax matters are relevant (as they often will be), it is likely to be the duty of the trustees, under their duty of skill and care, to take proper advice as to those matters."[103]

6.66 In Chapter 7 we outline the statutory duty on pension fund trustees to take appropriate advice.

---

[98] [1980] Ch 515 at 532, by Brightman J.

[99] Above, at 533, by Brightman J.

[100] Above, at 534, by Brightman J.

[101] G Thomas and A Hudson, *The Law of Trusts* (2nd ed 2010) para 54.81; see also *Lewin on Trusts* (18th ed 2012) para 34-50.

[102] *Martin v City of Edinburgh District Council* [1989] Pens LR 9 at [32], 1988 SLT 329 at 335.

[103] *Pitt v Holt* [2011] EWCA Civ 197 at [119] (affirmed on appeal [2013] UKSC 26 at [80]).

Hindsight

6.67 It is tempting to judge investment decisions with the benefit of hindsight. However, it is clear that this is the wrong approach – investment decisions need to be judged by reference to the state of things at the time the decision was made. This was made clear by Mr Justice Megarry in *Duchess of Argyll v Beuselinck*:

> In this world, there are few things that could not have been done better with hindsight. The advantages of hindsight include the benefit of having sufficient indication of which of the many factors present are important and which are unimportant. But hindsight is no touchstone of negligence. The standard of care to be expected of a professional man must be based on events as they occur, in prospect, and not in retrospect.[104]

TRUSTEES' EXEMPTION CLAUSES

The common law

6.68 The trust deed may include an exemption clause, excluding or limiting a trustee's liability for negligence. The English courts have upheld such clauses. *Armitage v Nurse*[105] decided that a trustee is free to contract out of all liabilities to beneficiaries, except for liability for fraud. Lord Justice Millett thought that the irreducible core of trustees' obligations related only to "the duty of the trustees to perform the trusts honestly and in good faith for the benefit of the beneficiaries", and did not extend to duties of care.[106]

6.69 In *Spread Trustee Co v Hutcheson*[107] the Privy Council confirmed that under English law a trustee could validly exclude liability, even for gross negligence. Lord Clarke was clear that "*Armitage v Nurse* correctly states English law as it stands at present".[108] This appears to differ from the law in Scotland, where liability for gross negligence cannot be excluded.[109]

---

[104] [1972] 2 Lloyd's Rep 172 at 185.

[105] [1998] Ch 241.

[106] Above, at 253.

[107] [2011] UKPC 13.

[108] Above, at [52].

[109] Above, at [48]. See, for example, *Lutea Trustees Ltd v Orbis Trustees Guernsey Ltd* 1997 SC 255. The law is discussed, but no reform suggested, in Breach of Trust (2003) Scottish Law Commission Discussion Paper No 123 paras 3.12-3.61. The Discussion Paper did suggest (at para 3.46) that professional trustees should be unable to exclude liability for breach of their duties of care and skill. See also D Cabrelli, "Scotland", in D Busch and D DeMott (eds), *Liability of Asset Managers* (1st ed 2012) paras 15.27-15.30.

6.70 A related issue arose in *Bogg v Raper*.[110] A testator's will included a clause exempting the trustees from any liability for breach of duty as trustees. The solicitors who drafted the will (and the exemption clause) were the trustees appointed under the will. The beneficiaries under the will alleged that by including the exemption clause the solicitors had conferred a benefit on themselves, and were thereby in breach of their fiduciary duties owed to the testator. The Court of Appeal held that the clause did not confer a benefit, but rather defined the extent of the trustees' liabilities.[111]

Statutory restrictions

6.71 By contrast, pension trustees may not exclude their liability for poor investment decisions. Section 33(1) of the Pensions Act 1995 states that pension trustees cannot exclude or restrict any liability for breach of an obligation under any rule of law to take care or exercise skill in the performance of investment functions.

6.72 *Adams v Bridge*[112] is a reported decision of the Pensions Ombudsman. The trustees of a pension fund sought to rely on exclusion clauses when beneficiaries brought claims against them.[113] The alleged breaches included self-investment; failing to reinvest cash once investments had been sold; and improper augmentations being made to trustees. The ombudsman held that the trustees were not entitled to rely on their exclusion clauses in respect of any of the breaches, as section 33(1) applied.

The Law Commission's views: our 2006 Report

6.73 The Law Commission undertook a project in the wake of the Trustee Act 2000 to review the use of clauses exempting trustees from liability. In the consultation paper, we provisionally proposed that no professional trustee should be permitted to exclude liability for negligence. The same restrictions were not to apply to lay (that is, non-professional) trustees.[114]

---

[110] (1998) 1 ITELR 267.

[111] Above, at [47]. The logic of this result has been questioned (see Trustee Exemption Clauses (2006) Law Com No 301 para 2.20), but it remains good law.

[112] [2009] Pens LR 153.

[113] The trust deed contained a clause exempting the trustees from some liabilities, and granting them an indemnity from the trust fund in the case of all others (except knowing breaches of trust).

[114] It was suggested in Breach of Trust (2003) Scottish Law Commission Discussion Paper No 123 para 3.46 that professional trustees should be unable to exclude liability for breach of their duties of care and skill.

6.74 The consultation process cast doubt on the practicality of the proposed approach. In the executive summary that accompanied our Report in 2006, we explained the outcome of our consultation as follows:

> There was widespread concern about the likely adverse impact of statutory regulation restricting reliance on trustee exemption clauses. Particular reference was made to the likelihood of increased indemnity insurance premiums and the possible unavailability of insurance; defensive trusteeship (in particular, a reluctance on the part of trustees to exercise discretionary powers expeditiously and without first taking legal advice); a decrease in the flexibility of the management of trust property; an increase in speculative litigation for breach of trust; and a possible reluctance to accept trusteeship.[115]

6.75 Consultation also revealed concern that our proposal would deter professional trustees from acting, as many now do, on an unpaid basis.[116]

6.76 As a result of these concerns, the report proposed a different approach to the regulation of trustee exemption clauses. The report emphasised the importance of increasing settlor awareness of the existence and effect of a clause. This would respect and possibly enhance settlor autonomy. The report proposed a "rule of practice", imposed and enforced by regulators, but not applicable to pension fund trustees:

> Any paid trustee who causes a settlor to include a clause in a trust instrument which has the effect of excluding or limiting liability for negligence must before the creation of the trust take such steps as are reasonable to ensure that the settlor is aware of the meaning and effect of the clause.[117]

That recommendation has been taken up by the main trust and regulatory bodies.

CONCLUSION

6.77 The law imposes a variety of duties on those who make investment decisions on behalf of others. First, a power must be used for the purpose for which it was given. It must be exercised properly: trustees and others should not act capriciously or fetter their discretion. Instead, they should consider matters which are relevant at the time the decision is reached.

6.78 In making a decision, trustees should also use reasonable care and skill. Professional trustees in England & Wales are held to a higher level of skill than others. For pension fund trustees, however, the statutory scheme imposes more prescriptive duties, which we consider in the following chapter.

---

[115] Trustee Exemption Clauses (2006) Executive Summary para 1.6(5).

[116] Trustee Exemption Clauses (2006) Law Com No 301 paras 4.24-4.25.

[117] Above, para 1.22.

CHAPTER 7
LEGISLATION GOVERNING PENSION TRUSTEES

7.1 We have considered how investment decisions are governed by fiduciary duties, duties applying to the exercise of a power and duties of care. For pension trustees, however, the starting point is the pensions legislation.

7.2 The investment decisions of pension trustees are governed by the Pensions Act 1995, the Pensions Act 2004 and by the various regulations made under these Acts. The most important are the Occupational Pension Scheme (Investment) Regulations 2005 (the Investment Regulations).[1] Here we provide a brief outline of these provisions.

7.3 The provisions are enforced by The Pensions Regulator (TPR), who may impose civil penalties for contraventions of various requirements. The maximum amount of the penalty is £5,000 in the case of an individual and £50,000 in any other case.[2] TPR may also prohibit an individual from being a trustee of a particular scheme, a particular type of scheme, or schemes in general.[3]

PENSIONS ACT 1995

The power to invest

7.4 Section 34 of the Pensions Act 1995 provides occupational pension scheme trustees with a wide investment power. It is said to be the same as if the trustees had been absolutely entitled to the scheme's assets. This is in addition to any powers granted by the trust deed but is subject to any restrictions in the trust deed and relevant case law.

7.5 The power is also constrained by the Investment Regulations.[4] Regulation 4 requires that:

   (1) investment of the scheme assets is in the best interests of the beneficiaries;[5]

   (2) the power of investment is exercised in a manner "calculated to ensure the security, quality, liquidity and profitability of the portfolio as a whole";[6]

   (3) assets held to cover the scheme's technical provisions are invested in a manner "appropriate to the nature and duration of the expected future retirement benefits payable under the scheme";[7]

---

[1] SI 2005 No 3378.

[2] Pensions Act 1995, s 10(2)(a).

[3] TPR must be satisfied that the individual is not a fit and proper person: see Pensions Act 1995, s 3.

[4] Pensions Act 1995, s 36(1); Occupational Pension Schemes (Investment) Regulations 2005 SI 2005 No 3378.

[5] Occupational Pension Scheme (Investment) Regulations 2005 SI 2005 No 3378, reg 4(2).

(4)   scheme assets consist predominantly of investments admitted to trading on regulated markets.[8] Other investments must be kept at a prudent level;[9]

(5)   the assets should be properly diversified to "avoid excessive reliance on any particular asset, issuer or group of undertakings and so as to avoid accumulations of risk in the portfolio as a whole";[10] and

(6)   investment in derivative instruments may only be made in so far as they contribute to a reduction of risks or facilitate efficient portfolio management.[11]

7.6   Schemes with fewer than 100 members are excluded from these requirements,[12] even though small schemes are common.[13] Where the regulation does not apply, the trustees have a more limited duty to have regard to the diversification of investments in so far as appropriate to the circumstances of the scheme.[14] If the regulations are breached, TPR may take action, including applying civil penalties under the Act.[15]

Delegation to an investment manager[16]

7.7   Under section 34(2), trustees may delegate their discretion to make a decision about investments to an investment manager who is authorised (or exempt from authorisation) under the Financial Services and Markets Act 2000 (FSMA).[17] Any investment manager to whom investment discretions have been delegated must also exercise their discretion in accordance with the Investment Regulations.[18]

---

[6]   Occupational Pension Scheme (Investment) Regulations 2005 SI 2005 No 3378, reg 4(3).

[7]   Occupational Pension Scheme (Investment) Regulations 2005 SI 2005 No 3378, reg 4(4).

[8]   Occupational Pension Scheme (Investment) Regulations 2005 SI 2005 No 3378, reg 4(5).

[9]   Occupational Pension Scheme (Investment) Regulations 2005 SI 2005 No 3378, reg 4(6).

[10]   Occupational Pension Scheme (Investment) Regulations 2005 SI 2005 No 3378, reg 4(7).

[11]   Occupational Pension Scheme (Investment) Regulations 2005 SI 2005 No 3378, reg 4(8).

[12]   Occupational Pension Scheme (Investment) Regulations 2005 SI 2005 No 3378, reg 7.

[13]   For example, Spence Johnson reports that, out of 45,295 defined contribution trust-based schemes, 43,804 (97%) had fewer than 100 members: *Defined Contribution Market Intelligence* (2013) p 16.

[14]   Occupational Pension Scheme (Investment) Regulations 2005 SI 2005 No 3378, reg 7(2).

[15]   See Pensions Act 1995, ss 10 and 36(8)(a).

[16]   The Pensions Act 1995 uses the language of "fund manager", but the terminology of "investment manager" has been preferred throughout.

[17]   Pensions Act 1995, s 34(2).

[18]   Pensions Act 1995, s 36(1).

7.8 Under section 47(2), trustees must appoint an investment manager in relation to "investments" within the meaning of FSMA. "Investments" appear to include not only shares and bonds but also collective investment schemes, such as unit trusts which are run by persons authorised under FSMA. [19]

7.9 Under section 47(3), trustees cannot rely on investment managers or asset custodians unless they have appointed them properly, in accordance with the provisions of the Occupational Pension Schemes (Scheme Administration) Regulations 1996.[20] Among other things, these require an investment manager to confirm they will declare any conflict of interest affecting their relationship with the trustees in accordance with the rules of the Financial Conduct Authority (FCA).[21]

No exclusion of the duty of care

7.10 Under section 33(1), pension trustees cannot exclude or restrict any liability for breach of an obligation under any rule of law to take care or exercise skill in the performance of investment functions. As we have seen, this marks a stark contrast to other forms of trustee who may exclude their duties.[22]

7.11 However, a trustee will not be liable where they have delegated their investment discretion to an investment manager, provided that they have taken reasonable steps to check that the investment manager is suitable and to monitor that they are carrying out their work competently.[23]

7.12 The investment manager to whom investment functions are delegated is also prohibited from excluding or limiting their liability for breach of their duty of care.[24]

Statement of investment principles (SIP)

7.13 A statement of investment principles is "a written statement of the investment principles governing decisions about investments for the purposes of the scheme".[25] Under section 36(5), the trustees, or the investment manager to whom any discretion has been delegated, must exercise their powers of investment in accordance with the SIP in "so far as reasonably practicable".

---

[19] Financial Services and Markets Act 2000 (Regulated Activities) Order 2001 SI 2001 No 544, Part III.

[20] SI 1996 No 1715.

[21] Occupational Pension Schemes (Scheme Administration) Regulations 1996 SI 1996 No 1715, reg 5(2)(b)(i).

[22] Trustee Exemption Clauses (2006) Law Com No 301.

[23] Pensions Act 1995, ss 34(4) and 34(6).

[24] Pensions Act 1995, s 33(1)(b).

[25] Pensions Act 1995, s 35(2).

7.14 The Investment Regulations provide further detail about the content of a SIP. Under regulation 2(3), the SIP must include a statement of the trustees' policy on:

(1) securing compliance with the rules on choosing investments in the pensions legislation;[26]

(2) the kinds of investments to be held;

(3) the balance between different kinds of investments;

(4) risk;

(5) the expected return on investments;

(6) the realisation of investments;

(7) the extent to which social, environmental or ethical considerations are taken into account in the selection, retention and realisation of investments; and

(8) the exercise of the rights (including voting rights) attaching to investments.

7.15 A leading pensions text suggests that the investment strategy set out in the SIP:

> Must accord with the general law ... and be devised to reflect the liability position of the scheme in question.[27]

7.16 Under section 35(1), trustees "must secure" that a SIP is "prepared and maintained", and that it is reviewed and "if necessary, revised". The obligation to review the SIP is clarified by regulation 2(1) of the Investment Regulations,[28] which provides that the SIP must be reviewed "at least every three years" and "without delay after any significant change in investment policy". Failure to do so exposes the trustees to civil penalties.[29]

---

[26] Regulation 2(3)(a) of the Investment Regulations requires that a SIP must state the trustees' policy for securing compliance with section 36 of the Pensions Act 1995. In particular, section 36(1) requires trustees (and any investment manager to whom discretion has been delegated) to exercise their powers of investment in accordance with regulations. This will include regulation 4 of the Investment Regulations.

[27] Nabarro Pensions Team, *Pensions Law Handbook* (11th ed 2013) para 10.26.

[28] SI 2005 No 3378.

[29] Pensions Act 1995, s 35(6).

7.17   Before preparing or revising a SIP, pension trustees must obtain and consider "proper advice", discussed below. They should also consult with the scheme's sponsoring employer.[30] Pension trustees must confirm in their annual report whether they have produced a SIP and include a statement of any investments which were not made in accordance with the SIP, giving the reasons why.[31]

Proper advice

7.18   Under section 36(3), the trustees must obtain and consider "proper advice" as to whether an investment is satisfactory, taking into account the criteria in regulation 4 of the Investment Regulations and the principles contained in the SIP. For existing investments, trustees should obtain advice periodically, when it is "desirable".[32]

7.19   Section 36(6) states that "proper advice" means advice from someone authorised under FSMA to provide a regulated activity,[33] or the advice:

> of a person who is reasonably believed by the trustees to be qualified by his ability in and practical experience of financial matters and to have the appropriate knowledge and experience of the management of the investments of trust schemes.

7.20   Under section 36(7), trustees will not be taken to have fulfilled their duty to obtain and consider "proper advice" unless the advice was given or confirmed in writing. Again, failure to comply with the advice requirements exposes trustees to civil penalties.[34]

PENSIONS ACT 2004

7.21   The Pensions Act 2004 was motivated in part by the Myners Review of 2001. It covers a wide range of areas, including setting up TPR[35] and the Pension Protection Fund.[36] Notably for our purposes, it also required trustees to know about pensions issues.

---

[30]   Occupational Pension Schemes (Investment) Regulations 2005, SI 2005 No 3378, reg 2(2)(b).

[31]   Occupational Pension Schemes (Disclosure of Information) Regulations 1996 SI 1996 No 1655, reg 6.

[32]   Pensions Act 1995, s 36(4).

[33]   This is discussed in para 8.9.

[34]   Pensions Act 1995, s 36(8).

[35]   Pensions Act 2004, Part 1.

[36]   Pensions Act 2004, Part 2.

The Myners Review

7.22 The Myners Review was published in March 2001. Many of its conclusions were similar to those of the Kay Review. For example, it noted that pension trustees are "centre stage" in making crucial investment decisions, but lack the resources or expertise necessary. They therefore relied on a narrow market of investment consultants. The report thought that the objectives set for investment managers were often artificial, leading to herding and short-termism.[37] Little appears to have changed in the decade between the two reports.

7.23 However, some practical change was made in light of the report's findings, including amendments to the 1995 Act. The 2004 Act also incorporated the Myners Review's recommendations to improve trustees' knowledge and understanding, which we explain briefly below.

Improving trustees' knowledge and understanding

7.24 Under the 2004 Act, trustees and directors of trustee companies are required to be familiar with the scheme trust deed and rules, the SIP, the statement of funding principles and any other documentation setting out the scheme's policy.[38]

7.25 TPR has prepared Code of Practice No 7 to give further detail. The Code states that "knowing the essential elements of the scheme's trust documentation will require every trustee to read it through thoroughly".[39] Trustees should have a working knowledge of the trust documents, so that they can use them effectively when carrying out their functions.[40]

7.26 Further, trustees must have an understanding of the law relating to pensions and trusts and the principles relating to the funding and investment of occupational pensions schemes, sufficient to enable them to exercise their functions properly.[41] Notably, they should know enough to ask relevant questions of their advisers. As one law firm notes, these obligations are "potentially very onerous".[42]

7.27 There is an exemption for small schemes.[43] Trustees are also exempt for six months from the date on which they are appointed.[44]

---

[37] P Myners, *Institutional Investment in the UK: A Review* (2001) p 1-2.

[38] Pensions Act 2004, ss 247(3) and 248(3).

[39] The Pensions Regulator, Code of Practice 07: Trustee knowledge and understanding, para 69.

[40] Nabarro Pensions Team, *Pensions Law Handbook* (11th ed 2013) para 3.23.

[41] Pensions Act 2004, ss 247(4) and 248(4).

[42] CMS Cameron McKenna, *Pensions Act 2004: Your plain English guide* (2008) para 97.

[43] Occupational Pension Scheme (Trustees' Knowledge and Understanding) Regulations 2006 SI 2006 No 686, reg 2.

[44] Occupational Pension Scheme (Trustees' Knowledge and Understanding) Regulations 2006, regs 3-4.

OVERLAP WITH THE TRUSTEE ACT 2000

7.28 In Chapter 6 we set out the background to the Trustee Act 2000 (Trustee Act). In relation to investment duties we explained how it incorporated existing case law and set out a duty of care. The Trustee Act also includes other provisions[45] such as:

(1) A new permitted range of investments which "liberalised"[46] the range of investments a trustee is permitted to invest in: subject to limited exceptions, a trustee may make any kind of investment that they could make if they were absolutely entitled to the assets of the trust.[47]

(2) An obligation to keep the portfolio under regular review.[48]

(3) An obligation to "have regard to the standard investment criteria",[49] which include the "suitability to the trust" of the type of investment in question and the specific asset in question and "the need for diversification of investments ... in so far as is appropriate to the circumstances of the trust".[50] The explanatory notes suggest that suitability in this context includes "any relevant ethical considerations as to the kind of investments which it is appropriate for the trust to make".[51]

(4) The ability to delegate certain functions.[52] This does not extend to decisions on how the trust assets should be distributed.

7.29 Many of the provisions of the Trustee Act do not apply to the trustees of occupational pension schemes. In most of these areas, the pensions rules are a more prescriptive version of the Trustee Act. For example, the Occupational Pension Scheme (Investment) Regulations 2005 are a more detailed version of the requirement under the Trustee Act to have regard to standard investment criteria. Similarly, the pension provisions on appointing agents are more detailed than the equivalent provisions in the Trustee Act.

---

[45] Broadly similar provisions can be found in the Charities and Trustee Investment (Scotland) Act 2005 Part 3, amending the Trusts (Scotland) Act 1921, s 4 and adding new sections 4A and 4C.

[46] R Thornton, "Ethical investments: a case of disjointed thinking" (2008) *Cambridge Law Journal* 396 at 397.

[47] Trustee Act 2000, s 3(1).

[48] Trustee Act 2000, s 4(2).

[49] Trustee Act 2000, s 4(1).

[50] Trustee Act 2000, s 4(3).

[51] Trustee Act 2000, Explanatory Note [23].

[52] Trustee Act 2000, s 11.

7.30   The exact overlap is complex. The provisions in Part I on the duty of care do not apply to occupational pension scheme trustees when carrying out investment functions,[53] but they may apply to other functions.[54] Similarly, the Trustee Act does not apply to pension trustees when they appoint nominees, custodians or, in relation to investment functions, an agent.[55] However, Part IV of the Trustee Act applies to allow pension trustees to delegate non-investment functions.[56]

7.31   It is not the purpose of this paper to give a full overview of the Trustee Act 2000. Instead we provide only a brief introduction to the standard investment criteria and the delegation of functions.

Standard investment criteria

7.32   The Trustee Act applies to a wide range of trusts, so the provisions are more flexible. The need to consider the "suitability" of an investment[57] is likely to differ according to the nature of the trust. For a small family trust with a weak risk appetite, the investments made should be safe. For a highly leveraged hedge fund, the trustees are permitted to take greater risks.[58]

7.33   It is suggested that where the trustee is regulated by the FCA's Conduct of Business Rules, which require a consideration of the suitability of an investment, the regulatory standards will guide the application of this rule. Where they are not, arguably the duty of care in section 1 of the Trustee Act 2000 will provide the guide.[59]

7.34   The requirement to have regard to "the need for diversification"[60] hinges on the notion that a diversified portfolio of investment lessens the impact of the fall in value of any individual market or investment. It is also specific to the particular trust. For example, a trust with only a small amount of capital is not expected to diversify as broadly as a large fund.

---

[53]   Trustee Act 2000, s 36(2)(a).

[54]   Similarly, under s 36(3) of the Trustee Act 2000, Parts II (investment) and III (acquisition of land) of the Trustee Act 2000 do not apply to pension trustees; see Trustee Act 2000, Explanatory Note [126].

[55]   Trustee Act 2000, s 36(2)(b).

[56]   Trustee Act 2000, ss 36(4)-(8).

[57]   Trustee Act 2000, s 4(3)(a).

[58]   See G Thomas and A Hudson, *The Law of Trusts* (2nd ed 2010) para 54.55.

[59]   Above, para 54.56.

[60]   Trustee Act 2000, s 4(3)(b).

Delegation

7.35   Under section 11(1) of the Trustee Act, trustees "may authorise any person to exercise any or all of their delegable functions as their agent".[61] Trustees are able to appoint a nominee[62] and a custodian[63] in relation to any of the assets of the trust. However, some functions may not be delegated. For non-charitable trusts, this includes "any functions relating to whether and in what way any assets of the trust should be distributed".[64]

7.36   In delegating their functions, trustees are subject to the statutory duty of care.[65] Once delegated, trustees are required to keep the activities of their agent under constant review.[66] More specifically, when delegating functions, the Act states that "unless it is reasonably necessary for them to do so" trustees should not:

   (1)   permit the agent to appoint a substitute;

   (2)   restrict the liability of the agent or their substitute to the trustees or any beneficiary; or

   (3)   permit the agent to act in circumstances giving rise to a conflict of interest.[67]

7.37   Whether or not an exclusion clause is "reasonably necessary" is "a question of fact and degree in each case".[68] Shortly after the Act came into force, one writer suggested that the "acceptance of exclusion clauses by trustees is likely to be one of the more contentious issues".[69]

7.38   In fact, it appears that exclusion clauses are commonplace: we have been told that investment consultants, actuaries and investment managers often place quite a low cap on their liability to the trust. Small trusts are unlikely to have market power to insist that terms excluding or heavily limiting the agents' duties are removed from agency agreements.

---

[61]   For Scots law see Trusts (Scotland) Act 1921, s 4C, inserted by the Charities and Trustee Investment (Scotland) Act 2005, s 94.

[62]   Trustee Act 2000, s 16(1). For Scots law see Trusts (Scotland) Act 1921, s 4B, inserted by the Charities and Trustee Investment (Scotland) Act 2005, s 94; and see further Supplementary and Miscellaneous Issues in the Law of Trusts (2011) Scottish Law Commission Discussion Paper No 148 ch 5.

[63]   Trustee Act 2000, s 17(1). On Scots law see Supplementary and Miscellaneous Issues in the Law of Trusts (2011) Scottish Law Commission Discussion Paper No 148 para 5.13.

[64]   Trustee Act 2000, s 11(2).

[65]   Trustee Act 2000, sch 1 para 3. See Trustees' Powers and Duties (1999) Law Com No 260; Scot Law Com No 172 para 4.15.

[66]   Trustee Act 2000, s 22(1).

[67]   Trustee Act 2000, s 14.

[68]   R Wilson, "The Tension Between Trustees and Investment Managers: Part 2" [2003] 2 *Private Client Business* 91 at 94.

[69]   Above, at 94.

7.39 Beneficiaries, however, are afforded some protection where trustees delegate. Trustees may not authorise a person to exercise investment management functions unless they have prepared a written policy statement as to how the functions should be exercised and the investment manager agrees to comply.[70] In our 1997 consultation paper on Trustees' Powers and Duties we felt that trustees should "retain their responsibilities for determining investment and management policy in accordance with their fiduciary obligations to act in the best interests of the beneficiaries".[71] We commented:

> What does seem to be required is that the trustees should define the policy within which the management of trust assets is then carried out. That policy *would* of course have to be settled in compliance with the trustees' fiduciary duties … . The execution of that policy could then be conducted by those with appropriate professional expertise.[72]

7.40 Accordingly, under the Act, in formulating the policy statement the trustees must ensure that investment management functions will be exercised in the best interests of the trust.[73] The explanatory notes to the Act state that this policy statement might include "any 'ethical' considerations relevant to the investment policy of the trust".[74] Where the trustees are the trustees of a pension scheme trust, however, the SIP *must* include the trustees' policy on how social, environmental or ethical considerations are taken into account.[75]

CONCLUSION

7.41 When considering the investment duties of pension scheme trustees, the starting point is the Pensions Act 1995, as amended. It provides trustees with wide investment powers, but these are subject to a variety of constraints. In particular, the Investment Regulations require that the power is exercised in a manner "calculated to ensure the security, quality, liquidity and profitability of the portfolio as a whole"[76] and that the assets are properly diversified.[77]

7.42 The legislation requires pension scheme trustees to prepare a written statement of investment principles (or SIP) governing how investment decisions will be made. This should include the pension scheme trustees' policy on how social, environmental or ethical considerations are taken into account. This policy, however, must be one permitted by the general law. In Chapter 10 we consider how far pension trustees may (or indeed must) take these factors into account.

---

[70] Trustee Act 2000, s 15; the Trustee Act 2000 uses the language of "asset management", but the terminology of "investment management" has been preferred throughout.

[71] Trustees' Powers and Duties (1997) Law Commission Consultation Paper No 146 para 5.16.

[72] Trustees' Powers and Duties (1997) Law Commission Consultation Paper No 146 para 5.13.

[73] Trustee Act 2000, s 15(3).

[74] See Trustee Act 2000, Explanatory Note [63].

[75] See para 7.14 above.

[76] Occupational Pension Schemes (Investment) Regulations 2005 SI 2005 No 3378, reg 4(3).

[77] Occupational Pension Schemes (Investment) Regulations 2005 SI 2005 No 3378, reg 4(7).

7.43   Unlike other trustees, pension scheme trustees may not exclude their liability to take care when making investment decisions. They may, however, delegate their investment functions to an investment manager. Provided that pension scheme trustees take reasonable steps to ensure the investment manager is suitable and monitor its work, the trustees will not be liable for any investments made by the investment manager.

CHAPTER 8
FINANCIAL CONDUCT AUTHORITY RULES

8.1   For many of the stakeholders we spoke to, the regulatory regime is of overriding concern. It is seen as the primary source of legal obligations for market participants.

8.2   The Financial Conduct Authority rules are complex, and we do not attempt a comprehensive explanation. Instead, we provide an overview of the rules most relevant to issues of fiduciary duty.

THE FINANCIAL CONDUCT AUTHORITY HANDBOOK

8.3   On 1 April 2013, the Financial Services Authority (FSA) was replaced with two separate bodies: the Financial Conduct Authority (FCA) and the Prudential Regulation Authority (PRA). The intention was to divide prudential supervision from conduct supervision and to provide more detailed prudential supervision for the largest and most important financial firms. The FCA focuses on conduct – that is, whether firms deal fairly with their clients. All financial services firms are regulated by the FCA for conduct supervision. Firms which pose less systemic risk are also prudentially regulated by the FCA.

8.4   Before the split, the FSA used its powers to create an extensive regulatory regime, set out in the FSA Handbook. When the FSA was replaced, the handbook was split into two, one each for the FCA and PRA.

8.5   Different paragraphs of the Handbook have different status. For example, the letter "R" indicates a rule, which imposes a binding obligation on authorised persons.[1] Breach of such a rule exposes a firm to the possibility of enforcement by the FCA and may give rise to a private claim to damages.[2] The letter "G" indicates guidance. This does not give rise to enforceable obligations, but suggests a way of securing compliance.

8.6   The FCA Handbook is often criticised for being overly detailed. It is important to note, however, that many FCA rules are statements of principle, designed to be broad enough to cover the many circumstances in which they apply. The FCA has stressed the need to stay clear of a more intrusive approach towards firm's management of regulated fiduciary duties, such as conflicts of interest.[3]

---

[1]   *McMeel and Virgo on Financial Advice and Financial Products: Law and Liability* (Release 10 2012) para I.4.221.

[2]   See para 8.72 below, where we discuss the scope of FSMA, s 138D, which provides a right of action for private individuals for breach of the FCA rules.

[3]   For example, FSA, *MiFID supervisory priorities – results of wholesale thematic review* (2009) para 2.48.

EUROPEAN DIRECTIVES

8.7 The Handbook implements several European directives. For our purposes the most important is the Markets in Financial Instruments Directive (MiFID).[4]

8.8 This directive is intended to harmonise the provision of investment services to achieve similar regulatory outcomes across member states. It works together with the MiFID Implementing Directive[5] and the MiFID Regulation,[6] collectively known as the "Level 2" legislation. Most recently the European Commission has published a draft of a proposed new Directive intended to repeal MiFID and replace it with an updated form (generally known as MiFID 2).

WHO IS SUBJECT TO THE RULES?

8.9 All persons and firms conducting "regulated activities" in the UK must be authorised by the FCA (unless they fall within an exemption) and must comply with the relevant FCA rules as set out in the Handbook.[7] There are three elements which make an activity a "regulated activity":

(1) It must be specified in the Financial Services and Markets Act 2000 (Regulated Activities) Order 2001.[8]

(2) It must be carried on "by way of business" as set out in the Financial Services and Markets Act 2000 (Carrying on Regulated Activities by Way of Business) Order 2001.[9]

(3) It must relate "to an investment of a specified kind" or be an activity specified as regulated in relation to "property of any kind".[10]

8.10 The FCA rules also distinguish in places between "MiFID or equivalent third country business" and "non-MiFID business." When incorporating MiFID into English law, the FCA decided that there were some situations that fall outside of MiFID where it was nonetheless appropriate to apply MiFID principles. There are other areas which fall outside MiFID entirely but where the FCA has created its own rules and principles.

---

[4] Markets in Financial Instruments Directive 2004/39/EC, Official Journal L145 of 30.4.2004 p 1.

[5] Markets in Financial Instruments Implementing Directive 2006/73/EC, Official Journal L241 of 2.9.2006 p 26.

[6] Markets in Financial Instruments Directive Regulation 1287/2006/EC, Official Journal L241 of 2.9.2006 p 1.

[7] Financial Services and Markets Act 2000, s 19.

[8] SI 2001 No 544.

[9] SI 2001 No 1177.

[10] Financial Services and Markets Act 2000, s 22.

8.11 Broadly speaking, MiFID business is business carried on by a MiFID investment firm.[11] A MiFID investment firm is "any legal person whose regular occupation or business is the provision of one or more investment services to third parties and/or the performance of one or more investment activities on a professional basis."[12] This definition is broad, and it is reined in by a list of exemptions under article 2. The exemptions are extensive and include:

(1) persons providing investment services exclusively in the administration of employee-participation schemes;[13]

(2) collective investment undertakings and pension funds;[14]

(3) persons providing investment advice in the course of providing another professional activity not covered by MiFID, where the provision of such advice is not specifically remunerated;[15] and

(4) persons whose business consists mainly of dealing on their own account.[16]

8.12 These exclusions are *only* relevant where the rules differ in their treatment of MiFID and non-MiFID business: the fact that something falls outside of MiFID does not mean that it falls outside the FCA rules. The applicability of the rules must always be determined by reference to the rules themselves rather than to MiFID.

8.13 Below we briefly turn to consider when the various intermediaries in a typical investment chain might be subject to the FCA Handbook rules.

Pension trustees

8.14 It is unlikely that pension trustees will fall under the FCA regulatory regime. However, several steps must be worked through to determine whether this is so in each case.

---

[11] FCA Handbook Glossary.

[12] Markets in Financial Instruments Directive 2004/39/EC, art 4(1)(1).

[13] Markets in Financial Instruments Directive 2004/39/EC, art 2(1)(e).

[14] Markets in Financial Instruments Directive 2004/39/EC, art 2(1)(h).

[15] Markets in Financial Instruments Directive 2004/39/EC, art 2(1)(j).

[16] Markets in Financial Instruments Directive 2004/39/EC, arts 2(1)(i),(k) and (l).

8.15 Managing investments belonging to another by way of business, in circumstances involving the exercise of discretion, is a regulated activity.[17] For the purposes of the Financial Services and Markets Act 2000 (FMSA 2000), trustees may be taken to be managing investments belonging to another despite the fact they will be the legal owners of the scheme's assets.[18] Under article 4 of the Financial Services and Markets Act 2000 (Carrying on Regulated Activities by Way of Business) Order 2001,[19] occupational pension scheme trustees will be taken to be managing the assets of their scheme by way of business unless a specific exception applies.

8.16 The key exception is where trustees delegate decision making to an investment manager. Under section 47(2) of the Pensions Act 1995, where an occupational pension scheme has assets including investments, an investment manager[20] *must* be appointed. Where the investment manager carries out all the "day-to-day" decisions relating to the management of securities or contractually-based investments and is authorised by the FCA, the trustees will fall within this exception.[21]

8.17 Unlike trust-based occupational schemes, the operation of a contract-based pension scheme is a regulated activity[22] and therefore within the scope of the FCA Handbook.

The investment consultant

8.18 In our meetings with stakeholders we were consistently told that investment consultants are not regulated by the FCA. This was said to be a particular concern. The provision of investment advice is only a regulated activity under FSMA where the advice is:

(1) given to the person in his capacity as investor or potential investor, or in his capacity as agent for an investor or a potential investor; and

(2) advice on the merits of his buying, selling, subscribing for or underwriting a *particular investment*, or exercising any right conferred by such an investment to buy, sell, subscribe for or underwrite such an investment.[23]

---

[17] Financial Services and Markets Act 2000, s 22 and sch 2 para 6; Financial Services and Markets Act 2000 (Regulated Activities) Order 2001 SI 2001 No 544, art 37.

[18] See D Frase, *Law and Regulation of Investment Management* (2nd ed 2011) para 9-025.

[19] SI 2001 No 1177.

[20] The Pensions Act 1995 uses the language of "fund manager", but the terminology of "investment manager" has been preferred throughout.

[21] Financial Services and Markets Act 2000 (Carrying on Regulated Activities by Way of Business) Order SI 2001 No 1177, art 4(1)(b).

[22] Financial Services and Markets Act 2000 (Regulated Activities) Order 2001 SI 2001 No 544, art 52.

[23] Financial Services and Markets Act 2000 (Regulated Activities) Order 2001 SI 2001 No 544, art 53.

8.19 "Advice on the merits" has been construed liberally. *Martin v Britannia Life*[24] involved a claim for damages for negligent financial advice. Advice had been given to enter into a package of transactions which included a re-mortgage of the claimants' home. The court held that "investment advice" included not only financial advice relating to an investment, but also any ancillary or associated transaction:

> Advice as to the "merits" of buying or surrendering an "investment" cannot sensibly be treated as confined to a consideration of the advantages or disadvantages of a particular "investment" as a product, without reference to the wider financial context in which the advice is tendered ... It must follow that the concept of "investment advice" will comprehend all financial advice given to a prospective client with a view to or in connection with the purchase, sale or surrender of an "investment", including advice as to any associated or ancillary transaction.[25]

8.20 Regulated investment advice must, however, relate to one or more transactions in specific investments, as opposed to generic advice.[26] In 2009, the Committee of European Securities Regulations[27] published a consultation paper on what constitutes generic advice and gave the following as examples:

(1) advice on the merits of investing in one geographical zone rather than another;

(2) advice on the merits of investing in certain asset classes rather than in others;

(3) advice on different types of investments, for example, whether it would be best for a client to invest directly or through a collective investment scheme; and

(4) advice to become the client of a particular firm or to use its services in a certain way, provided it does not relate to one or more specific investments.[28]

8.21 Accordingly, consistent with the concerns of stakeholders, it appears that investment consultants will not fall within the FCA regulatory regime so long as they only give "generic advice".

---

[24] [1999] All ER (D) 1495.

[25] [1999] All ER (D) 1495 at [5.2.5], by Parker J.

[26] D Frase, *Law and Regulation of Investment Management* (2nd ed 2011) para 3-026; see also Markets in Financial Instruments Implementing Directive 2006/73/EC, recital 81.

[27] The predecessor of the European Securities and Markets Authority.

[28] Committee of European Securities Regulations, *Understanding the definition of advice under MiFID* CESR/09-665 paras 32 and 39-41.

The investment manager

8.22 Investment managers operating in the UK must be authorised and regulated by the FCA, unless they are exempt persons.[29] This is because the management of investments constitutes a regulated activity, provided that it involves the exercise of discretion.[30]

Platform service providers

8.23 Whilst providing access to a platform is not in itself a regulated activity, it may involve carrying out a regulated activity. For example, it may involve:

    (1)   dealing in investments as agent;[31]

    (2)   arranging deals in investments;[32]

    (3)   safeguarding and administering assets;[33] or

    (4)   sending dematerialised instructions.[34]

The custodian

8.24 Custody is defined in article 40 of the Financial Services and Markets Act 2000 (Regulated Activities) Order 2001 as the activity consisting of both:

    (1)   the safeguarding of assets belonging to another; and

    (2)   the administration of those assets,

    or arranging for one or more other persons to carry on that activity.[35]

8.25 Where the assets are "investments" within the terms of the Order, custodians must be authorised.[36]

---

[29] Financial Services and Markets Act 2000, s 19(1).

[30] Financial Services and Markets Act 2000 (Regulated Activities) Order 2001 SI 2001 No 544, art 37.

[31] Financial Services and Markets Act 2000 (Regulated Activities) Order 2001 SI 2001 No 544, art 21.

[32] Financial Services and Markets Act 2000 (Regulated Activities) Order 2001 SI 2001 No 544, art 25.

[33] Financial Services and Markets Act 2000 (Regulated Activities) Order 2001 SI 2001 No 544, art 40.

[34] Financial Services and Markets Act 2000 (Regulated Activities) Order 2001 SI 2001 No 544, art 45.

[35] Both elements of the activity have to be conducted together, and conducted in relation to the same investments: M Yates and G Montagu, *The Law of Global Custody* (4th ed 2013) para 7.4.

[36] See Financial Services and Markets Act 2000 (Regulated Activities) Order 2001 SI 2001 No 544, art 40(2).

8.26 Custody services will not automatically fall within the scope of the current MiFID regime.[37] This may change under the MiFID 2 proposals.[38] The significance of this distinction is that firms holding client money in a non-MiFID context for a professional client are permitted to agree with the client that the FCA's Client Money Rules do not apply.[39] MIFiD firms cannot opt-out of the rules.

WHAT DO THE RULES REQUIRE?

8.27 The FCA Handbook is split into various sections known as sourcebooks or manuals. Different sections of the Handbook will apply depending on the specific activity that is being carried out and the categorisation of the client. For our purposes, we discuss the following sections of the Handbook:

(1) Principles for Business (PRIN) – these form part of the "High Level Standards" which apply to all regulated entities. These High Level Standards "act as a general embodiment of the FSA's regulatory approach"[40] and are not intended to create third party rights.[41]

(2) Senior Management Arrangements, Systems and Controls (SYSC) – like PRIN, these form part of the "High Level Standards" which apply to all regulated entities.

(3) Conduct of Business Sourcebook (COBS) – or "Business Standards". The specific rules often depend on how a client is categorised under the rules, which we discuss at paragraphs 8.42 to 8.52 below.

Principles for business

8.28 The FCA imposes certain fundamental obligations on all authorised persons.[42] These include:

(1) A firm must conduct its business with due skill, care and diligence (Principle 2).

(2) A firm must take reasonable care to organise and control its affairs responsibly and effectively, with adequate risk management systems (Principle 3).

(3) A firm must observe proper standards of market conduct (Principle 5).

[37] MiFID only applies to "investment firms", which are defined as legal persons "whose regular occupation or business is the provision of one or more investment services to third parties and/or the performance of one or more investment activities on a professional basis": Markets in Financial Instruments Directive 2004/39/EC, art 4(1)(1).

[38] M Yates and G Montagu, *The Law of Global Custody* (4th ed 2013) para 7.14.

[39] Above, para 7.22.

[40] M Blair QC and G Walker, *Financial Services Law* (1st ed 2006) para 3.74.

[41] Rights to damages have been disapplied under Financial Services and Markets Act 2000, s 138D(3); see FCA, *Principles for Businesses* (2013) para 3.4.4.

[42] "Authorised persons" are defined in s 31 of the Financial Services and Markets Act 2000, and include persons who have permission to carry on regulated activities under Part 4A of the Financial Services and Markets Act 2000.

(4)   A firm must pay due regard to the interests of its customers and treat them fairly (Principle 6).

(5)   A firm must pay due regard to the information needs of its clients, and communicate information to them in a way which is clear, fair and not misleading (Principle 7).

(6)   A firm must manage conflicts of interest fairly, both between itself and its customers and between a customer and another client (Principle 8).

(7)   A firm must take reasonable care to ensure the suitability of its advice and discretionary decisions for any customer who is entitled to rely upon its judgment (Principle 9).

(8)   A firm must arrange adequate protection for clients' assets when it is responsible for them (Principle 10).[43]

8.29   The PRIN rules are enforceable by the FCA, but they do not give a cause of action to a private person (discussed below).

Senior Management Arrangements, Systems and Controls Sourcebook 10

8.30   Detailed FCA rules on conflicts of interest are contained in SYSC 10, which largely replicates the equivalent provisions of MiFID. These rules apply to all clients regardless of classification.[44] However, the specific requirements differ for a "firm", a "common platform firm" and a "management company". As an overview, we set out the general rules that apply to a "firm" below.

8.31   Some commentators suggest that the SYSC 10 rules will only apply where there is a fiduciary relationship recognised in equity.[45] This is because:

> The starting point of SYSC 10 is the concept of a conflict, not the concept of a fiduciary, and although the existence of a conflict presupposes the existence of a fiduciary relationship, this is consistent with the idea that a conflict does not arise outside the scope of a fiduciary relationship.[46]

However, this approach is far from clear. SYSC 10.1.1R states the section applies to regulated firms carrying on regulated activities.

8.32   The SYSC 10 rules provide three key controls to deal with conflicts of interest. First, they require a firm to identify any conflicts that arise or may arise. Second, they require a firm to manage those conflicts. Finally, if a firm is unable to manage conflicts to sufficiently protect the interests of its client, the rules require the firm to disclose the conflict. As we discuss, these rules fall below the fiduciary standards on which they are loosely based.

---

[43]   FCA Handbook PRIN 2.1.1R.

[44]   FCA Handbook SYSC 10.1.2G.

[45]   D Frase, *Law and Regulation of Investment Management* (2nd ed 2011) para 8-041.

[46]   Above, para 8-041.

Identifying conflicts

8.33   SYSC 10.1.3R requires a firm to take all reasonable steps to identify conflicts between the firm and a client, or one client of the firm and another client. The term "conflict of interest" is not defined. Instead, SYSC 10.1.4AG and SYSC 10.1.4BG list five[47] situations that a firm should take into account, "as a minimum", to identify whether a conflict of interest may arise (or has arisen). These are where the firm, a relevant person[48] or a person linked to the firm:

(1)   is likely to make a financial gain, or avoid a financial loss, at the expense of the client;[49]

(2)   has an interest in the outcome of a service provided to the client, or of a transaction carried out on behalf of the client, which is distinct from the client's interest in that outcome;

(3)   has a financial or other incentive to favour the interest of a client or group of clients over another;

(4)   carries on the same business as the client; or

(5)   receives or will receive from a person other than the client an inducement in relation to a service provided to the client, other than the standard commission or fee for that service.

8.34   The concept of a conflict of interest under SYSC 10 differs from the fiduciary rules. For example, an individual will breach their fiduciary duty where they make a secret profit, regardless of the effect on the principal.[50] Under SYSC 10, a gain to the firm is not a breach of the conflict duty unless there is (or there is the potential for) actual disadvantage to the client. This is confirmed by SYSC 10.1.5G, which states:

> It is not enough that the firm may gain a benefit if there is not also a possible disadvantage to a client, or that one client to whom the firm owes a duty may make a gain or avoid a loss without there being a concomitant possible loss to another such client.[51]

---

[47]   A sixth criterion applies specifically to management companies providing collective portfolio management services for a UCITS scheme; see 10.1.4R(2A).

[48]   As defined in article 2(3) of the Markets in Financial Instruments Implementing Directive 2006/73/EC.

[49]   The fact that a firm charges for its services is not in itself a conflict of interest. On the contrary, there is an implied contractual right to reasonable remuneration. See D Frase, *Law and Regulation of Investment Management* (2nd ed 2011) para 8-053.

[50]   *Regal (Hastings) Ltd v Gulliver* [1967] 2 AC 134, by Lord Russell at 145. However, a fiduciary will not be liable for breach of their fiduciary duty not to make a profit if the principal gives consent after a full and proper disclosure has been made to them.

[51]   FCA Handbook SYSC 10.1.5G, replicating recital 24 of the Markets in Financial Instruments Implementing Directive 2006/73/EC. For discussion, see D Frase, *Law and Regulation of Investment Management* (2nd ed 2011) para 8-059.

8.35 In a briefing paper, Slaughter and May comment on this provision:

> The fiduciary obligation, on the other hand, is more stringent; it is that the fiduciary may not make a profit from its position as such. This can be illustrated by reference to the case of dealing errors, where an investment manager may mistakenly buy securities for the account of a client but in breach of the investment limits agreed with the client. If the manager sells down the holding to restore the agreed limits a profit may be made in a rising market – but for whose account is that profit? If the securities are re-sold before formal allocation to the client, then the firm could argue that the profit is not made at the expense of the client, because the client was not supposed to become the owner of the surplus securities in the first place. However, the position under fiduciary law is clear. Unless the client expressly consents to it, the firm cannot retain any profit it makes from its position as investment manager, even in respect of dealing mistakes. It is not enough, for example, for a firm which absorbs any losses arising on dealing errors to claim that its retention of profits means that the position is neutral in the long run.[52]

Managing conflicts

8.36 As we set out in Chapter 5, fiduciary duties will be breached whenever a person acts where their personal interests conflict with those of their principal or where their duty to one principal conflicts with their duty to another. The SYSC 10 rules impose a lesser standard. They require a firm to:

> Maintain and operate effective organisational and administrative arrangements with a view to taking all reasonable steps to prevent conflicts of interest ... from constituting or giving rise to a material risk of damage to the interests of its clients.[53]

This is treated as a duty to manage conflicts, rather than avoid conflicts altogether.

Disclosing conflicts

8.37 SYSC 10.1.8R provides that if the arrangements made by a firm to manage conflicts of interest are insufficient to prevent the risk of damage to the client, the firm must clearly disclose the general nature and/or source of conflicts to the client before undertaking business for the client. Further, such disclosure must be made in a durable medium and in sufficient detail, taking into account the nature of the client, to enable the client to make an informed decision.

---

[52] Slaughter and May, *Briefing paper: Conflicts of interest – MiFID and the General Law* (2008) p 3.

[53] FCA Handbook SYSC 10.1.7R.

8.38 The emphasis that the FCA Handbook places on organisational requirements has been said to reflect the intention that it "should be preventative rather than simply reacting to actual breaches of duty".[54] SYSC 10.1.9G clarifies that the disclosure by a firm should not exempt it from the obligation to maintain and operate the organisational arrangements mandated by SYSC 10.1.7R. It has been suggested that SYSC 10.1.9G actively discourages the use of disclosure as opposed to conflict management.[55] The FSA has said:

> This test applies in relation to specific conflicts of interest, rather than generally, and that the purpose of disclosure is to give the client an opportunity to consider whether or not to accept the service offered by the firm. These proposals do not imply that disclosure cannot be the appropriate tool for a firm to employ. But a firm must consider whether other reasonable measures would be effective to reduce the potential damage to the client's interests before making a disclosure.[56]

Chinese walls

8.39 As a way of managing conflicts a firm may use a "Chinese wall". This is an arrangement that requires information held by a person in the course of carrying on one part of the business to be withheld from, or not to be used for, persons with whom it acts in the course of carrying on another part of its business. Where a Chinese wall is operating, SCYC 10 recognises that the duty of a firm to utilise all the information available to it for the benefit of the client does not apply.[57]

Conduct of Business Sourcebook

8.40 COBS sets out rules designed to ensure firms adhere to certain minimum standards in dealing with their clients.[58] Much of COBS implements MiFID, although in certain respects it goes further.[59]

8.41 Many rules depend on how a client is classified. For example, some rules do not apply where a client is classified as an eligible counterparty and a firm carries out "eligible counterparty business".[60] We therefore begin by explaining the highly complex system of client categorisation for the purpose of COBS.[61]

---

[54] D Frase, *Law and Regulation of Investment Management* (2nd ed 2011) para 8-060.

[55] Above, para 8-073.

[56] FSA, *Consultation Paper 06/09* (2006) para 9.10.

[57] FCA Handbook SYSC 10.2.2R.

[58] L Van Setten, *The Law of Institutional Investment Management* (1st ed 2009) para 2.02.

[59] *McMeel and Virgo on Financial Advice and Financial Products: Law and Liability* (Release 10 2012) para VI.1.237.

[60] See para 8.61 below.

[61] Here we explain the categorisation for the purpose of COBS; categorisation may differ depending on the section of the Handbook that is in issue.

Client categorisation

8.42 COBS 3 provides for the classification of clients into two main categories: retail and professional.[62] A third category of "eligible counterparty" exists, but is relevant only in relation to "eligible counterparty business".[63]

8.43 These rules are largely derived from MiFID. The "retail client" classification is the default. A firm is classified as a "retail client" where they are neither a "professional client", nor an "eligible counterparty".[64]

8.44 Professional clients are either "elective" professional clients or "per se" professional clients.[65]

8.45 There are detailed rules on when a firm may treat a client as an elective professional client.[66] Generally, a firm must undertake an adequate assessment of the expertise, experience and knowledge of the client which provides reasonable reassurance that the client is capable of managing their own investment decisions and understands the risk. The client must request the categorisation in writing and the firm must then provide a clear written warning of the protections the client might lose. The client must confirm in writing that they are aware of the consequences of the categorisation. In relation to MiFID business, further criteria must be satisfied such as the number of transactions and size of transactions that the client has carried out.

8.46 The rules also provide a list of per se professional clients.[67] The list includes any entity required to be authorised or regulated to operate in the financial markets, which includes investment firms, pension funds, collective investment schemes, insurance companies and "any other institutional investor".[68] There is no definition given of "pension fund", and the same words appear in MiFID itself.[69] We have been told that there has been no guidance forthcoming from the European Commission or the FCA on what "pension fund" means in this context. There could be important implications for treatment of clients by intermediaries if, for example, a small five member pension scheme is treated as a per se professional client.

8.47 A further category of per se professional clients are "large undertakings". There are two definitions of "large undertaking", depending on whether the business is within or outside the scope of MiFID.

---

[62] FCA Handbook COBS 3.3.1R(1).

[63] FCA Handbook COBS 3.6.1R(2).

[64] FCA Handbook COBS 3.4.1R.

[65] FCA Handbook COBS 3.5.1R.

[66] FCA Handbook COBS 3.5.3R.

[67] FCA Handbook COBS 3.5.2R.

[68] FCA Handbook COBS 3.5.2R(1).

[69] Markets in Financial Instruments Directive 2004/39/EC, Annex 2, para 1(1)(f).

8.48   For MiFID business, a client is classified as a per se professional client if it meets two of the following criteria:

(1)   a balance sheet of €20 million or more;

(2)   a net turnover of €40 million or more; or

(3)   own funds of €2 million or more.[70]

8.49   The slightly more complex criteria relating to non-MiFID business are set out at COBS 3.5.2R(3). When engaging in non-MiFID business, the trustees of an occupational pension scheme, or the trustees or operators of a personal pension or stakeholder pension scheme, will be treated as per se professional clients if the scheme meets two conditions. Firstly, the scheme has (or had at any time during the previous two years) at least 50 members; and, secondly, the assets under management total at least £10 million.[71] Other trustees (that is, non-pension trustees) will be treated as per se professional clients if the trust has (or had at any time during the previous two years) assets of over £10 million.[72]

8.50   Eligible counterparties are a sub-category of professional client. A client may be categorised as an eligible counterparty if:

(1)   they are listed as a per se eligible counterparty in COBS 3.6.2R; or

(2)   they may be treated as an elective eligible counterparty. The list of per se eligible counterparties is similar to the list of per se professional clients.[73]

8.51   Like professional client categorisations, there are detailed rules on when a firm may choose to treat a client as an elective eligible counterparty.[74] We do not rehearse them here.

8.52   A firm must allow a professional client or an eligible counterparty to request re-categorisation as a client that benefits from a higher degree of protection.[75] Such re-categorisation may, for example, be on a general basis or on a trade-by-trade basis.[76] The responsibility for such a request rests with the client.[77] However, this does not preclude a firm acting of its own volition. COBS 3.7.3R provides that a firm may, either on its own initiative or at the request of the client:

(1)   treat as a professional client or a retail client a client that might otherwise be categorised as a per se eligible counterparty;

---

[70]   FCA Handbook COBS 3.5.2R(2).

[71]   FCA Handbook COBS 3.5.2R(3)(e).

[72]   FCA Handbook COBS 3.5.2R(3)(d).

[73]   FCA Handbook COBS 3.6.2R.

[74]   FCA Handbook COBS 3.6.4R.

[75]   FCA Handbook COBS 3.7.1R.

[76]   FCA Handbook COBS 3.7.7G.

[77]   FCA Handbook COBS 3.7.2G.

(2)   treat as a retail client a client that might otherwise be categorised as a per se professional client.

Generally applicable rules

8.53   Here we discuss the limited rules which will apply regardless of the categorisation of a client. COBS 9 imposes "know-your-customer" requirements. This is one of the rules that differs in application depending on whether the business is MiFID or non-MiFID business. It applies to all business falling within MiFID, regardless of client classification.[78] However, it only applies to non-MiFID business where the client is a retail client, or where the firm is managing the assets of an occupational pension scheme, stakeholder pension scheme or personal pension scheme.[79]

8.54   Principally, "know-your-customer" requires a firm to take reasonable steps to ensure that the advice it gives and investment management decisions it takes are suitable for its client.[80] It applies to firms that manage investments on behalf of a client[81] or make personal recommendations about particular investments.[82]

8.55   Firstly, COBS 9 requires that, when making a personal recommendation or managing a client's investments, a firm must obtain the necessary information regarding the client's:

(1)   knowledge and experience in the investment field relevant to the specific type of designated investment or service;

(2)   financial situation; and

(3)   investment objectives;

so as to enable the firm to make the recommendation, or take the decision, which is suitable for the client.[83]

---

[78]   FCA Handbook COBS 9.1.3R.

[79]   FCA Handbook COBS 9.1.4R.

[80]   FCA Handbook COBS 9.2.1R(1).

[81]   FCA Handbook COBS 9.1.3R.

[82]   Financial Services and Markets Act 2000 (Regulated Activities) Order 2001, SI 2001 No 544. This only applies if their recommendations fall within the definition of "advice on investments" as set out in art 53 of the Regulated Activities Order. Because this requires advice on particular investments, investment consultants are unlikely to be subject to COBS 9.

[83]   FCA Handbook COBS 9.2.1R(2).

8.56   There are further highly detailed rules about the extent of the information which must be obtained.[84] It includes matters such as the length of time the client wishes to hold an investment,[85] their financial status[86] and the nature, volume and frequency of previous transactions.[87] If a firm does not obtain this information, it must not make a personal recommendation to the client or take a decision to trade for them.[88]

8.57   Second, COBS 9 provides guidelines on how firms should assess suitability. COBS 9.3.1G states:

(1)   A transaction may be unsuitable for a client because of the risks of the designated investments involved, the type of transaction, the characteristics of the order or the frequency of the trading.

(2)   In the case of managing investments, a transaction might also be unsuitable if it would result in an unsuitable portfolio.

8.58   COBS 9 is not applicable to "execution only" type business (that is, business which does not involve the provision of advice or the exercise of discretion over investments). All firms which provide "investment services" in the course of MiFID business which are not subject to COBS 9 are subject to "appropriateness" requirements in COBS 10.[89]

8.59   The appropriateness requirement requires a firm to ask their client to provide information regarding their knowledge and experience in the relevant investment field, so as to enable the firm to assess whether the service or product is appropriate for the client.[90] Where the client is classified as a professional client, the firm is entitled to assume that they have the necessary knowledge and experience.[91]

8.60   An exception applies where the firm is only transmitting orders in respect of non-complex financial instruments, at the initiative of the client. In order to avoid the requirement of assessing appropriateness, the firm must warn the client that suitability and appropriateness assessments have not been made.

Non-eligible counterparty business rules

8.61   The rules we discuss in the following paragraphs do not apply where a firm carries out "eligible counterparty business".[92]

---

[84]   FCA Handbook COBS 9.2.2R(1)-(3).

[85]   FCA Handbook COBS 9.2.2R(2).

[86]   FCA Handbook COBS 9.2.2R(3).

[87]   FCA Handbook COBS 9.2.3R(2).

[88]   FCA Handbook COBS 9.2.6R.

[89]   FCA Handbook COBS 10.1.1R.

[90]   FCA Handbook COBS 10.2.1R.

[91]   FCA Handbook COBS 10.2.1R(2)(b).

[92]   FCA Handbook COBS 1 Annex 1.

ACT HONESTLY, FAIRLY AND PROFESSIONALLY

8.62 Under COBS 2.1.1R, a firm must act honestly, fairly and professionally in accordance with the best interests of its client in relation to designated investment business carried on:

(1) for a retail client, whether the business is MiFID business or not; and

(2) for any other client in relation to MiFID business.

DISCLOSURE OF COSTS AND RISKS

8.63 Firms must provide, under COBS 2.2.1R, appropriate information in a comprehensible form to a client about:

(1) the firm and its services;

(2) designated investments and proposed investment strategies;

(3) execution venues; and

(4) costs and associated charges.

8.64 COBS 14.3.2R states that:

A firm must provide a client with a general description of the nature and risks of designated investments, taking into account, in particular, the client's categorisation as a retail client or a professional client.

INDUCEMENTS: "COMMISSIONS, FEES AND NON-MONETARY BENEFITS"

8.65 In broad terms, COBS 2.3.1R states that a firm must not pay or accept any fee or commission, or provide or receive any non-monetary benefit, in relation to designated investment business carried on for a client other than:

(1) those paid or provided to or by the client (or a person on behalf of the client); or

(2) those paid or provided to or by a third party (or a person acting on behalf of a third party) if:

(a) they do not impair compliance with the firm's duty to act in the best interests of the client; and

(b) the existence, nature and amount of the fee, commission or benefit is clearly disclosed to the client in a manner that is comprehensive, accurate and understandable, before the provision of the service. Where the amount cannot be ascertained, the firm can disclose the method of calculating that amount.

8.66 COBS 11.6 sets additional rules for investment managers when they execute customer orders. An investment manager must not accept goods or services from brokers and others when it:

(1) executes its customer orders through a broker or another person;

(2)   passes on the broker's or other person's charges to its customers; and

(3)   is offered goods or services in return for the charges referred to in (2).[93]

8.67   However, this prohibition does not apply where the broker provides the investment manager with research. The investment manager can accept an inducement if it has reasonable grounds to be satisfied that the goods or services received in return for the charges:

(a)   are related to the execution of trades on behalf of the investment manager's customers, or comprise the provision of research; and

(b)   will reasonably assist the investment manager in the provision of its services to its customers and do not, and are not likely to, impair compliance with the duty of the investment manager to act in the best interests of its customers.[94]

8.68   Therefore, the only services which may be paid for out of dealing commission are execution and research. This is important because investment managers may pay brokers for corporate access through dealing commission. The Investment Management Association has commented, in light of the rules, that:

Many managers have informed brokers that they consider themselves unable now to pay for corporate access through dealing commission. The IMA understands that many will now ensure that corporate access is not a factor used in voting on how dealing commissions are allocated to brokers. A fear remains that brokers may still recover costs associated with corporate access through bundled content services: this is something that must be dealt with commercially.[95]

BEST EXECUTION

8.69   MiFID imposes a duty of best execution on market intermediaries, which has been implemented by the FCA in COBS 11.2. COBS 11.2.1R states that:

A firm must take all reasonable steps to obtain, when executing orders, the best possible result for its clients taking into account the execution factors.

8.70   The execution factors are price, costs, speed, likelihood of execution and settlement, size, nature or any other consideration relevant to the execution of an order.[96]

---

[93]   FCA Handbook COBS 11.6.3R(1).

[94]   FCA Handbook COBS 11.6.3R(2).

[95]   Investment Management Association, *Use of Dealing Commission: Corporate Access / Research Services* (2013) p 5.

[96]   FCA Handbook COBS Glossary.

ENFORCEMENT

Enforcement by the FCA

8.71 Where the rules are breached, the FCA has a wide range of disciplinary, civil and criminal enforcement powers. These include powers to:

(1) withdraw authorisation;[97]

(2) prohibit an individual from operating in all or some regulated financial activities;[98]

(3) publicly censure firms and individuals;[99]

(4) impose financial penalties;[100]

(5) seek injunctions, including asset-freezing injunctions;[101]

(6) seek restitution orders;[102] and

(7) prosecute firms and individuals.[103]

Remedies available to private persons

8.72 In some limited circumstances, a private person may bring an action, if they have suffered loss as a result of breach of FCA rules. This is set out in section 138D of FMSA, which states:

> A contravention by an authorised person of a rule made by the FCA is actionable at the suit of a private person who suffers loss as a result of the contravention, subject to the defences and other incidents applying to actions for breach of statutory duty.

8.73 The section has no effect on any other causes of action a claimant may have at common law (for example, negligence).

---

[97] Financial Services and Markets Act 2000, s 63.

[98] Financial Services and Markets Act 2000, s 56.

[99] Financial Services and Markets Act 2000, s 66(3)(b).

[100] Financial Services and Markets Act 2000, s 66(3)(a).

[101] Financial Services and Markets Act 2000, s 380.

[102] Financial Services and Markets Act 2000, s 382.

[103] Financial Services and Markets Act 2000, ss 401 and 402.

8.74 This right, however, is extremely limited:

(1) The claimant must be a private person, as defined in the Right of Action Regulations.[104] Generally, the claimant must be an individual. Corporate persons may only use this provision if they were not "conducting business of any kind".[105] As we shall see,[106] *Titan Steel Wheels Ltd v Royal Bank of Scotland plc*[107] gave a limited definition to "conducting business".

(2) The FCA must not have removed the availability of a right of action for the rule in question.[108] Among those rules which are not actionable are:

(a) the PRIN rules;[109]

(b) SYSC 10;[110] and

(c) the fair, clear and not misleading rule under COBS 4.2.1R if, in relation to a particular communication or financial promotion, a firm takes reasonable steps to ensure it complies with the fair, clear and not misleading rule.[111]

8.75 The private person must have suffered loss as a result of the contravention. In *Rubenstein v HSBC Bank plc*, Lord Justice Rix said that the approach to causation, foreseeability and remoteness will be "guided by the focus and purpose of the statutory provisions".[112] In this way, "whereas the underlying principles [of causation, foreseeability and remoteness] may be the same, they may operate in different ways".[113]

8.76 Finally, in Appendix B we describe the FCA's powers to implement consumer redress schemes. We explain that the 1994 review of personal pension mis-selling was a prototype for these powers.

---

[104] Financial Services and Markets Act 2000 (Rights of Action) Regulations 2001, SI 2001 No 2256, reg 3.

[105] Financial Services and Markets Act 2000 (Rights of Action) Regulations 2001, SI 2001 No 2256, reg 3(1)(b).

[106] See para 11.89 below.

[107] [2010] EWHC 211.

[108] See Financial Services and Markets Act 2000, s 138D(3).

[109] FCA Handbook PRIN 3.4.4R.

[110] FCA Handbook SYSC 1 Annex 1.2.19R.

[111] FCA Handbook COBS 4.2.6R.

[112] *Rubenstein v HSBC Bank plc* [2012] EWCA Civ 1184 at [46].

[113] Above, at [45], by Rix LJ.

CONCLUSION

8.77 Market participants are subject to an extensive regime of regulatory rules. The rules aim to ensure that firms deal fairly with their clients. Firms must act with due care, skill and diligence. They should manage any conflicts between their client's interests and their own, or those of others. They should take reasonable care to ensure that any advice they give or decisions they make are suitable.

8.78 These rules are complex and different rules apply to different market participants. Where clients are classified as "professional", such as pension funds, market participants are exempt from some requirements. In some cases regulatory rules sit uneasily with the other legal duties of market participants. Rules such as those about conflicts of interest differ from what fiduciary duties require. In Chapter 11 we consider how far the courts are influenced by FCA rules in formulating the civil duties of market participants.

PART 4

ANALYSIS

CHAPTER 9
APPLYING THE LAW TO THE INVESTMENT CHAIN: OUR TERMS OF REFERENCE

9.1 Having set out the law in general terms, in Part 4 we now apply the law to the questions we have been asked to consider.

OUR TERMS OF REFERENCE

9.2 Our terms of reference ask the Law Commission to form a view on how the current law of fiduciary duties applies to investment intermediaries and their advisers. Specifically, we are asked:

   (1) To investigate the extent to which, under existing law, fiduciary duties apply to:

      (a) intermediaries (including investment managers and pension scheme trustees) investing on behalf of others;

      (b) those providing advice or other services to those undertaking investment activity.

   (2) To evaluate what fiduciary duties permit or require such persons to consider when developing or discharging an investment strategy in the best interests of the ultimate beneficiaries: in particular, the extent to which fiduciaries may, or must, consider:

      (a) factors relevant to long-term investment performance which might not have an immediate financial impact, including questions of sustainability or environmental and social impact;

      (b) interests beyond the maximisation of financial return;

      (c) generally prevailing ethical standards, and / or the ethical views of their beneficiaries, even where this may not be in the immediate financial interest of those beneficiaries.

   (3) To consult relevant stakeholders in the equity investment chain on their understanding of what the content and application of fiduciary duties in this context is, or should be, and to consider their responses;

   (4) To consider whether fiduciary duties, as established in law or as applied in practice, are conducive to investment strategies that are in the best interests of the ultimate beneficiaries. We are asked to consider this against listed criteria.

9.3 Finally, we are asked to identify any areas where changes are needed and to make recommendations.

9.4 In this Part we give our initial view of how the law currently applies to financial markets. In Chapter 14, we ask stakeholders whether the law is satisfactory.

PENSION TRUSTEES' INVESTMENT STRATEGIES

9.5 Our initial meetings were dominated by the concerns of pension trustees. They focused on which factors they should (or should not) take into account when investing assets on behalf of members. In particular, should a pension fund investment strategy take into account environmental or social factors, and how far might it go beyond maximising long-term return?

9.6 We deal with this issue in Chapter 10. The case of *Cowan v Scargill* is quoted as saying that fiduciaries should exercise their powers in the best interests of their beneficiaries.[1] We discuss this difficult case and other cases in the field. Similarly, the Occupational Pension Scheme (Investment) Regulations 2005 require the investment of pension members' assets in the best interests of the scheme members and beneficiaries.[2] These regulations apply not only to pension trustees but also to the immediate investment managers when pension trustees delegate decisions to them.

9.7 We consider five factors which pension trustees and their investment managers may wish to take into account when making investment decisions. These are:

(1) wider factors relevant to long-term investment performance;

(2) wider systemic considerations;

(3) beneficiaries' quality of life;

(4) ethical issues; and

(5) the views of the beneficiaries.

9.8 We consider stakeholders' views and reach a tentative conclusion on how far pension trustees may, or indeed must, take each factor into account.

OTHERS IN THE INVESTMENT CHAIN

9.9 We then turn our attention to other intermediaries in the investment chain and those who provide advice or services to them. Our terms of reference ask us to investigate how far fiduciary duties apply to them.

9.10 Chapter 11 outlines the courts' general approach. As we shall see, the courts have been reluctant to override the contractual arrangements made between sophisticated parties, or to add new duties to the detailed rules imposed by the regulators. The courts have tended to confine fiduciary duties to those who act on behalf of individuals, at the lower rungs of the investment chain. Although it is difficult to be definitive, it appears unlikely that the courts would intervene to impose fiduciary duties on sophisticated commercial players further up the chain.

---

[1] [1985] Ch 270 at 287.

[2] SI 2005 No 3378, reg 4(2).

9.11 Chapter 12 addresses specific issues. We start by looking at the fiduciary duties of those involved in contract-based pensions. During discussions, consultees frequently said that contract-based pension providers were not subject to fiduciary duties. We think this may be an over-simplification. On the other hand, the law in this area is far from clear. It is particularly uncertain how often scheme providers must review the suitability of their schemes.

9.12 We then look at how fiduciary duties might apply to others in the scheme, including investment consultants, brokers, collective investment schemes and custodians. We consider some areas of controversy, including conflicts of interest for investment consultants and whether custodians should rebate stock lending fees. There is uncertainty about how the courts would decide these issues, as the outcome of any litigation is highly fact dependent.

WORKPLACE DEFINED CONTRIBUTION PENSIONS: PROBLEMS IN PRACTICE

9.13 Our terms of reference ask us not only to evaluate fiduciary duties as established in law but also to consider their effect in practice. Recently, a series of reports has highlighted problems with the way that the interests of beneficiaries are safeguarded in workplace defined contribution (DC) pensions. In Chapter 13 we summarise the evidence, drawing particularly on a market study by the Office of Fair Trading published in September 2013.

9.14 For contract-based pensions, we conclude that the law is unduly uncertain. For trust-based schemes, it is clearly established that trustees owe fiduciary duties to act in the best interests of beneficiaries. However, the law may not be enough. The duties need good enforcement mechanisms. They also need to be embedded in industry structures which ensure that those charged with safeguarding beneficiaries' interests have the expertise and resources to carry out their duties effectively.

THE MEANING OF FIDUCIARY DUTIES

9.15 As we saw in Chapter 5, the courts have given the phrase "fiduciary duty" a narrow legal meaning. Several cases have emphasised that not every breach of duty by a fiduciary is a breach of fiduciary duty.[3] Fiduciary duties sit alongside the duties that attach to the exercise of a power and duties of care.

9.16 We have not interpreted our terms of reference in this narrow legalistic way. Instead we have looked at all the duties which require a trustee, adviser or other market participant to put the interests of another above their own. Many of these duties are "judge-made", so we start with the case-law. The cases, however, must be read in conjunction with the pensions legislation outlined in Chapter 7, and the Financial Conduct Authority (FCA) Handbook. In this Part we draw on the various sources of rules outlined in Part 3, including fiduciary duties in the narrow sense, duties attached to the exercise of a power, duties of care, the pensions legislation and the FCA Handbook.

---

[3] See paras 5.52 to 5.54 above.

CHAPTER 10
PENSION TRUSTEES' DUTIES TO INVEST IN THE "BEST INTERESTS" OF OTHERS

10.1 The case of *Cowan v Scargill*[1] stated that the "starting point" for a fiduciary is to exercise their powers in the best interests of their beneficiaries. Where the purpose of a trust is to provide financial benefits this usually means their best financial interests.[2] As we discuss below, this case has proved controversial. It has become the focus of the debate about what those subject to fiduciary duties are entitled to take into account when making investment decisions.

10.2 Here we consider *Cowan v Scargill* and three other cases which have been prominent in this debate: *Harries v Church Commissioners*;[3] *Martin v City of Edinburgh District Council*;[4] and *Buttle v Saunders*.[5] Drawing on these cases, we set out the main principles.

10.3 We then consider five factors which pension trustees may wish to take into account when making investment decisions. We summarise the views expressed on these issues, and reach a tentative conclusion on how far pension trustees may, or indeed must, take them into account. Finally, we consider the role of investment managers when trustees delegate decisions to them.

10.4 We concentrate on pension trusts because they are at the centre of the debate. They are large and significant funds, focused on long-term outcomes. However, at the end of the chapter we discuss how similar principles would apply in general terms to other trustees.

COWAN V SCARGILL

The facts

10.5 *Cowan v Scargill* was a dispute between the trustees of a mineworkers' pension scheme. Five trustees appointed by the National Union of Mineworkers (NUM) refused to approve an investment plan unless it was amended to prohibit investments in overseas companies or in oil and gas. The other trustees claimed that this was a breach of fiduciary duty. The leading NUM trustee, Arthur Scargill, argued the case in person. He said that such investments were against union policy, would damage the coal industry and would be against beneficiaries' interests.[6] He argued that he could maintain this objection, even if it was to the fund's financial detriment.[7]

---

[1] [1985] Ch 270.

[2] Above, at 287.

[3] [1992] 1 WLR 1241.

[4] [1989] Pens LR 9, 1988 SLT 329.

[5] [1950] 2 All ER 193.

[6] [1985] Ch 270 at 282.

[7] Above, at 284-285.

The decision

10.6 The court held the NUM trustees were in breach of their fiduciary duties. Their duty was to put the interests of their beneficiaries first, and normally this meant their best financial interests.[8] The court recognised there may be circumstances in which financially disadvantageous arrangements may be in the beneficiaries' best interests, but the burden of proving this would rest very heavily on the trustees.[9] Fiduciaries could take social and political factors into account when making investment decisions, but would be open to criticism if that meant the investment was less beneficial.[10] Further, fiduciaries should not be influenced by their personal views and may even have to act dishonourably (although not illegally) to obtain the best result for their beneficiaries.[11]

10.7 On the facts, the court found the proposed exclusion of certain investments was not in the beneficiaries' best interests. In particular, the interests of retirees, and the widows and children of deceased miners, differed from the interests of the union and the industry as a whole. The connection between the coal mining industry and the beneficiaries was "too remote and insubstantial",[12] so the trustees should not have based their investment decisions on the effect on the industry.

10.8 Sir Robert Megarry VC stated the applicable law:

> The starting point is the duty of trustees to exercise their powers in the best interests of the present and future beneficiaries of the trust, holding the scales impartially between different classes of beneficiaries. This duty of the trustees towards their beneficiaries is paramount. They must, of course, obey the law; but subject to that, they must put the interests of their beneficiaries first. When the purpose of the trust is to provide financial benefits for the beneficiaries, as is usually the case, the best interests of the beneficiaries are normally their best financial interests. In the case of a power of investment, as in the present case, the power must be exercised so as to yield the best return for the beneficiaries, judged in relation to the risks of the investments in question; and the prospects of the yield of income and capital appreciation both have to be considered in judging the return from the investment.[13]

---

[8] [1985] Ch 270 at 287.

[9] Above, at 288.

[10] Above, at 287.

[11] Above, at 287-288.

[12] Above, at 292.

[13] Above, at 286-287.

10.9 Arthur Scargill said that trustees could not be criticised for excluding some investments for social or political reasons. The judge did not accept this assertion "in its full width". He continued:

> If the investment in fact made is equally beneficial to the beneficiaries, then criticism would be difficult to sustain in practice, whatever the position in theory. But if the investment in fact made is less beneficial, then both in theory and in practice the trustees would normally be open to criticism.[14]

The debate

10.10 *Cowan v Scargill* has sparked great debate.[15] The statement that "the best interests of the beneficiaries are normally their best financial interests" could be seen as precluding pension schemes from taking into account environmental, social and governance issues when making investment decisions.[16] However, many believe that the case would not be interpreted in this way today.[17]

10.11 The 2005 Freshfields Report[18] said *Cowan v Scargill* was "not a reliable legal authority".[19] Scargill "represented himself", so the case was "not properly argued" and it should be "limited to its particular facts".[20] Freshfields quote a lecture given by Megarry VC after he decided *Cowan v Scargill*, in which he described it as "a dull case" that should not be taken as saying profit must be maximised at all costs.[21] The report comments that, read carefully, the case merely confirms that fiduciary powers must be exercised "carefully and fairly for the purposes for which they are given and not so as to accomplish any ulterior purpose".[22]

---

[14] [1985] Ch 270 at 287.

[15] See, for example, P Watchman, J Anstee-Wedderburn and L Shipway, "Fiduciary duties in the 21st century: a UK perspective" (2005) 19(3) *Trust Law International* 127 at 127 where it was stated that the view that profit maximisation is the fundamental fiduciary duty is "based on a fundamental misunderstanding of the law" and should not be followed. See also S Hulme, "The basic duty of trustees of superannuation trusts - fair to one, fair to all?" (2000) 14(3) *Trust Law International* 130 and X Frostick, "Is there a duty to act in the best interests of the beneficiaries?" (2000) 83(Feb) *Pension Lawyer* 2.

[16] C Scanlan, *Socially Responsible Investment: A Guide for Pension Schemes and Charities* (1st ed 2005) p 79.

[17] P Watchman, J Anstee-Wedderburn and L Shipway, "Fiduciary duties in the 21st century: a UK perspective" (2005) 19(3) *Trust Law International* 127 at 127-128; Freshfields Bruckhaus Deringer, *A legal framework for the integration of environmental, social and governance issues into institutional investment* (2005) p 89; FairPensions (later known as ShareAction), *Protecting our best interests: rediscovering fiduciary obligation* (2011) p 19-20.

[18] Freshfields Bruckhaus Deringer, *A legal framework for the integration of environmental, social and governance issues into institutional investment* (2005).

[19] Above, p 89.

[20] Above, p 89.

[21] Above, p 9.

[22] Above, p 89.

10.12 This was also the view of Lord Nicholls. Commenting extra-judicially, he thought that the duty to act in a beneficiary's best interests was a formulation in different words of a fiduciary's duty to promote the purpose for which the trust was created.[23]

OTHER RELEVANT CASES

Martin v City of Edinburgh District Council

10.13 In the Scottish case of *Martin v City of Edinburgh District Council*,[24] a group of councillors challenged the decision of Edinburgh District Council to disinvest its trust funds from South Africa at the time of the apartheid regime. This followed the Council's policy to be "an apartheid-free authority" in all its dealings.

10.14 The Court of Session found that the Council had failed in its duty as trustees. This was not because the decision to disinvest in South Africa was necessarily wrong, but because the Council had made the decision in the wrong way. The Council had applied a pre-existing policy: it did not consider whether it was in the best interests of the beneficiaries or seek professional advice on the issue.[25] Lord Murray held that "trustees have a duty not to fetter their investment discretion for reasons extraneous to the trust purpose, including reasons of a political or moral nature".[26]

10.15 Notably, the court explicitly reached this conclusion on "the general principles of law applicable to trusts in Scotland" and not on *Cowan*, should this differ.[27] However, in a non-binding comment as to the meaning of *Cowan*, Lord Murray stated that:

> I accept that the most profitable investment of funds is one of a number of matters which trustees have a duty to consider. But I cannot conceive that trustees have an unqualified duty ... simply to invest trust funds in the most profitable investment available. To accept that without qualification would, in my view, involve substituting the discretion of financial advisers for the discretion of trustees.[28]

---

[23] Lord Nicholls, "Trustees and their Broader Community: Where Duty, Morality and Ethics Converge" (1996) 70 *Australian Law Journal* 205 at 211.

[24] [1989] Pens LR 9, 1988 SLT 329.

[25] [1989] Pens LR 9 at [24], [32], 1988 SLT 329 at 331-2, 334.

[26] [1989] Pens LR 9 at [33], 1988 SLT 329 at 334.

[27] [1989] Pens LR 9 at [32], 1988 SLT 329 at 333, by Lord Murray.

[28] [1989] Pens LR 9 at [33], 1988 SLT 329 at 334.

10.16 Lord Murray recognised that it may not be possible for a fiduciary to "divest himself of all personal preferences, of all political beliefs, and of all moral, religious or other conscientiously held principles".[29] Nevertheless, they must do their "best to exercise fair and impartial judgment" in the interests of the beneficiaries.[30] Trustees should genuinely apply their minds to the merits of a particular trust decision and, if they are not able to exercise fair and impartial judgment, must abstain from participating in deciding the issue.

Harries v Church Commissioners

10.17 In *Harries v Church Commissioners*[31] the Bishop of Oxford and other members of the clergy challenged the investment policy of the Church commissioners who managed the substantial trust funds of the Church of England. They claimed the commissioners attached undue importance to financial considerations in making investment decisions and failed to take into account the underlying purpose for which the assets were held – the promotion of the Christian faith.

10.18 The court held that although the commissioners were in law a charity, the main purpose of the trustees' investment powers was to make money: "most charities need money and the more of it there is available, the more the trustees can seek to accomplish".[32] Charitable trustees could restrict investments which conflicted with the work of a charity; for example, a cancer charity could refuse to invest in tobacco. They could also exclude investments which would alienate their supporters. But trustees should not lose sight of the purpose of their investment powers.[33] They should not make financially detrimental investment decisions based on moral concerns where there were differing views among their supporters.

10.19 On the facts, the commissioners exercised an "ethical" policy, which excluded around 13% of listed UK companies (by value), including alcohol, tobacco and armaments firms. The judge, Sir Donald Nicholls VC, found that the trustees did not err in law by adopting this ethical policy. On the other hand, the claimants' proposed plan would have excluded around 37% of listed UK companies. The judge commented:

> Not surprisingly, the commissioners' view is that a portfolio thus restricted would be much less balanced and diversified, and they would not regard it as prudent or in the interest of those for whom they provide.[34]

---

[29] [1989] Pens LR 9 at [33], 1988 SLT 329 at 334.

[30] [1989] Pens LR 9 at [33], 1988 SLT 329 at 334.

[31] [1992] 1 WLR 1241.

[32] Above, at 1246.

[33] Above, at 1247.

[34] Above, at 1251.

The judge held that, given the "endless argument and debate" over what Christian ethics require, the commissioners were "right not to prefer one view over the other beyond the point at which they would incur a risk of significant financial detriment".[35]

Buttle v Saunders: a duty to gazump?

10.20 It is sometimes said that fiduciary duties are concerned with maintaining "the highest standards of probity".[36] The American judge Chief Justice Cardozo classically stated that:

> A trustee is held to something stricter than the morals of the market place. Not honesty alone, but the punctilio of an honor the most sensitive, is then the standard of behavior.[37]

10.21 The case of *Buttle v Saunders*[38] is a reminder that the duty is to act in the interests of the beneficiary – not to act morally in a general sense. Trustees under a will had entered into negotiations for the sale of trust property. Draft contracts had been prepared but not concluded. At this stage, the trustees received a higher offer but refused it on the basis that they felt honour-bound not to withdraw from the initial negotiations. The beneficiaries challenged this decision. The court held that there may be legitimate circumstances in which trustees could refuse a higher offer, such as the certainty of the original offer. However, the trustees had only considered the honour of withdrawing from existing negotiations. This was incorrect.

10.22 In *Cowan v Scargill* the court endorsed the idea that fiduciaries should act dishonourably (although not illegally) if the interests of their beneficiaries require it.[39]

THE DUTIES ON PENSION TRUSTEES

10.23 When a pension trustee considers an investment strategy it is necessary to consider different duties drawn from several sources, including the trust deed, pensions legislation, duties attached to the exercise of a power and duties of care.

---

[35] [1992] 1 WLR 1241 at 1251.

[36] D Hayton, *The Law of Trusts* (4th ed 2003) p 37; see also J Langbein, "The Contractarian Basis of the Law of Trusts" (1995-1996) 105 *Yale Law Journal* 625 at 658.

[37] *Meinhard v Salmon* (1928) 164 NE 545 (NY) at 546.

[38] [1950] 2 All ER 193.

[39] [1985] Ch 270 at 288.

Acting for the purpose for which the power is given

10.24 Following Lord Nicholls, we think that the core duty of a trustee is to promote the purpose for which the trust was created.[40] A trustee should start with the trust deed: what is the purpose of the power I have been given, and how can I use the power to promote that purpose?

10.25 In the case of a pension scheme, the simple answer is that the purpose is to provide pensions. Contributions should be invested to earn returns so as to provide members with retirement and other benefits. As many stakeholders stressed to us, this is not an easy task. For some defined contribution (DC) schemes with low contributions and low returns, the chances of providing employees with adequate incomes in old age may be low. Without a sustained focus on the objective, the chances of success reduce further.

The investment regulations

10.26 Next, trustees must act within the confines of the legislation. In Chapter 7 we highlighted the Occupational Pension Scheme (Investment) Regulations 2005 (the Investment Regulations),[41] which require an investment power to be exercised in a manner "calculated to ensure the security, quality, liquidity and profitability of the portfolio as a whole".[42] The aim is to balance risk against returns.

10.27 The regulations also require the portfolio to be properly diversified to "avoid excessive reliance on any particular asset, issuer or group of undertakings".[43] *Harries v Church Commissioners*[44] provides examples of when a negative screening strategy might hamper diversification by leaving too small a class of companies in which a fund could invest.

Exercising discretion

10.28 Within these broad parameters, trustees must exercise their own discretion. There are no right answers: no-one knows what will produce a good return in twenty years' time. It is not simply a matter of applying a mechanical calculation, such as a price to earnings multiple. Trustees have been given the task of guiding general investment strategy because it is thought they are best placed to understand the interests of the beneficiaries. They are certainly better placed than the courts.

10.29 The courts will not second guess the decision itself. Instead, the law requires that trustees go through the right procedure to reach their decision, keeping the purpose of the trust at the front of their minds. In practice, the more unusual the decision, the more trustees will need to show that they reached their decision in the right way.

---

[40] Lord Nicholls, "Trustees and their Broader Community: Where Duty, Morality and Ethics Converge" (1996) 70 *Australian Law Journal* 205.

[41] SI 2005 No 3378.

[42] Occupational Pension Scheme (Investment) Regulations 2005 SI 2005 No 3378, reg 4(3).

[43] Occupational Pension Scheme (Investment) Regulations 2005 SI 2005 No 3378, reg 4(7).

[44] [1992] 1 WLR 1241 at 1251.

The procedure

10.30   We listed the various procedural duties in Chapter 6. Three are particularly relevant.

(1)   Most importantly, trustees must not fetter their discretion. They must genuinely consider how to achieve a pension for their members and must not simply apply a pre-existing moral or political judgment. This was the basis of the decision in *Martin*. The NUM trustees in *Cowan v Scargill* also fettered their discretion in that they simply applied union policy to narrow the scope of the investment options for the trust's portfolio. They did not consider the effect on the diversity of the portfolio.

(2)   The trustees should consider relevant circumstances. This is not necessarily an onerous duty. As the court said in *Pitt v Holt*, there will not necessarily be a breach of duty even if the trustees' deliberations have fallen short of the highest possible standards.[45] But trustees should exercise fair and impartial judgment, regardless of their own political, moral or religious views.[46]

(3)   As the court stressed in *Martin*, pension trustees should take advice. This is now specifically required by section 36 of the Pensions Act 1995.

The duty of care

10.31   Overlying these various duties, trustees should act "with such care and skill as is reasonable in the circumstances".[47] This must be judged at the time the decision was made, not with hindsight.

A bundle of duties

10.32   Overall, we think that the requirement on pension trustees to act in the best interests of beneficiaries is best seen as a bundle of duties. It is a short-hand for all the duties we have set out above.

THE STATEMENT OF INVESTMENT PRINCIPLES (SIP)

10.33   As we saw in Chapter 7, pension trustees must prepare a SIP stating their policy on such things as the kinds of investments to be held and the extent (if at all) to which social, environmental or ethical considerations are taken into account. This does not give trustees special authority to consider social, environmental or ethical issues. Any investment strategy in the SIP must accord with the general law.[48]

---

[45]   [2013] UKSC 26 at [73].

[46]   *Martin v City of Edinburgh District Council* [1989] Pens LR 9 at [33], 1988 SLT 329 at 334.

[47]   Trustee Act 2000, s 1.

[48]   Nabarro Pensions Team, *Pensions Law Handbook* (11th ed 2013) para 10.26.

10.34 Trustees must exercise their powers with a view to giving effect to those principles "so far as reasonably practicable".[49] This is not a fetter of discretion, since trustees must consider policy in general terms before applying it (or asking investment managers to apply it). It is important to note, however, that the legislation also requires trustees to review and, if necessary, revise the SIP.[50] A SIP might be considered an unacceptable fetter if it was applied blindly after circumstances had changed.

10.35 The Investment Regulations require trustees to consult the employer in drawing up the SIP.[51] However, the SIP may not require trustees to seek the employer's consent.[52] Pension trustees may consider the views of the employer but are not required to act in accordance with them. They must exercise independence of thought and use their powers for the purpose for which they were given them.

STEWARDSHIP

10.36 We are not only concerned with decisions to buy or sell shares and other investments. As shareholders, trustees may also guide their investee companies by entering into dialogue with them and considering whether and how to exercise voting rights. As we saw in Chapter 6, this may be an element of a trustee's duty of care.

10.37 The Financial Reporting Council publishes the UK Stewardship Code which encourages all institutional investors to publicly disclose how they will discharge their stewardship responsibilities.[53] The Financial Conduct Authority (FCA) requires authorised investment managers to report on whether or not they comply with the code.[54] Some stakeholders argued that stewardship should be "an explicit part of fiduciary duty".[55]

10.38 At present, however, only a tiny minority of pension schemes conduct stewardship activities. Research by Tilba and McNulty of a sample of 35 of the largest 100 UK pension schemes found that only 2 exhibited "engaged ownership behaviour" such as company research, voting and face-to face meetings with senior management.[56] Our discussions with stakeholders confirmed that all but the very largest schemes lacked the internal resources or the financial clout to have much effect.

---

[49] Pensions Act 1995, s 36(5).

[50] Pensions Act 1995, s 35(1)(b).

[51] Occupational Pension Schemes (Investment) Regulations 2005 SI 2005 No 3378, reg 2(2)(b).

[52] Pensions Act 1995, s 35(5).

[53] Financial Reporting Council, *The UK Stewardship Code* (2012) Principle 1.

[54] FCA Handbook COBS 2.2.3R. The rule does not apply to venture capital firms.

[55] Mark Goyder, speech in March 2011. See also Lord Myners' evidence to the BIS Select Committee, The Kay Review of Equity Markets and Long-Term Decision Making, Third Report of the Select Committee on Business, Innovation and Skills (2013-14) HC 603 at Ev 27.

[56] A Tilba and T McNulty, "Engaged versus disengaged ownership: the case of pension funds in the UK" (2013) 21(2) *Corporate Governance: An International Review* 165 at 171.

10.39   The courts have held that where the trust owns a controlling interest in a small private company, professional trustees should take an interest in what the company is doing.[57] However, this does not necessarily apply to shares in public listed companies, where small and medium funds lack the resources needed for stewardship activities.

10.40   For large funds, stewardship is one possible tool. Where a company is in danger of making poor long-term decisions it may be more effective to engage with the company to influence the decision, rather than simply sell the shares. In other words, "voice" may be used before "exit". In the discussion below, we look both at "voice" and "exit" decisions.

FACTORS RAISED WITH US

10.41   During our initial discussions, stakeholders raised many possible factors which trustees may wish to consider in the course of their investment decisions. We have grouped these factors into five broad categories:

(1)   wider investment factors aimed at securing financial returns, including environmental, social and governance factors;

(2)   macroeconomic factors, where accepting a lesser return in some areas may be justified by the benefits to the portfolio as a whole;

(3)   quality of life factors, which may bring non-financial benefits to the beneficiaries;

(4)   ethical factors; and

(5)   the views of beneficiaries.

10.42   For each, we report on what has been said to us, and reach a tentative conclusion on whether trustees may (or must) take the factor into account.

1. WIDER FACTORS AIMED AT SECURING FINANCIAL RETURNS

10.43   Investment decisions involve predicting the future, and therefore defy objective quantification. Conventional investment decision-making has always been guided by subjective opinion. For example, in deciding whether to invest in the shares of an electronics firm, a traditional investment manager may look at likely future innovations, the firm's plans to expand into new markets and the competition it faces from its rivals.

---

[57]   See the discussion of *Bartlett v Barclays Bank* [1980] Ch 515 at para 6.60 above.

The use of environmental, social and governance factors

10.44 Many firms now look at a broader range of issues, often referred to as "environmental, social and governance" (ESG) factors. This does not fundamentally alter the traditional approach; it merely expands it by taking a more holistic approach to valuing a company.[58] As AXA Investment Managers put it:

> What we are doing is capturing more signals about a company... Why would you ignore something that could give you a fuller picture of the company in which you are investing?[59]

10.45 A ratings agency provided us with an example of how ESG factors may be used. GMIRatings judge companies on 150 separate issues. These range from traditional governance factors (such as board composition, pay, ownership and control), through environmental impact (such as carbon emissions and water use) to social concerns (including human rights violations and child labour). The use of such data is now common. A 2011 international survey of institutional investors found that almost half that considered wider investment factors obtained information from specialist ratings agencies.[60]

10.46 ESG factors can be used in a variety of ways, including to:

(1) negatively screen – excluding investment in particular companies or sectors, such as tobacco companies or pesticide manufacturers;

(2) positively screen – selecting firms engaged in what are considered to be desirable practices, such as renewable energy supply; or

(3) select "best of sector" or "best of class" companies – choosing companies that perform best in their industry sector against specified indicators.[61]

10.47 These strategies can be used in both passive and active strategies. For example, a passive mandate might track an index such as the FTSE4Good series (managed by a policy committee using complex inclusion criteria) or one of the S&P DJSI Diversified indices (which adopt a "best of sector" approach). An active mandate might select an investment manager or fund on the basis of their stated policy on wider investment factors. Alternatively, it might specify precisely how the investment manager ought to take wider investment matters into account.

---

[58] See for example, A Gore and D Blood, "A Manifesto for Sustainable Capitalism: How businesses can embrace environmental, social and governance metrics" (14 December 2011) *The Wall Street Journal*.

[59] See AXA Investment Managers, *White Paper: Piloting ESG Integration* (2012) p 9.

[60] The survey was of 259 institutional investors in 11 countries, including the UK: BNP Paribas Investment Partners, *SRI Insights: Adding value to investments* (2012) vol 2 pp 60-61.

[61] The BNP Paribas survey showed that of those who considered wider investment factors used a combination of approaches. 43% adopted a normative negative screening approach, 59% adopted a sector screening approach and 66% adopted a positive screening approach. BNP Paribas Investment Partners, *SRI Insights: Adding value to investments* (2012) vol 2 p 58.

The link with better returns

10.48　The use of ESG factors in this way is aimed at increasing returns. At its most basic, taking account of ESG factors is designed to reduce risks. The Kay Review highlights how poor safety procedures, together with a lack of environmental concern, may lead to disastrous and expensive mistakes. For example, the Deepwater Horizon saga significantly reduced the value of BP shares.[62] ESG failings may also cause reputational harm to companies, and in a sentiment-driven market, such impacts might be substantial.[63] When realised, these risks also take up board and management time, distracting from the company's performance. [64]

10.49　However, an ESG driven approach is not simply about avoiding the next company crisis. It works on the basis that companies do better in the long term if they are well-run and sustainable, and have loyal suppliers, customers and employees. Thus ESG factors in this context are about improving financial outcomes for the beneficiaries: they are not about ethical preferences.

---

[62]　J Kay, *The Kay Review of UK Equity Markets and Long-Term Decision Making: Final Report* (2012) para 1.22.

[63]　See BNP Paribas Investment Partners, *SRI Insights: Adding value to investments* (2012) vol 2 p 60.

[64]　Responsible Investor and MSCI, *ESG Risks and Financial Implications, Sustainability themes: how and when they become financially material to institutional investors* (2013) p 10.

10.50 Many studies have found a link between ESG factors and company performance.[65] In June 2012 a report by Deutsche Bank Group reviewed over 100 academic studies and 56 research papers and concluded that ESG factors do have positive financial impacts.[66] Over the medium[67] to long[68] term, companies that scored well for ESG factors outperformed or yielded comparative returns to others and were a lower risk as measured by the cost of equity and debt capital.[69] This was particularly so for environmental and governance ratings.[70] The report did find, however, that negative screening on the basis of socially responsible investing generally had neutral or mixed results.[71]

10.51 Other studies have reported similar findings of a link. For example, a study by Business in the Community and Legal & General found that companies that consider ESG factors show reduced share price volatility against the FTSE 350.[72] Similarly, Harvard Business School noted that "High Sustainability" companies significantly outperform their peers over the long term, in both stock market and accounting performance.[73] Mercer Investment Consulting and the United Nations Asset Management Working Group conclude that "the argument that integrating ESG factors into investment analysis and decision-making will only lead to underperformance simply cannot be made".[74]

---

[65] For example, Deutsche Bank Group, DB Climate Change Advisors, *Sustainable Investing: Establishing Long-Term Value and Performance* (2012); R Eccles, I Ioannou and G Serafeim, *The Impact of Corporate Sustainability on Organizational Processes and Performance* Harvard Business School Working Paper 12-035 (2013); J Margolis, H Elfenbein and J Walsh, *Does it pay to be good?: A meta-analysis and redirection of research on the relationship between corporate social and financial performance* (2007); B Gordon, S Hine and N Alam, EIRIS, *The state of responsible business: Global corporate response to environmental, social and governance (ESG) challenges* (2007); Environment Agency, *Corporate Environmental Governance: A study into the influence of Environmental Governance and Financial Performance* (2004).

[66] The study included 100 academic studies of sustainable investing, 56 research papers, two literature reviews and four meta-studies. See Deutsche Bank Group, DB Climate Change Advisors, *Sustainable Investing: Establishing Long-Term Value and Performance* (2012) p 8.

[67] 3 to 5 years.

[68] 5 to 10 years.

[69] See Deutsche Bank Group, DB Climate Change Advisors, *Sustainable Investing: Establishing Long-Term Value and Performance* (2012) p 5 and p 38.

[70] Above, p 39.

[71] Above, p 5.

[72] Business in the Community and Legal & General, *Conscious capital: bridging the gap between business and investors* (2013) p 16.

[73] R Eccles, I Ioannou and G Serafeim, *The Impact of Corporate Sustainability on Organizational Processes and Performance* Harvard Business School Working Paper 12-035 (2013) p 18.

[74] Mercer LLC, *Shedding light on responsible investment: Approaches, returns and impacts* (2009).

10.52   We were told that the integration of ESG factors may well become the norm. AXA Investment Managers said that there was "good reason to think that ESG considerations will go mainstream".[75] Similarly, Paul Todd, head of investment policy at the National Employment Savings Trust, stated:

> In future we suspect that the ESG debate will stop being a separate discussion and become just another element of long-term investing, in the same way that market and liquidity risk would not be separated out from the overall investment process.[76]

May pension trustees use wider factors?

10.53   We have been asked whether fiduciaries may consider factors relevant to long-term investment performance, including questions of sustainability or environmental and social impact.

10.54   As we have explained, the requirement for a trustee to act "in the best interests of the beneficiary"[77] refers to a bundle of duties connected to the exercise of a power and duties of care. The core duty is the duty to exercise a power for the purpose for which it was intended. For an occupational pension set up under trust, investment powers are conferred for the purpose of generating risk-adjusted financial returns. In each case it is necessary to ask "why should we consider this factor?" and the answer must be "because it is authorised by and furthers the purpose for which the power was granted". Trustees should also be careful that the connection between the investment factor being considered and the furthering of the power's purpose is not "too remote and insubstantial".[78] The policy in the SIP on the extent to which ESG factors can be considered should be consistent with this obligation.

10.55   Given the evidence that ESG factors can lead to better returns in the long run, the answer is clearly that pension trustees *may* use wider factors. There can be no objection to using ESG factors as a way of increasing long-term performance.

10.56   We agree with previous advice given on this issue. For example, we endorse the advice DLA Piper gave to the Universities Superannuation Scheme (USS):

> Where any ethical, social, environmental, corporate governance issue can be regarded as having a current or potential impact on actual or contemplated investment, whether from the point of view of the return to be expected of that investment, its liquidity and/or its underlying capital value, it is in my view wholly consistent with the duties of the Trustee Company referred to above to take those considerations into account.[79]

---

[75]   AXA Investment Managers, *White Paper: Piloting ESG Integration* (2012) p 6.

[76]   Above, p 6.

[77]   See *Cowan v Scargill* [1985] Ch 270 at 286-287, by Sir Robert Megarry VC.

[78]   Above, at 292, by Sir Robert Megarry VC.

[79]   DLA Piper, *Responsible Investment Policy and Exclusions* (8 September 2006) para 3.2, http://www.uss.co.uk/Documents/Legal%20advice%20to%20USS%20on%20RI%20from%20DLA%20Piper%20Sept06.pdf.

10.57 In 2005, the Freshfields Report concluded:

> The links between ESG factors and financial performance are increasingly being recognised. On that basis, integrating ESG considerations into an investment analysis so as to more reliably predict financial performance is clearly permissible and is arguably required in all jurisdictions.[80]

10.58 Again, we agree that ESG factors are clearly permissible. We discuss whether they are required below.

10.59 ShareAction told us that the Freshfields Report "has been influential in building support" for the view that fiduciary duties are compatible with taking into account ESG considerations where they may be financially material.[81] However, uncertainty remains. ShareAction argue that this is "partly down to the persistence of myths and misconceptions about fiduciary duty".[82] We hope that we can finally remove this misconception.

Must pension trustees use wider factors?

10.60 This is a more difficult question. If the evidence suggests that ESG factors increase long-term performance, must all pension trustees use them in their investment decisions?

10.61 Several stakeholders told us it would be a breach of fiduciary duties to ignore ESG factors.[83] As *Tomorrow's Company* put it:

> It is precisely the lack of awareness of new potential risks that environmental and social impacts may have on pension funds' assets that could be interpreted as a breach of fiduciary duties.[84]

10.62 Richard Keery, an investment manager for the Strathclyde Pension Fund, said:

> The Fund also believes that ESG issues can impact value and therefore we would be failing in our fiduciary duty if we did not actively pursue an ESG policy.[85]

---

[80] Freshfields Bruckhaus Deringer, *A legal framework for the integration of environmental, social and governance issues into institutional investment* (2005) p 13.

[81] ShareAction, Response to "Fiduciary Duties of Investment Intermediaries: Initial Questions" (July 2013).

[82] Above.

[83] Tomorrow's Company, *Tomorrow's Value, Achieving sustainable financial returns: A guide for pension trustees* (forthcoming) p 33; UNEP Finance Initiative, *Fiduciary responsibility, Legal and practical aspects of integrating environmental, social and governance issues into institutional investment* (2009); see also B Richardson, "Do the Fiduciary Duties of Pension Funds Hinder Socially Responsible Investment?" (2007) 22(2) *Banking and Finance Law Review* 145 at 149.

[84] Tomorrow's Company, *Tomorrow's Value, Achieving sustainable financial returns: A guide for pension trustees* (forthcoming) p 33.

[85] AXA Investment Managers, *White Paper: Piloting ESG Integration* (2012) p 7.

10.63   The Kay Review also took this approach:

> Institutional investors acting in the best interests of their clients should consider the environmental and social impact of companies' activities.[86]

10.64   We do not think that the law is this prescriptive. Considering a wide range of factors costs money, and smaller schemes in particular may decide that their members' interests are best served by reducing costs. They may decide, for example, simply to track an index. There is no right way to make money. Views legitimately differ, and the decision is ultimately one for trustees rather than judges. As we note, the courts have stressed that there are limits to what are considered "relevant considerations", which the trustees must take into account. Trustees have considerable latitude to use their own discretion. As *Pitt v Holt* stressed:

> It is not enough to show that the trustees' deliberations have fallen short of the highest possible standards, or that the court would, on a surrender of discretion by the trustees, have acted in a different way.[87]

10.65   In 2005, the Freshfields Report suggested that pension trustees should at least consider whether to take wider investment factors into account, even if they then reject this approach:

> Even where ESG considerations are ultimately rejected as having negligible weight (because they have little effect on the relative value of an investment, for example), we think they should form part of the basket of considerations to which a decision-maker has regard.[88]

10.66   We think that this is a sensible conclusion. Even if the duty of adequate consideration does not require this, trustees are also under a duty of care. As part of this duty, we think that trustees should consider, in general terms, whether their policy will be to take account of ESG factors in their decision-making, bearing in mind the resources available to them. The law, however, allows trustees discretion not to take an ESG approach if after due consideration they consider that another strategy would better serve the interests of their beneficiaries.

---

[86]   J Kay, *The Kay Review of UK Equity Markets and Long-Term Decision Making: Final Report* (2012) para 10.20.

[87]   [2013] UKSC 26 at [73].

[88]   Freshfields Bruckhaus Deringer, *A legal framework for the integration of environmental, social and governance issues into institutional investment* (2005) p 94.

2. MACROECONOMIC FACTORS

10.67 It is argued that since many pension funds hold such diverse portfolios, they are essentially interested in the performance of the economy as a whole. Their returns depend on the growth of the stock market which in turn depends on the growth of the economy. Therefore, to maximise returns, they need to make decisions that provide the foundations of a stable, sustainable and successful economy.[89] We have called these wider systemic considerations "macroeconomic factors".

10.68 In their response to our short paper, UNISON pointed out that fund fiduciaries "are owners not of just a handful of assets, but of a slice of the economy as a whole". As the performance of investment funds "is directly correlated to the overall performance of the British and world economy", fiduciaries ought to consider macroeconomic factors when making their investment decisions. As one writer comments:

> It would seem a zero-sum game for an investor to favour a profitable but polluting fossil fuel business if it created risks and costs for other economic sectors the investor has a stake in.[90]

10.69 This theory is often described as "Universal Ownership" and is strongly promoted by Hawley and Williams. They contend that:

> ... the time has come for institutional investors to explicitly recognize that economy-wide, macroeconomic issues heavily influence the returns they will earn on their investments.[91]

10.70 Gifford explains that pension funds:

> Generally prefer indexing strategies, in which they invest in almost every stock in the market to match a major market index. Therefore, if one company causes environmental damage, another company will often suffer, and that company will also be in the fund's portfolio so it is a zero sum game for the fund ... Similarly, if the environmental cost is externalised onto the taxpayer (ie to clean up a toxic waste site), those taxpayers will most likely also be members of the fund.[92]

---

[89] B Richardson, "Do the Fiduciary Duties of Pension Funds Hinder Socially Responsible Investment?" (2007) 22(2) *Banking and Finance Law Review* 145 at 163.

[90] Above, at 163-164.

[91] J Hawley and A Williams, *The Rise of Fiduciary Capitalism: How Institutional Investors Can Make Corporate America More Democratic* (1st ed 2000) p 22.

[92] J Gifford, "Measuring the Social, Environmental and Ethical Performance of Pension Funds" (2004) 53 *Journal of Australian Political Economy* 139 at 140-141.

10.71   This view was reflected in the Network for Sustainable Financial Markets' response to our short paper. They noted:

> Nearly universal adoption of broadly diversified investment strategies tied to capital weighted market indices has resulted in economic health and institutional investor success becoming mutually interdependent.[93]

10.72   In their response to our short paper, ShareAction suggested the banking crisis offered a good example:

> Major banks' excessive leverage and risky lending strategies had systemic impacts which have been devastating for pension fund returns. However, far from reining in these risky strategies in the run-up to 2008, most institutional investors actively encouraged them, on the basis that they were good for the short-term profitability of the individual banks. In the aftermath of the crisis, indications are of a return to business as usual. There appears to be limited recognition by fiduciary investors that what is good for individual banks may not be good for their portfolios as a whole.[94]

10.73   We have been told that fiduciaries may be uncomfortable acting on such macroeconomic factors. For example, whilst some feel they are able to take into account the impact an environmental disaster may have on the performance of a company share price, they would not consider the wider impacts that it may have on their entire portfolio.[95] ShareAction noted that "fiduciary duty is equated solely with seeing 'the most commercially competitive assets' regardless of their wider impact, and is therefore regarded as a constraint on investments to mitigate climate change".[96]

May pension trustees take macroeconomic factors into account?

10.74   Again, the duty to exercise a power for the purpose it was given is likely to be most relevant. The aim of a pension fund is to secure returns across the whole portfolio. Therefore there can be no legal objection to making a decision which, on a due consideration of the factors, is designed to provide financial benefits to the portfolio as a whole. The anticipated benefits should outweigh the likely costs. Trustees should also ensure the financial benefit is not "too remote and insubstantial".[97]

---

[93]   Network for Sustainable Financial Markets, Response to "Fiduciary Duties of Investment Intermediaries: Initial Questions" (July 2013).

[94]   ShareAction, Response to "Fiduciary Duties of Investment Intermediaries: Initial Questions" (July 2013).

[95]   Above.

[96]   Above.

[97]   *Cowan v Scargill* [1985] Ch 270 at 292.

10.75 Often the problem is not a legal one but a practical one. Whatever the benefits of combating climate change, it is unlikely that one pension fund acting alone can make an appreciable difference to the problem. Each fund's individual interests may run counter to the general interest. In their 2011 Report, ShareAction described this as a "tragedy of the commons":[98]

> It might be difficult to use universal owner arguments to justify a climate-based stock-picking policy, since disinvestment from an environmentally damaging company by a single fund will not, by itself, protect the rest of that fund's portfolio from the negative externalities the company creates.[99]

10.76 Macroeconomic objectives may be better met through stewardship activities (such as engagement and voting) rather than through stock-picking. For example, to use ShareAction's earlier example, in retrospect, pension funds might have protected their portfolios by asking more questions about banks' excessive leverage. Even here, however, it is difficult for any but the largest pension funds to justify the costs of monitoring firms' complex decision-making. Macroeconomic factors are usually better addressed through collaborative initiatives, where both costs and benefits are shared across many investors. Where the benefits are universal and the costs fall disproportionately on a single fund, trustees could consider how costs can be reduced through collaborative working.

Must pension trustees take macroeconomic factors into account?

10.77 The same arguments apply as with wider investment factors. The courts allow flexibility and discretion and impose only a base-line standard. No court would find pension fund trustees liable for having failed to prevent the banking crisis or global warming.

10.78 We do not think it is right to say that trustees *must* take macroeconomic factors into account. However, good practice suggests that pension trustees should consider, in general terms, whether they will take account of macroeconomic factors in their decision-making.

3. QUALITY OF LIFE FACTORS

10.79 It is suggested that investors should be able to take into account the beneficiaries' quality of life now and in the future. For example, one writer argues:

> Apart from a good retirement income, pension fund members also desire a clean, safe and secure world. Given the ubiquity of pension fund membership, the interests of members should be broadly consistent with those of the society in which members live.[100]

---

[98] FairPensions (later known as ShareAction), *Protecting our Best Interests: Rediscovering Fiduciary Obligation* (2011) p 92.

[99] Above, p 93.

[100] B Richardson, "Do the Fiduciary Duties of Pension Funds Hinder Socially Responsible Investment?" (2007) 22(2) *Banking and Finance Law Review* 145 at 170.

10.80 We have called these "quality of life factors". Several stakeholders raised issues about the human cost of environmental degradation and climate change. The Freshfields Report commented:

> Many people wonder what good an extra percent or three of patrimony are worth if the society in which they are to enjoy retirement and in which their descendants will live deteriorates. Quality of life and quality of the environment are worth something, even if, or particularly because, they are not reducible to financial percentages.[101]

10.81 "Quality of life" may also be a factor in deciding whether to invest in local infrastructure and social projects. Some local authority pension funds invest in infrastructure projects partly on this basis. For example, Strathclyde Pension Fund puts a proportion of its investment into a New Opportunities Fund which aims to create local jobs or benefits to the local community while delivering returns. However, pension trustees will aim to receive at least equally beneficial financial returns. For example, a study of 100 local authority pension funds by the Smith Institute showed that none would be prepared to accept lower returns in exchange for achieving social benefit; they saw "finance first" as their overriding duty.[102]

The tie-break principle

10.82 The courts have held that non-financial factors may be used as a "tie-breaker": in other words, they may be used when choosing between two equally beneficial investments. Pension fund trustees should not, however, make investments which are likely to produce lower financial returns.

10.83 In *Harries*, Sir Donald Nicholls VC stressed that the purpose of investment was to generate money. Other factors could be accommodated, but only "so long as the trustees are satisfied that the course would not involve a risk of significant financial detriment".[103] Lord Nicholls later expanded on the principle, arguing that:

> The inclusion or exclusion of particular investments or types of investment will often be possible without incurring the risk of a lower rate of return or reducing the desirable spread of investments.[104]

---

[101] Freshfields Bruckhaus Deringer, *A legal framework for the integration of environmental, social and governance issues into institutional investment* (2005) p 3.

[102] The Smith Institute, *Local authority pension funds: investing for growth* (2012) p 18.

[103] [1992] 1 WLR 1241 at 1247.

[104] Lord Nicholls, "Trustees and their Broader Community: Where Duty, Morality and Ethics Converge" (1996) 70 *Australian Law Journal* 205 at 212.

Is the tie break principle compatible with modern portfolio theory?

10.84   The tie-break principle has been subject to academic criticism. Rosy Thornton argues that "any restriction adopted on ethical or other grounds will necessarily have an effect, however small, upon efficiency".[105] She points out that the tie-break principle is not compatible with the sophisticated quantification of modern portfolio theory. The principle is based on an unreality; "trustees are never likely to face the artificially constructed choice" suggested in *Cowan*.[106]   It is also very unlikely another investment will be "an exact twin".[107]

10.85   Further, any decision to invest should consider the need to diversify the portfolio. Rosy Thornton argues that diversification is always beneficial: even if it cannot reduce systemic risk it will reduce firm-specific risk. Thus "by increasing the number of assets in the investment portfolio and by ensuring that they are as independent as possible", the "efficiency frontier" can be improved.[108] It becomes possible to reduce risk for the same returns, or to increase returns for the same risk. On this basis, she argues that in the unlikely event of two investments appearing equally beneficial, the correct answer is to split the investment and invest in both.[109]

A broader approach

10.86   The debate is between those who see investment decisions as made on the basis of precisely quantified returns, co-variance and risk, and those who see it as a broad subjective evaluation, depending largely on the sustainability and stability of the economy as a whole. The first focuses on firm-specific risks, the second on systemic risk.

10.87   The courts have not required trustees to restrict themselves to the metrics of modern portfolio theory. They do not demand that an efficiency frontier is improved through greater and greater diversification. As we have seen, trustees may instead make broad judgments based on a wide range of factors, including ESG factors and the effect of investments on the economy as a whole. On this basis it makes sense to say that two investments may appear equally beneficial.

10.88   The Investment Regulations require that assets should be properly diversified to "avoid excessive reliance on any particular asset, issuer or group of undertakings and so as to avoid accumulations of risk in the portfolio as a whole".[110]   However, increasing diversification is not necessarily an unmitigated good. Increased diversification leads to increased costs, and it becomes more and more difficult to monitor investee companies. Shareholders lose the ability to notice obvious risks in what a company is doing.

---

[105]   R Thornton, "Ethical investments: a case of disjointed thinking" (2008) 67(2) *Cambridge Law Journal* 396 at 407.

[106]   Above, at 405.

[107]   Above, at 405.

[108]   Above, at 401.

[109]   Above, at 406.

[110]   Occupational Pension Schemes (Investment) Regulations 2005 SI 2005 No 3378, reg 4(7).

10.89   The courts do not require a portfolio to be diversified to the fullest extent possible. Instead trustees should avoid excessive reliance on any particular asset, and the strategy as a whole should not exclude too much of the market. It is a question of degree in each case. As we saw, in *Harries* the Church commissioners reached the view that excluding 13% of the market would be acceptable, while excluding 37% would not be. The court held that this decision did not err in law. It was the trustees' discretion and the court would not interfere.

Taking quality of life factors into account: conclusion

10.90   Trustees may decide that investments which improve people's quality of life are likely to be good long-term investments while those which degrade the environment or lead to inevitable public outcries may involve risk. On this basis, the effect of an investment on quality of life may be seen as an investment factor.

10.91   However, trustees should not accept a lower return from an investment simply because it will improve members' quality of life. Furthermore, trustees must ensure that the portfolio remains adequately diversified. This follows from the purpose of the powers: trustees are required to invest to provide financial benefits, not to combat climate change or to improve local infrastructure.

10.92   This is important to remember where trustees face pressure to invest in "the issue of the day". As one commentator notes:

> Schemes are being regarded, following the collapse of our banking framework, as the magic porridge pot out of which the money for the roads and railways we need can be found.[111]

10.93   Ros Altmann also comments that private pensions may become "a piggy bank for politicians to raid in tough times", referring to moves in Poland, Portugal, Ireland and France to use pension assets or the Pension Reserve Fund to reduce visible levels of Government debt.[112] It may be helpful to trustees to use the law of fiduciary duties to resist external pressure to do the next fashionable thing.

10.94   Quality of life objectives "have to remain a subordinate investment objective".[113] That said, trustees may still look for good infrastructure schemes which will both improve quality of life *and* provide good financial returns. And, in the rare circumstances in which two projects appear equally beneficial but one has to be selected over the other, trustees may choose the investment which will most improve beneficiaries' quality of life.

---

[111] R Ellison, "Pointing the finger" (July 2013) *Pensions World* 14 at 14.

[112] R Altmann, "Private pensions have become a piggy bank for spendthrift states" (11 September 2013) *City AM*.

[113] B Richardson, "Do the Fiduciary Duties of Pension Funds Hinder Socially Responsible Investment?" (2007) 22(2) *Banking and Finance Law Review* 145 at 161.

10.95   In the course of our initial discussions it was said that pension scheme members were not simply concerned with a pension but had other concerns. For example, it was suggested that people would be prepared to forgo the opportunity to drive a car or take foreign holidays in retirement to combat the effects of climate change. We do not think that trustees should make this decision for others. If a pension fund is invested on this basis, the scheme member should have made a fully informed choice.

10.96   ShareAction presented us with a more difficult scenario. How should a large multi-employer fund vote on a take-over bid in a company in which the fund held shares? Could the fund take account of the fact that some of their beneficiaries might lose their jobs? Or could the fund only consider whether they were receiving a good price for the shares?

10.97   The law appears to be that trustees should only take into account the fact that some members would lose their job where this would not cause financial detriment to the fund. Otherwise, trustees are in the invidious position of prioritising some members' interests over others. In *Cowan v Scargill*, it was said that trustees should hold "the scales impartially between different classes of beneficiaries".[114] Where one group's quality of life factors will be another group's financial loss, the law appears to be that trustees should concentrate on financial returns.

4. ETHICAL FACTORS

10.98   Another element of uncertainty is the extent to which trustees may take account of ethical factors in making investment decisions.

Religious and affinity groups

10.99   Ethical investment is most commonly raised by those investing on behalf of religious groups. It is not simply about religion, however. In *Harries*, it was pointed out that similar issues also arise for other groups whose members may be expected to have the same strong moral views. Cancer research companies may not wish to invest in tobacco; temperance charities may not wish to invest in breweries.

10.100   The issue has recently been highlighted by the criticism of the Church of England's indirect investment in Wonga, a payday loan lender.[115] It has been pointed out, however, that the Church of England cannot disinvest from every potentially unethical company and still diversify its funds. As one commentator put it:

> The trouble is that, wherever you look, there are pitfalls to ethical investment. Almost everything, from tax avoidance to environmental failings, is a potential banana skin for the Church.[116]

---

[114] [1985] Ch 270 at 287, by Sir Robert Megarry VC.

[115] See D Kennedy and R Gledhill, "Welby's assault on Wonga falls into pension trap" (26 July 2013) *The Times*.

[116] H Ebrahimi, "CNBC Comment: Ethical vigilance isn't easy for Church" (30 July 2013) *City AM*.

10.101 Instead, the Church commissioners stress the importance of engaging with the companies in which they invest to improve the ethics of the company. For example, between April 2012 and March 2013 the Church of England met with 50 companies on topics including:

> Access to medicines in developing countries, arctic drilling, banking ethics and practice, carbon emissions management and reporting, corporate governance, country-specific risks, defence sales, executive remuneration, the Groceries Code Adjudicator Bill, human rights, labour relations, oil sands, pharmaceutical ethics, relationships with communities, responsibility in the marketing and retailing of alcohol, safety/operational risk, and sustainable housing.[117]

The Church of England Ethical Investment Advisory Group notes that "institutional investors do not always find scrutiny of this kind easy".[118]

Ethical considerations in general funds

10.102 Outside affinity groups, it becomes more difficult to achieve consensus on what ethical issues are. As Lord Nicholls put it, permitting investment on ethical grounds "would mean moving the boundary of the law into adjacent moral territory where right-thinking people differ widely in their views".[119] Rosy Thornton notes that one individual:

> Might consider vivisection to be immoral, for instance, and refuse to invest in companies which engage in animal experimentation, while another might applaud any activity which advances medical science. Some may be opposed to nuclear power on grounds of safety or of its potential links to the arms industry; others may actively prefer it to other forms of power generation because of its lower impact in carbon emissions.[120]

10.103 When the motivation for an investment decision is purely moral, rather than the belief that it produces better returns, it is difficult for a trustee to act for another without a clear framework; decisions may be guided by the trustee's ethics rather than the beneficiary's ethics.

10.104 Furthermore, once trustees start to exclude companies for ethical reasons, investment opportunities can narrow rapidly. It has been estimated that ethical grounds of some kind could be found for excluding as many as half of all companies on the FTSE 100 share index.[121]

---

[117] The Church of England, Ethical Investment Advisory Group, *Annual Review 2012/13* (2013) p 4.

[118] Above, p 2.

[119] Lord Nicholls, "Trustees and their Broader Community: Where Duty, Morality and Ethics Converge" (1996) 70 *Australian Law Journal* 205 at 211.

[120] R Thornton, "Ethical investments: a case of disjointed thinking" (2008) 67(2) *Cambridge Law Journal* 396 at 418.

[121] G Watt, *Trusts and Equity* (2nd ed 2006) p 436.

Acting monstrously?

10.105 In his evidence before the BIS Select Committee, Professor Kay advocated a middle ground between behaving monstrously and pursuing one's own moral beliefs at the expense of the beneficiary:

> You do not have to behave monstrously and unethically in order to make more money for your beneficiaries, which – to caricature a bit – is one suggestion of how the law is interpreted. Equally, you may not pursue your own particular moral, ethical or political purposes with the beneficiaries' money. We want to define the middle ground between the two: that is, that the morality and ethics that you apply should essentially be those that would be appropriate to the beneficiary.[122]

10.106 Others have also suggested that some common core of what is "ethical" can be found:

> While disagreements will most likely permeate traditional ethical or religious issues, such as alcohol or gambling, substantial agreement in other areas may readily arise. For instance, members of a pension fund probably rarely favour deliberate environmental degradation or human rights' violations.[123]

10.107 Trustees are entitled to conclude that a firm which is deliberately damaging the environment should be avoided on risk grounds rather than moral ones: it is unlikely to be a sustainable business model in the long term. Similarly a firm which is carrying out human rights violations may present reputational and regulatory risks. We think it will be rare for such a company to be excluded on ethical grounds alone. As we discuss below, however, there may be examples where members have shared ethical beliefs which may be used to decide between two equal investments.

Can trustees take ethical issues into account?

10.108 As the court stated in *Harries,* trustees "must not use property held by them for investment purposes as a means for making moral statements".[124] The case of *Buttle v Saunders*[125] (discussed earlier) is a useful reminder that the obligation on trustees is to act in the interests of their beneficiaries, not to act honourably in some generic sense.

10.109 Professor Kay is therefore right in both policy and legal terms to highlight that trustees should not pursue their own particular moral, ethical or political purposes with their beneficiaries' money. Nor should trustees be swayed by the many views urged on them by narrow interest groups. In some cases, it may be useful for trustees to be able to cite the law of fiduciary duties to free themselves from unhelpful pressure from others.

---

[122] The Kay Review of Equity Markets and Long-Term Decision Making, Third Report of the Select Committee on Business, Innovation and Skills (2013-14) HC 603 at Ev 12.

[123] B Richardson, "Do the Fiduciary Duties of Pension Funds Hinder Socially Responsible Investment?" (2007) 22(2) *Banking and Finance Law Review* 145 at 166.

[124] *Harries v Church Commissioners* [1992] 1 WLR 1241 at 1247.

[125] [1950] 2 All ER 193.

10.110   We think that there are only three circumstances when trustees should be swayed by general ethical issues, unrelated to risks, returns or the interests of beneficiaries.

Affinity groups

10.111   The first is where the pension fund is set up by a religious group, other charity or political organisation. As was stated in *Harries*, trustees should not be required to make investments which conflict with the aims of the charity. Nor should they be required to make investments which would reduce support for the group by alienating the organisation's donors or recipients. This is in line with the guidance of the Charity Commission.[126]

10.112   However, this exception is likely to be construed narrowly. As was remarked wryly in *Harries*, not all members of the Church of England eschew gambling, alcohol or tobacco. Similarly, other organisations may employ staff who take a relaxed view of their employer's moral stance. Ideally, the limitations imposed on trustees in these specialists schemes should be written into the trust deed and made explicit to all concerned.

Consent

10.113   In DC schemes it is common to allow members a choice of fund. For example, in Chapter 3 we gave a case history of a large trust-based hybrid scheme. The DC "offering" consisted of 12 funds, including ethical and Shariah options. We think it is acceptable to offer members an ethical pension which will or may produce a lower return, provided that that the scheme has been explained fully and each member has given informed consent.

A tie-breaker

10.114   Finally, where trustees think that scheme members would hold a particular moral view, they may use this as a tie breaker. They may avoid investments which they consider scheme members would regard as objectionable, so long as they make equally advantageous investments elsewhere.

---

[126] Charity Commission, *Charities and Investment Matters: A guide for trustees* (CC14) (2011), section C3.

10.115   This endorses the views of the 1993 Pension Law Review Committee, which said that pension trustees:

> Are perfectly entitled to have a policy on ethical investment and to pursue that policy, so long as they treat the interests of the beneficiaries as paramount and the investment policy is consistent with the standards of care and prudence required by law. This means that trustees are free to avoid certain kinds of prudent investment which they consider the scheme members would regard as objectionable, so long as they make equally advantageous investments elsewhere, and that they are entitled to put funds into investments which they believe the members would regard as desirable, so long as these are proper investments on other grounds. What trustees are not entitled to do is to subordinate the interests of the beneficiaries to ethical or social demands and thereby deprive the beneficiaries of investment income or opportunities they would otherwise have enjoyed.[127]

10.116   Note, however, that this is subject to two limitations. Firstly, trustees must have good reason to think that scheme members would share the moral viewpoint. Secondly, the decision must not be to the financial detriment of the scheme. Again, we endorse the views of DLA Piper in their advice to the USS:

> It is important to draw a distinction between (a) an assessment of the likely financial impact the failure to meet particular ESG standards will have on the return or value of an actual or contemplated investment and (b) the ethical or moral aspects of that failure in the absence of any such financial impact… it is not the role of the Trustees of a pension scheme or other trust whose objects are to produce financial benefits for the beneficiaries to seek to exclude the making of investments on moral or other non investment grounds.[128]

5. THE VIEWS OF THE BENEFICIARIES

10.117   Some argue for greater dialogue with scheme beneficiaries to enable investments to be made according to their preferences. This may enable subjective choices about ethics to be taken into account in investment decisions. One article suggests:

> Where it is practicable to survey the moral or social preferences of beneficiaries in order to arrive at an investment strategy that reflects their interests, we think that may assist trustees to justify a particular approach.[129]

---

[127]   Report of the Pension Law Review Committee (1993) Cm 2342-I para 4.9.18 (footnotes omitted).

[128]   DLA Piper, *Responsible Investment Policy and Exclusions* (8 September 2006) para 3.2, http://www.uss.co.uk/Documents/Legal%20advice%20to%20USS%20on%20RI%20from%20DLA%20Piper%20Sept06.pdf.

[129]   P Watchman, J Anstee-Wedderburn and L Shipway, "Fiduciary duties in the 21st century: a UK perspective" (2005) 19(3) *Trust Law International* 127 at 142.

10.118 Others were acutely aware of the responsibilities of the role they had been given to look after the investments of others. Chris Hitchen, Chief Executive of the Railways Pension Trustee Company told the BIS Committee that the fiduciary duty which "goes to the core" of his job is:

> not the same thing as doing what your members want you to do; it is about doing what is in their best interests, and those two things are not always the same.[130]

May trustees take into account the views of beneficiaries?

10.119 We have seen that a pension fund must not require the employer's consent to trustees' investment decisions.[131] Equally trustees should not act under the dictation or instructions of the beneficiaries.[132] Academic commentators have noted that donees of powers must not act as "another's puppet".[133] Nor do investors "have the right to dictate the design and implementation of the fund's investment strategy to the fiduciary".[134]

10.120 Furthermore, trustees may not delegate investment decisions to members. As explained in Chapter 7, under the pensions legislation, trustees may only delegate their investment powers to an investment manager authorised to carry out investment activities under the Financial Services and Markets Act 2000 (FSMA).[135] Scheme members are unlikely to be authorised under FSMA.

10.121 However, this does not mean that trustees may not consult their beneficiaries[136] so long as they make the ultimate decision.[137] Our conclusion is that trustees may consider the views of the beneficiaries when making their investment decisions, but there is no need for them to do so.

---

[130] The Kay Review of Equity Markets and Long-Term Decision Making, Third Report of the Select Committee on Business, Innovation and Skills (2013-14) HC 603 at Ev 58.

[131] See para 10.35 above.

[132] See for example *Selby v Bowie* (1863) 8 LT 372 (instruction to accept a particular offer to purchase trust property) and *Re Brockbank* [1948] Ch 206 (instruction to appoint a particular person as trustee).

[133] P Finn, *Fiduciary Obligations* (1st ed 1977) para 42.

[134] P Ali & K Yano, *Eco-finance: the legal design and regulation of market-based environmental instruments* (1st ed 2004) p 140.

[135] This requirement is reinforced by article 4 of the Financial Services and Markets Act 2000 (Carrying on Regulated Activities by Way of Business) Order 2001 SI 2001 No 1177 which provides that anyone who manages investments belonging to another person in circumstances involving discretion for an occupational pension scheme is generally to be regarded as undertaking a business activity and therefore requires authorisation under FSMA.

[136] See for example, *Re Agricultural Industries* [1952] 1 All ER 1188 at 1190.

[137] *Re Poole* (1882) 21 Ch D 397 at 404; *Re Smith* (1886) 17 QBD 488.

INVESTMENT MANAGERS TO WHOM POWERS ARE DELEGATED

The power to delegate

10.122 As we discussed in Chapter 7, pension trustees may delegate their discretion to make decisions about investments to an investment manager[138] who is authorised (or exempt from authorisation) under FSMA.[139] Where trustees have delegated discretion in this way, they are not liable for what the investment manager does, provided that they have taken all reasonable steps to check that the investment manager is suitable[140] and to monitor that they are carrying out their work competently and complying with the Investment Regulations.[141]

10.123 Meanwhile the investment manager to whom investment discretion is delegated in this way becomes subject to duties under the pensions legislation. In particular:

(1) Investment managers must exercise their discretion in accordance with the Investment Regulations.[142] This includes the requirement in Regulation 4(2) that the investment of scheme assets is in the best interests of the beneficiaries.

(2) Investment managers are prohibited from excluding or limiting their liability to take care or exercise skill in the performance of any investment functions.[143] This is in contrast to investment managers in other circumstances, who may limit liability.

10.124 We think that the requirement to invest assets in the best interests of beneficiaries has the same meaning for investment managers as it has for trustees. In other words, investment managers must exercise their delegated powers for the purpose for which they have been given them. If they do not do so, they will incur the same liabilities as pension trustees would incur if the trustees had made the decision.

10.125 Investment managers will also owe duties of care to act with reasonable skill and will be subject to FCA rules. Principle 2 confirms that an investment manager, like other firms, "must conduct its business with due skill, care and diligence".

---

[138] The Pensions Act 1995 uses the language of "fund manager", but the terminology of "investment manager" has been preferred throughout.

[139] Pensions Act 1995, s 34(2).

[140] Section 34(4) of the Pensions Act 1995 requires trustees to take all reasonable steps to satisfy themselves that an investment manager has the appropriate knowledge and experience for managing the investments of the scheme.

[141] Pensions Act 1995, ss 34(4), 34(6). Section 34(6) requires trustees to take all reasonable steps to satisfy themselves that an investment manager is complying with section 36 of the Pensions Act 1995. Section 36 requires the trustees (and any investment manager to whom discretion has been delegated) to exercise their powers of investment in accordance with regulations.

[142] Pensions Act 1995, s 36(1).

[143] Pensions Act 1995, s 33(1)(b).

May trustees delegate their power to set a scheme strategy?

10.126   A more difficult question is how far trustees may delegate all strategic decisions to an investment manager. Under section 35(1) of the Pensions Act 1995, pension trustees "must secure" that a SIP "is prepared and maintained", and that it is reviewed and "if necessary, revised". The reference to "securing" that a SIP is prepared suggests that trustees need not do it themselves. Trustees are required to take advice about the SIP and the words of the legislation suggest that the adviser may draft the SIP for them. Section 36(5) requires the investment manager to exercise their investment powers with a view to giving effect to the SIP in so far as reasonably practicable.

10.127   However, under regulation 2(3)(a) of the Investment Regulations, the SIP must cover "the trustees' policy for securing compliance with" the rules on choosing investments in the pensions legislation.[144] The policy is owned by the trustees, which suggests that trustees should consider the contents of the SIP and take responsibility for it. It is clearly good practice for trustees to consider the overall investment strategy of the fund, and it may be regarded as a legal requirement. Trustees should also ensure that the mandate given to the investment manager is satisfactory, consistent with the law and gives effect to the principles in the SIP.[145]

Where the investment manager invests in funds managed by others

10.128   It is common for the primary investment manager to invest at least some of the scheme's assets in a variety of different collective investment vehicles. The investment managers of the collective investment vehicles will be given power to pick stocks and other investments, in accordance with the terms of the contract governing the relationship.

10.129   At this stage, the various duties we have set out in this chapter become heavily modified by the terms of the contract. The conclusions set out in this chapter cease to apply.

10.130   This is partly a matter of practice. An investment manager of a collective investment undertaking will not have an overview of the scheme as a whole, and is not in a position to see if the portfolio is adequately diversified. If for example, the fund invests only in technology shares, the investment manager cannot tell how this may sit alongside the scheme's other assets. It is also a matter of law: the courts tend to give precedence to the terms of the contract over other fiduciary duties. We consider the investment duties of others in the chain in Chapters 11 and 12.

---

[144]   Regulation 2(3)(a) of the Investment Regulations requires that a SIP must state the trustees' policy for securing compliance with section 36 of the Pensions Act 1995. In particular, section 36(1) requires trustees (and any investment manager to whom discretion has been delegated) to exercise their powers of investment in accordance with regulations. This will include regulation 4 of the Investment Regulations.

[145]   Pensions Act 1995, s 36(5) requires both trustees and the investment manager to exercise their powers to give effect to the SIP principles "so far as reasonably practicable".

HOW FAR DO THESE PRINCIPLES APPLY TO OTHER TRUSTS?

10.131   In broad terms, these principles apply in similar ways to other trusts, including charitable trusts and family trusts. There are a few differences, however.

10.132   Firstly, the purpose may differ. Charities, in particular, may invest purely for a financial return; but they may also spend the charity's resources to further its charitable purposes. In some cases, the use of money in direct pursuit of the charity's purposes may give rise to a financial return, even though that is not the main purpose: for example, a charity might make a long-term loan at a low rate of interest to an initiative which directly furthers one of the charity's aims (known as "programme-related investment"). In some cases a charity may be able to justify laying out funds on a mixed basis, where the purpose is a combination of achieving a financial return and furthering the charity's purposes ("mixed-purpose investment") – for example, a charity for the relief of poverty considering an investment in a low-cost housing scheme. This is the subject of Charity Commission guidance.[146]

10.133   Secondly, the requirements on general trusts are often less prescriptive. For example, pension trustees are required to take advice. Other trustees are required, by section 5 of the Trustee Act 2000, to obtain and consider proper advice unless they reasonably conclude that this is unnecessary or inappropriate. We described these differences in more detail in Chapter 7.

10.134   Finally, other trustees are able to exclude their liability for negligence, including gross negligence.[147] Furthermore, the investment manager to whom investment functions are delegated by such trustees may also exclude or limit their liability.[148] We have been told that investment managers often include limitation clauses in their contracts.

CONCLUSION

10.135   Trustees must use their powers for the purpose for which they are given. In the case of a pension scheme, investment powers are granted to trustees so that they can earn returns to provide a pension. Within these broad parameters, however, trustees are given considerable discretion, so long as trustees reach the decision in the right way. In particular:

(1)   trustees must not fetter their discretion by, for example, applying a pre-existing moral or political judgment;

(2)   trustees must consider the relevant circumstances; and

(3)   pension trustees must take advice.

---

[146] Charity Commission, *Charity and Investment Matters: A guide for trustees* (CC14) (2011), in particular sections J and K. See para 1.37 above.

[147] See para 6.68 and following above.

[148] Pensions Act 1995, s 33(1)(b).

10.136 Stakeholders raised five possible factors which trustees may wish to take account of in making investment decisions. We summarise our conclusions on these issues in Chapter 14 and ask consultees whether they think that the law is right. In particular, is it conducive to investment strategies in the best interests of pension scheme members?

CHAPTER 11
DUTIES ON OTHERS IN THE INVESTMENT CHAIN: THE COURTS' GENERAL APPROACH

11.1 In Chapter 3 we described some of the complex "chains of intermediation" between the original saver and the company in which they invest.[1] In the pensions context, for example, the trustees will use an investment manager who may purchase units in collective investment funds, using brokers and custodians. And the chain is often subject to oversight by actuaries and consultants. We have been asked to consider who in this line-up is subject to fiduciary duties, and in respect of which of the tasks they undertake.

11.2 Specifically, our terms of reference ask us to investigate the extent to which, under existing law, fiduciary duties apply to:

(a) intermediaries (including investment managers and pension scheme trustees) investing on behalf of others; and

(b) those providing advice or other services to those undertaking investment activity.

11.3 In Chapter 10 we considered the duties of pension scheme trustees and their immediate investment managers. Here we begin to consider how far the courts might apply fiduciary duties or duties of care to intermediaries and their advisers.

11.4 This is a difficult question to answer. As we have seen, the law of fiduciary duties is extremely flexible. In theory, many of those in the investment chain might be considered fiduciaries, for example if one acts as an agent for another or if there is a combination of power to act, discretion and vulnerability. However, the content of those duties is highly fact-specific.[2] Similarly, the courts are prepared to extend duties of care to new circumstances, outside contractual relationships, but they do so cautiously, bearing in mind issues of public policy and whether the actor has "assumed responsibility".[3] It is impossible to know how the courts will apply these fluid principles to the myriad of participants in financial markets, or the many problems which might arise.

11.5 In this chapter, we do not attempt to provide specific answers. Instead, we outline some of the general principles which guide the courts in deciding whether to apply fiduciary duties or duties of care to participants in financial markets. We start with a short description of these principles. We then illustrate how they have been applied in some recent cases.

---

[1] See para 3.5 and following above.

[2] See para 4.13 above.

[3] See para 6.43 above.

11.6 As we have seen, "fiduciary duty" is a term which may be used narrowly, to refer just to duties peculiar to fiduciaries, or widely to embrace all the various duties owed by a fiduciary to their principal. In this chapter, we look widely at both fiduciary duties and duties of care. It is noticeable that when investors sue financial intermediaries following disastrous investments they tend to frame their claims as generally as possible, often alleging breach of contract, negligence, misrepresentation, and breach of fiduciary duty alongside each other. In this chapter we attempt to discern the general approach of the courts to these claims.

11.7 This chapter is intended to outline some of the broad themes which run through court decisions. In the next chapter, Chapter 12, we look at some of the specific issues which stakeholders have brought to our attention, and attempt to reach some tentative conclusions.

The Kay Review's recommendation

11.8 Professor Kay recommended that all those in financial markets should apply fiduciary standards in their dealings with each other whenever they exercise discretion over the investments of others or give advice on investment decisions. He thought that fiduciary standards "required that the client's interests are put first, that conflicts of interest should be avoided, and that the direct and indirect costs of services provided should be reasonable and disclosed". Furthermore, he thought that these obligations should be independent of the classification of the client, and should not be capable of being contractually overridden.[4] He said that intermediaries' legal responsibilities should be directed to the interests of end savers:

> The fiduciary obligation is not relieved by the identification of the immediate client as a professional or wholesale investor. The economic interest in all monies in the investment chain lies with savers, and it is to the interests of these savers that the legal and regulatory responsibilities of equity investment intermediaries must be directed.[5]

He thought that this was essential to improve trust, confidence and respect in the markets as a whole, as the chain is only as strong as its weakest link.[6] We have interpreted this as suggesting that fiduciary duties should be owed by all intermediaries not only to their immediate client but also to the end saver.

---

[4] J Kay, *The Kay Review of UK Equity Markets and Long-Term Decision Making: Final Report* (2012) Recommendation 7.

[5] Above, para 9.9.

[6] Above, para 9.11.

11.9   In its response to the Kay Review the Government set out a principle for all participants in the equity investment chain, which we reproduce in Chapter 1.[7] Among other things, it states that participants "should act in the best long-term interests of their clients or beneficiaries". As with Professor Kay's recommendations, the principle should be "independent of the classification of the client" and "should not be contractually overridden". It says that "this means ensuring that the direct and indirect costs of services provided are reasonable and disclosed".

11.10   These principles differ from the approach that the courts currently take. As we shall see, the courts are influenced by client classifications: they have been reluctant to override the contractual arrangements made between sophisticated parties, or to add new duties to the detailed rules imposed by the regulators. Instead, the courts have tended to confine fiduciary duties to those who act on behalf of individuals, at the lower rungs of the investment chain. Although it is difficult to be definitive, they would be unlikely to intervene to impose fiduciary duties on sophisticated commercial players further up the chain, who may be removed from and have little knowledge of the ultimate beneficiaries.

11.11   The courts require that charges are disclosed, but they do not assess whether those charges are reasonable. There is some limited power under the Unfair Terms in Consumer Contracts Regulations 1999 to assess the fairness of price terms in consumer contracts where those terms are not in plain, intelligible language. As we discuss below, this provision has led to litigation over bank charges for unauthorised overdrafts and has been interpreted restrictively by the Supreme Court.

GENERAL PRINCIPLES

Fiduciary duties may apply to contractual relationships

11.12   As we saw in Chapter 5, fiduciary duties may apply in a wide range of circumstances. They are not confined to trust-based relationships, but may also be owed, for example, by an agent to a principal. The courts may also apply the principles outside established categories where there is "discretion, power to act, and vulnerability".[8] Further, cases such as *Reading v Attorney General*[9] illustrate that the courts may hold a relationship to be fiduciary for some purposes where they feel it is right to do so – this is the prerogative of equity-based rules and remedies.

---

[7]   Department for Business, Innovation and Skills, *Ensuring equity markets support long-term growth, The Government Response to the Kay Review* (2012) para 2.8. For the full principle see para 1.10 above.

[8]   Law Commission, Fiduciary Duties and Regulatory Rules (1992) Law Commission Consultation Paper No 124 para 2.4.6.

[9]   [1951] AC 507.

11.13　The leading textbook on agency law emphasises that fiduciary duties may arise in contractual relationships. The authors stress:

> Even where the relationship is contractual (as it normally will be), the matter is too important to be left entirely to the agreement of the parties and the interpretation of that agreement ... A too casual failure to recognise the requirements of a fiduciary position, and sometimes a short-sighted assumption that all relevant duties are prescribed in a contract, can be and has been responsible for serious misbehaviour in the financial markets and elsewhere, as is shown by many litigated cases in the last quarter-century.[10]

11.14　However, the fact that the courts could develop the law to impose fiduciary duties on financial markets does not mean that they have. As we shall see, judges have often been reluctant to intervene. They have been heavily influenced by three interrelated considerations: namely, their respect for commercial relationships, for regulatory decision-making and for contract terms.

The courts respect commercial relationships

11.15　There is some reluctance to assign fiduciary obligations to a commercial relationship. The reason for this was well put by the Australian judge, Justice Kennedy:

> It would seem that part of the reluctance to find a fiduciary duty within an arm's length commercial transaction is due to the fact that the parties in that situation have an adequate opportunity to prescribe their own mutual obligations, and that the contractual remedies available to them to obtain compensation for any breach of those obligations should be sufficient.[11]

11.16　The New Zealand case of *DHL International (NZ) Ltd v Richmond Ltd* explained that commercial relationships often preclude the existence of fiduciary obligations:[12]

> Arm's length commercial transactions rarely give rise to fiduciary obligations. They are matters of contract where the parties reasonably expect their contract to govern, rather than matters of conscience.[13]

---

[10]　*Bowstead & Reynolds on Agency* (19th ed 2010) para 6-034. For Scots law see L Macgregor, *The Law of Agency in Scotland* (1st ed 2013) paras 6.11-6.13.

[11]　Kennedy J "Equity in a Commercial Context" in P Finn *Equity and Commercial Relationships* (1st ed 1987) p 15. Scottish examples of this include *Lothian v Jenolite* 1969 SC 111 and *Raymond Harrison & Co's Trustee v North West Securities* 1989 SLT 718.

[12]　[1993] 3 NZLR 10.

[13]　Above, at 22.

11.17 Similarly, Justice Dawson in *Hospital Products Ltd v United States Surgical Corporation*[14] stated that fiduciary relationships will not be used to overcome the shortcomings in the arrangements between the parties. One commentator suggests:

> It would not be reasonable for the party seeking to claim that a fiduciary obligation was owed to it to expect a higher degree of obligation than that which it bargained for.[15]

The courts respect regulatory rules

11.18 As we shall see, several court cases have interpreted the obligations owed by the parties in tort in line with the rules set out by the Financial Conduct Authority (FCA) and its predecessors. Judges are conscious that regulators have been charged with setting standards, and they are often reluctant to interfere with those decisions.

11.19 There are several ways in which regulatory rules can be actionable between the parties (rather than just left to regulators to enforce).

Breach of statutory duty

11.20 In Chapter 8 we saw that in some circumstances, a private person may bring an action under section 138D of the Financial Services and Markets Act 2000, if they have suffered loss as a result of the breach of FCA rules. However, this is a limited right. It only applies to private persons, and only to some rules.[16]

Contractual incorporation

11.21 In our 1995 report on fiduciary duties,[17] we looked in detail at whether regulatory rules could be incorporated into contracts, to take effect as contract terms. We thought that the courts might be inclined to give regulations the status of contract terms, so that contravention of the rules becomes actionable at common law as a breach of contract.[18]

---

[14] (1984) 156 CLR 41 at 147.

[15] P Hood, "Fiduciary obligation in a contractual/commercial context: DHL International (NZ) Ltd v Richmond Ltd (1994) *Journal of Business Law* 285 at 290.

[16] See para 8.72 and following above.

[17] Fiduciary Duties and Regulatory Rules (1995) Law Com No 236.

[18] See *Jackson & Powell on Professional Liability* (7th ed 2011) para 15-021.

11.22 There are some cases where this has happened. For example, in *Larussa-Chigi v CS First Boston Ltd*,[19] Mr Justice Thomas suggested that even if the parties had not (as he held) expressly incorporated the London Code of Conduct,[20] the Code would have been incorporated as an implied term since it was not intended that the foreign exchange transactions in question be unregulated.[21] However, most cases reject this approach.[22]

Informing duties of care

11.23 Rather than turn regulatory duties into contract terms, the courts have tended to interpret duties of care in line with regulatory standards. Leading textbook writers, McMeel and Virgo, summarise the courts' approach:

> Where an independent common law cause of action is established, or a common law duty is held to co-exist with a statutory duty, any applicable FSA rules or guidance will be highly influential in shaping the common law standard of care. The standard of liability at common law is likely to mirror precisely the statutory regime.[23]

11.24 Similarly, another leading textbook on professional negligence stresses that in a financial context, the "first main issue that needs to be addressed is one of regulatory application".[24] The authors conclude that:

> In particular the standard of the duty of care in negligence is likely to be largely co-extensive with that imposed by the regulatory rules.[25]

11.25 As we shall see, this is a guideline rather than a rule. As the judge put it in *Gorman v British Telecommunications plc*, the courts should "attach considerable weight" to the content of codes drafted by "those concerned with the maintenance of proper standards", but they are not excluded from making their own assessment of the situation.[26]

---

[19] [1998] CLC 277.

[20] The London Code of Conduct is a regulatory regime, applying to trading in the wholesale markets, published by the Bank of England until 1999 and thereafter by the FSA.

[21] [1998] CLC 277 at 295.

[22] See *Redmayne Bentley Stockbrokers v Isaacs* [2010] EWHC 1504; *Wilson v MF Global UK Ltd* [2011] EWHC 138 and *Clarion Ltd v National Provident Institution* at [2000] 1 WLR 1888.

[23] *McMeel and Virgo on Financial Advice and Financial Products: Law and Liability* (Release 10 2012) para V.1.20.

[24] *Jackson & Powell on Professional Liability* (7th ed 2011) para 15-012.

[25] Above, para 14-072.

[26] [2000] 1 WLR 2129 at 2141.

The courts respect contractual terms

11.26 The courts treat the contract as the starting point, and will usually interpret the parties' duties to each other in line with the contract terms. This is well-established in tort law, where duties of care can be modified by the terms of the contract.[27] The test is said to be:

> Whether the tortious duty is so inconsistent with the applicable contract that, in accordance with ordinary principle, the parties must be taken to have agreed that the tortious remedy is to be limited or excluded.[28]

11.27 The more difficult question is how far the terms of the contract modify fiduciary duties where there is an established fiduciary relationship. When the Law Commission considered this issue in our 1992 Consultation Paper[29] we said there were two possible ways of analysing the issue.

11.28 The first approach saw fiduciary duties as having primacy, arising from the nature of the relationship and independent of any contractual arrangement. This was termed the "status based approach". It would mean that terms of a contract which were incompatible with fiduciary duties would be of no effect.[30]

11.29 The second approach stated that the contract came first, and that fiduciary duties arose from the contract (or trust deed or other instrument). This meant that the court must look first to the contractual (or similar) relationship between the parties. This would determine whether the relationship was fiduciary in character and, if so, what fiduciary duties attached. In other words:

> The parties to a consensual relationship would be free to set out the parameters of their respective rights and duties by contract or other instrument, subject to any statutory provisions to the contrary.[31]

11.30 We preferred the second approach, although we thought that the position was unclear.

11.31 Following the consultation paper, but before our 1995 report, the case of *Kelly v Cooper*[32] was decided. We commented that this confirmed the "contract first" approach: express terms would be central to the court's assessment of the existence and scope of any fiduciary duties. Below we look at the *Kelly* case in more detail and consider how far it is modified by statutory protections.

---

[27] *Henderson v Merrett Syndicates Ltd* [1995] 2 AC 145, 193-194. For discussion of Scots law see J Thomson, *Delictual Liability* (4th ed 2009) paras 4.10-4.29.

[28] Above, at 193-194, by Lord Goff. See also *South Australian Asset Management Corporation v York Montague* [1997] AC 191 at 211.

[29] Fiduciary Duties and Regulatory Rules (1992) Law Commission Consultation Paper No 124.

[30] Above, para 3.3.9

[31] Above, para 3.3.10

[32] [1993] AC 205. For a discussion of the significance of this case in Scots law, see L Macgregor, *The Law of Agency in Scotland* (1st ed 2013) paras 6.55-6.56.

Kelly v Cooper

11.32   This was an appeal to the Privy Council from the Court of Appeal of Bermuda. The claimant instructed the defendant estate agent to sell his house. The owner of the adjacent house also instructed the same estate agents. The agent received an offer for both houses, but did not inform the claimants that their purchaser was also interested in buying the house next door. The claimants argued that they could have obtained a higher price for their house if they had known the purchaser was interested in both houses. They said that the defendants had created a conflict of interest by accepting instructions to act as agent for two parties without disclosing the fact.

11.33   Lord Browne-Wilkinson thought that the contract came first:

> First, agency is a contract made between principal and agent; second, like every other contract, the rights and duties of the principal and agent are dependent upon the terms of the contract between them, whether express or implied. It is not possible to say that all agents owe the same duties to their principals: it is always necessary to have regard to the express or implied terms of the contract.[33]

11.34   The final sentence is a strong statement in support of the "contract-first" approach. It suggests that, rather than arising from the nature of a relationship, fiduciary duties must be derived from the totality of the relationship in a way that is compatible with any contract between the parties.

11.35   Lord Browne-Wilkinson noted that estate agents would not be able to perform their function if they could not act for competing principals: it was in the nature of their business that they would at times act for purchasers and vendors whose interests would necessarily conflict.[34] He thought that estate agency contracts included an implied contract term that the agent is entitled to act for other vendors selling competing properties and to keep confidential the information obtained from each. The court therefore rejected the claim.

The effect of Kelly

11.36   *Kelly* has been taken as authority for the proposition that, where necessary for the functioning of the relationship, terms can be implied into the contract limiting the scope of fiduciary duties in exactly the same way as express terms.[35]

---

[33]   [1993] AC 205 at 213-214 (emphasis added).

[34]   [1993] AC 205 at 214.

[35]   D Frase, *Law and Regulation of Investment Management* (2nd ed 2011) para 8-069.

11.37 In our 1995 Report we said that the court would not give effect to a "mere sham".[36] We cited the case of *Glynwill Investments NV v Thompson McKinnon Futures Limited*,[37] where a foreign exchange dealer who was clearly acting as an agent pointed to a contract which described it as a principal. The court nevertheless looked at the substance of the relationship to find that it was a fiduciary relationship.

11.38 On the other hand, we said that a clearly worded clause which defined a party's duties or excluded their liability "will circumscribe the extent of the fiduciary duties owed to the other party."[38] We said that after *Kelly* there was "virtual unanimity" amongst consultees that express terms were effective in excluding, limiting or modifying fiduciary obligations.[39]

Statutory controls on unfair terms

11.39 There are two main forms of statutory controls on unfair terms:

(1) The Unfair Contract Terms Act 1977 (UCTA) applies to a wide range of contracts (including business-to-business contracts) but controls only a narrow range of terms. Broadly, UCTA focuses on terms which exclude liability for negligence or breach of contract.

(2) The Unfair Terms in Consumer Contracts Regulations 1999 (UTCCR)[40] apply only to consumer contracts but apply to all the terms of a contract (with a limited exception for the price and the main subject matter of the contract).

11.40 These provisions are discussed at length in previous Law Commission publications.[41] Here we provide a very brief summary.

CONTRACTS BETWEEN TWO BUSINESSES

11.41 In financial contracts where both parties are businesses, the most important protection is in section 2(2) of UCTA, which states that "a person cannot exclude or restrict his liability for negligence" unless the term is fair and reasonable.[42]

---

[36] Fiduciary Duties and Regulatory Rules (1995) Law Com No 236 para 3.42, citing *Ex parte Delhasse* (1877) 7 Ch 511 at 526, by James LJ; at 532, by Baggallay LJ.

[37] 13 February 1992 (unreported, Tuckey QC). This is discussed in more detail in para 12.34 and following above.

[38] Fiduciary Duties and Regulatory Rules (1995) Law Com No 236 para 3.29.

[39] Above, para 7.3.

[40] SI 1999 No 2083. The UTCCR apply to the whole of the UK.

[41] See Unfair Terms in Contracts (2005) Law Com No 292; Scot Law Com No 199; and Law Commission and Scottish Law Commission, Unfair Terms in Consumer Contracts: Advice to the Department for Business, Innovation and Skills (2013).

[42] Section 2(2) applies to England, Wales and Northern Ireland. In Scotland, the equivalent section is section 16(1) which covers terms which "restrict liability for breach of duty". However, under section 2(1), a person cannot by reference to any contract term exclude or restrict liability for death or personal injury resulting from negligence.

11.42 For standard term contracts, section 3 of UCTA also provides protection against exclusions for breach of contract and, more widely, any term which purports to allow the other party "to render a contractual performance substantially different from that which was reasonably expected".[43]

11.43 The question of whether a term is reasonable is a matter for the judge. However, schedule 2 of UCTA lists relevant factors to which the court may have regard, including: the strength of the bargaining position of the parties; whether the customer received an inducement; and whether the customer knew or ought to have known of the term.[44]

11.44 In *JP Morgan Bank v Springwell Navigation Corp* (discussed below),[45] the court found that UCTA applied to the term in question, but held that the term was reasonable, given the sophistication of the parties.

CONTRACTS BETWEEN A CONSUMER AND A BUSINESS

11.45 The UTCCR define a consumer as "any natural person who, in contracts covered by these Regulations, is acting for purposes which are outside his trade, business or profession."[46]

11.46 In *Standard Bank London Ltd v Apostolakis (No 1)*,[47] the court considered whether wealthy private individuals are consumers. A couple had entered into contracts with the claimant bank for large foreign exchange trades, worth in all several million dollars. The couple were sophisticated investors, having deposited over $1 million on margin with the bank. The bank argued that the couple were not consumers but in the business of trading foreign exchange contracts. Mr Justice Longmore disagreed. He said that the defendants:

> were disposing of income which they had available. They were using the money in a way which they hoped would be profitable but merely to use money in a way one hopes would be profitable is not enough, in my view, to be engaging in a trade... They were not trading in foreign exchange contracts in the sense that a bank or dealer can be said to trade.[48]

---

[43] For England, Wales and Northern Ireland, see s 3(2)(b)(i)). For Scotland, see s 17(1)(b).

[44] Technically these factors apply only to part of the Act, but they are frequently regarded as being of general application. See *Chitty on Contracts* (31st ed 2012) para 14-085.

[45] [2010] EWCA Civ 1221. See para 11.78 and following above.

[46] UTCCR 1999, reg 3(1).

[47] [2002] CLC 933.

[48] Above, at 937.

11.47 Therefore the UTCCR applied. It was later held that an exclusive jurisdiction clause was unfair.[49] The judge accepted that in this case the arrangements were "at the 'business' end of the scale" but "the purpose of the regulations is to protect consumers".[50]

11.48 The *Standard Bank* case shows that the UTCCR can apply to private investors, even sophisticated ones. However, the UTCCR only apply to natural persons.[51] They are of no use where an investor invests through a private investment vehicle (such as a limited company set up for the purpose of investing) or indeed a pension fund.

Should prices be reasonable?

11.49 One feature of the Government's principle for the functioning of equity markets set out in its response to the Kay Review is that "the direct and indirect costs of services provided" should be "reasonable and disclosed".[52]

11.50 The price of a service is not an area where the courts will generally intervene. There is no common law duty on providers to keep prices reasonable. Instead, the courts consider that this is an issue best left to the market. The only power the courts have to intervene over unreasonable prices relates to consumer contracts, where non-transparent charges may be assessed for fairness under the UTCCR.

11.51 Under the UTCCR, all terms in consumer contracts may be assessed for fairness, unless the term falls within one of the exemptions. The most important exemption is set out in regulation 6(2), which states that:

> In so far as it is in plain intelligible language, the assessment of fairness of a term shall not relate....
>
> (b) to the adequacy of the price or remuneration, as against the goods or services supplied in exchange.

---

[49] *Standard Bank London Ltd v Apostolakis (No 2)* [2002] CLC 939. This was the second of the two *Standard Bank* cases. Both raised preliminary issues on an application for summary judgment.

[50] Above, at [51].

[51] UTCCR 1999, reg 3(1).

[52] Department for Business, Innovation and Skills, *Ensuring equity markets support long-term growth, The Government Response to the Kay Review* (2012) para 2.8.

11.52   This provision has generated considerable litigation, particularly over whether bank charges for unauthorised overdrafts could be assessed for fairness. This culminated in the 2009 decision of the Supreme Court in *Office of Fair Trading v Abbey National plc*.[53] The Supreme Court held that whether a term was the "price" must be assessed objectively.[54] Provided that a term was "in plain intelligible language", the courts were not entitled to assess whether a price term was appropriate in relation to the goods or services supplied in exchange.[55] The decision reflects the courts' reluctance to intervene with the mechanisms of the market in setting prices.

11.53   The case has proved particularly difficult to interpret, as we discussed at length in our 2012 Issues Paper on Unfair Terms in Consumer Contracts.[56] It is clear that the courts have no powers to consider the reasonableness of "core bargains", where consumers are aware of price terms and take them into account in their decision-making. The difficulty lies in determining how far the courts may consider the fairness of ancillary or hidden charges, which are not subject to competition.

11.54   The courts may look at the fairness of any price term which is not in plain and intelligible language. The more difficult question is whether the term also has to be sufficiently clear and prominent that consumers would be aware of the term. Regulation 6(2) implements a European Directive,[57] and it is not clear what approach the Court of Justice of the European Union would take to the issue.

11.55   In 2013, the Law Commission and Scottish Law Commission recommended that the exemption should be clarified, to apply only to charges which are transparent and prominent. By transparent we meant charges which are in plain intelligible language and legible. By prominent, we meant charges presented in such a way that the average consumer would be aware of the term.[58] We are pleased to see that these recommendations have been included in the Draft Consumer Rights Bill, published by BIS in June 2013.[59]

A SUMMARY OF RECENT CASES

11.56   To illustrate the courts' approach, we look at some recent cases which consider the duties owed by investment intermediaries to their clients and others. As we explained above, these cases do not necessarily focus on "fiduciary" duties. Rather they tend to consider contractual, tortious and fiduciary duties in the round, and examine the nature of a "duty of care".

---

[53]   [2009] UKSC 6.

[54]   Above, at [113].

[55]   Above, at [95].

[56]   Law Commission and Scottish Law Commission, Unfair Terms in Consumer Contracts: a new approach?, Issues Paper (2012).

[57]   Unfair Terms Directive 93/13/EEC, Official Journal L 95 of 21.04.1993 p 29.

[58]   Law Commission and Scottish Law Commission, Unfair Terms in Consumer Contracts: Advice to the Department for Business, Innovation and Skills (2013).

[59]   Draft Consumer Rights Bill (June 2013) Cm 8657, cl 67.

11.57 We start by looking at claims brought by retail clients and other unsophisticated parties. In these cases, the courts have been prepared to adapt fiduciary duties and duties of care to provide the necessary protection. We then look at claims brought by sophisticated parties. Here the courts have been much less sympathetic to those who have made bad investments, and have tended to see the contractual terms as paramount.

11.58 "Sophistication" is not a defined term. Various regulatory protections have attempted to encapsulate those in need of protection, using defined terms such as "consumer" or "retail client". Here we use "sophistication" to refer to the concept in a broader, more impressionistic way. The sophistication of the parties is not necessarily an explicit factor in the courts' reasoning. However, as Lord Justice Fletcher Moulton said in 1911, "there is no class of case in which one ought more carefully to bear in mind the facts of the case" than cases relating to fiduciary duties.[60] We think it is helpful to put the explicit principles into their factual context.

CLAIMS BROUGHT BY UNSOPHISTICATED CLIENTS

11.59 Recently, the issue of fiduciary duties has arisen in two circumstances: as a protection against undisclosed commissions; and to impose duties on financial intermediaries to advise on the suitability of investments. The courts have imposed duties on financial intermediaries in both areas, but these duties are often interpreted as co-extensive with FCA rules.

Are undisclosed commissions a breach of fiduciary duty?

11.60 In Chapter 5 we described the case of *Wilson v Hurstanger Ltd*,[61] where a mortgage lender had paid a mortgage broker a fee of £250. The court found that because the borrowers were "vulnerable and unsophisticated", the broker should have disclosed the precise amount. It was "necessary to bring home to such borrowers the potential conflict of interest".[62] This is a powerful illustration of how the courts may adapt fiduciary duties to protect vulnerable consumers in financial markets.

11.61 However, the courts have been reluctant to extend duties further than the FCA rules. In *Harrison v Black Horse Ltd*[63] the issue was whether the failure of lenders to tell borrowers that they had received commission for selling them payment protection insurance amounted to unfairness in the relationship between lender and borrower for the purposes of the Consumer Credit Act 1974.

11.62 On appeal to the Court of Appeal, the claimant borrower's submission was that the size of the commission was so egregious that it amounted to a conflict of interest which had to be disclosed. The defendant lender relied on the Insurance Conduct of Business Rules (ICOB), part of what was then the FSA Handbook, and the absence of any disclosure requirement in those rules.

[60] *Re Coomber* [1911] 1 Ch 723 at 729.

[61] [2007] EWCA Civ 299. See para 5.36 above.

[62] Above, at [36].

[63] [2011] EWCA Civ 1128.

11.63 The Court of Appeal found it decisive that the ICOB regime did not require the disclosure of the receipt of the commission.[64] Lord Justice Tomlinson held:

> The touchstone must in my view be the standard imposed by the regulatory authorities pursuant to their statutory duties, not resort to a visceral instinct that the relevant conduct is beyond the Pale. In that regard it is clear that the ICOB regime after due consultation and consideration does not require the disclosure of the receipt of commission. It would be an anomalous result if a lender was obliged to disclose receipt of a commission in order to escape a finding of unfairness under s.140A of the [Consumer Credit] Act but yet not obliged to disclose it pursuant to the statutorily imposed regulatory framework under which it operates.[65]

A duty of care to advise on the suitability of investments

11.64 As we have seen, the FCA imposes various "know-your-customer" requirements. The Conduct of Business Sourcebook (COBS) requires a firm to take reasonable steps to ensure that the advice it gives and investment management decisions it takes are suitable for its client.[66] The courts have found that a failure to advise a retail client on the suitability of investments may also amount to a breach of a duty of care.

Duties of care to retail clients: an example

11.65 In *Loosemore v Financial Concepts*,[67] a nurse opted out of her employer's occupational pension scheme and subsequently took out a personal pension scheme, following a meeting with an independent financial adviser (IFA). The IFA had breached the regulatory rules applicable at the time. The judge found that this constituted negligence; the IFA was therefore liable to compensate the claimant. HHJ Raymond Jack QC held:

> The skill and care to be expected [from the IFA] would ordinarily include compliance with the rules. I should add that in comparison with what many financial advisers and companies were doing at this time – which was to encourage people to opt out and transfer, Mr Wischhusen did well. For he did give some warning. It was not, however, enough. The Financial Services Act 1986 and the rules made under it by the supervisory agencies brought in radically new standards.[68]

11.66 This principle has been followed on subsequent occasions.[69]

---

[64] [2011] EWCA Civ 1128 at [43]-[47].

[65] Above, at [58].

[66] FCA Handbook COBS 9.2.1R(1).

[67] [2001] Lloyd's Rep PN 235.

[68] Above, at 241-242.

[69] See, for example *Rubenstein v HSBC Bank* [2011] EWHC 2304. *Rubenstein* was reversed in part on appeal ([2012] EWCA Civ 1184) but on other grounds.

Duties of care to clients' dependants

11.67 It has been held that IFAs also owe duties to their clients' widows and other dependants. Thus the duty is not confined to the contracting parties but may extend more widely.

11.68 In *Gorham v British Telecommunications plc*,[70] the claimant was the beneficiary under her husband's personal pension. Her husband had received negligent pension advice about his occupational scheme and had been sold an unsuitable personal pension plan. The Court of Appeal held that where the intermediary knew that advice about pensions was central to the interests of the customer's dependants, a duty of care was owed not just to the immediate customer but also to the intended beneficiaries.

11.69 At first sight, this would appear to uphold Professor Kay's view that financial intermediaries not only owe duties to their immediate clients but also to other beneficiaries. However, the case has been given limited application, as we shall see from our discussion of the *Seymour* case below.

No duty on those who advise IFAs to the end client

11.70 In *Seymour v Caroline Ockwell & Co*,[71] a husband and wife sold their farm for £1.4 million and consulted an IFA, Miss Ockwell, about how best to invest the money. Miss Ockwell then consulted an "executive consultant" employed by a major insurance group, ZIFA. ZIFA recommended an offshore fund, which proved to be disastrous. The claimants sued both the IFA and ZIFA, in negligence and under the Financial Services Act 1986.[72] The defendant brought an additional claim against ZIFA seeking an indemnity in the event she was found liable.

11.71 In the High Court, HHJ Havelock-Allen held that:

(1) The IFA had acted negligently and in breach of the Financial Services Act 1986.

(2) ZIFA did not owe a duty of care to the claimants.

(3) ZIFA owed a duty of care to Miss Ockwell in respect of any misstatements made to her. She successfully argued that ZIFA should indemnify her for two-thirds of the claimant's lost capital claim.

---

[70] [2000] 1 WLR 2129.

[71] [2005] EWHC 1137.

[72] The predecessor to the Financial Services and Markets Act 2000.

11.72 On the first point, the judge went through the relevant rules:

> I accept that whilst the ambit of the duty of care owed by a financial adviser at common law is not necessarily co-extensive with the duties owed by that adviser under the applicable regulatory regime, the regulations afford strong evidence as to what is expected of a competent adviser in most situations.[73]

He found that Miss Ockwell tried hard to follow the regulatory requirements, but "failed to see the wood for the trees".[74] Looked at in the round, it should always have been evident that the fund was unsuitable for her clients.

11.73 As to the second point, the claimants used *Gorham v British Telecommunications plc*[75] to argue that ZIFA owed a duty of care directly to the claimants when giving advice to the IFA. However, the judge rejected this argument:

> I accept that the *Gorham* case illustrates that the existence of a regulatory regime is not preclusive of a common law liability not duplicated by that regime. But if the consequence is to impose a duty on another professional or organisation running parallel to the duties of others, caution is salutary.[76]

11.74 The judge found that ZIFA did not owe a duty directly to the claimants – only to their immediate client, Miss Ockwell. He outlined policy reasons against imposing duties between parties who had no direct dealings with each other:

> It would be a duty which by-passed the regulatory regime and side-stepped the contractual remedy. Whilst not of itself fatal, it is significant that the relevant provisions of the Adopted FIMBRA Rules … place responsibility for recommendations and information squarely on the shoulders of the professional whose clients are relying on the advice being given. Mr and Mrs Seymour were not ZIFA's clients. They were the clients of Miss Ockwell. This structure would be avoided if a direct duty was to be imposed.[77]

11.75 Thus the *Seymour* case addresses the question of whether those who give advice to professional clients in the investment chain owe duties of care to ultimate beneficiaries. The courts appear reluctant to impose such duties. We believe they are likely to follow a similar approach in relation to fiduciary duties.

11.76 We have considered what would happen if, for example, an investment consultant gave negligent advice to pension trustees. This case suggests that only the pension trustees could sue. It would be difficult for the pensioner beneficiaries themselves to succeed in an action for compensation.

---

[73] [2005] EWHC 1137 at [77]. The judge cites *Lloyd Cheyham & Co Ltd v Eversheds* (1985) 2 Lloyds PN 154 in support of this proposition.

[74] Above, at [79].

[75] [2000] 1 WLR 2129.

[76] [2005] EWHC 1137 at [142].

[77] Above, at [143].

CLAIMS BROUGHT BY SOPHISTICATED CLIENTS

11.77 Here we consider cases in which sophisticated investors have been sold unsuitable investments by an intermediary. Where the contractual documents state that the intermediary is not giving advice about suitability, the courts have been extremely reluctant to impose any liability on the intermediary, whether through fiduciary duties or duties of care.

JP Morgan Bank v Springwell Navigation Corp[78]

11.78 *Springwell* was an investment vehicle for the wealthy Polemis family, who owned a large Greek shipping fleet. The company invested heavily in emerging markets and they used JP Morgan (formerly Chase Manhattan Bank or "Chase") to acquire a portfolio of debt instruments.

11.79 The main investor on behalf of Springwell had a close relationship with an employee of Chase (JA), and the two men spoke regularly on the phone. During these conversations, JA recommended that Springwell buy derivatives linked to Russian bonds. JA was a persuasive salesman: Springwell made 42 separate purchases of these bonds, to the tune of $87 million. When in 1998 Russia defaulted on some of its financial obligations, Springwell's portfolio collapsed.

11.80 Among the many claims in this complex case, Springwell sought damages or other compensation from Chase for breach of contract, negligence, breach of fiduciary duty, negligent misstatement and/or misrepresentation.

11.81 Following a 68 day trial in the High Court, Mrs Justice Gloster dismissed Springwell's claims. Springwell appealed to the Court of Appeal who also rejected the claims. The Court of Appeal upheld the trial judge's finding that JA was a salesman rather than an adviser: his statements were no more than expressions of opinion. Furthermore, Chase had no duty to advise Springwell about the suitability of the investments. The relationship had to be understood in the context of the contractual documentation between Springwell and Chase, which clearly stated that the relationship was not advisory.

No fiduciary duties

11.82 For our purposes the decision is interesting for the comprehensive way in which the trial judge dismissed the argument that the relationship was subject to fiduciary duties – so much so that the matter was not raised before the Court of Appeal.

---

[78] [2008] EWHC 1186 (Comm). This was the first of two judgments. Gloster J dealt with another point at [2008] EWHC 1793 (Comm). Certain points from both of these judgments were appealed to the Court of Appeal at [2010] EWCA Civ 1221. Only the first judgment raises relevant points.

11.83 Mrs Justice Gloster accepted that, in its capacity as custodian of securities, Chase may have had some limited fiduciary obligations, but then said:

> This is a far cry from the wide-ranging fiduciary relationship which Springwell asserted ... The mere fact that one party to a commercial relationship "trusts" the other does not predicate a fiduciary relationship. The word "trust", like the word "advice" has a variety of meanings... Springwell no doubt "trusted" Chase to conduct itself in a commercially appropriate manner. But I do not consider that Springwell had any legitimate expectation that, in its commercial dealings with Springwell, Chase would subordinate its interests to those of Springwell.[79]

The significance of client classification

11.84 As we have seen, under FCA rules, where a client elects to be treated as a professional client, the client must request the categorisation in writing and the firm must then provide a clear written warning of the protections the client might lose.[80] In the High Court, Mrs Justice Gloster placed significance on these letters:

> I accept that, on the evidence, the [client classification] letters were of particular significance, because they reflected a regulatory classification consciously undertaken by Chase in the absence of which Springwell would not have been permitted access to the Margin Forward Programme or, subsequently, the repurchase programme.[81]

11.85 On appeal, Lord Justice Aikens agreed with this conclusion.[82]

The signficance of contractual documents

11.86 Finally, Chase's various terms and conditions included statements that "the holder has not relied on ... any representation or warranty with respect to the advisability of purchasing this note". The terms went further and said that Springwell acknowledged that Chase had not made any such representations. Springwell argued that this was not true: Chase had made representations about the advisability of buying the bonds and Springwell had relied on them.

---

[79] [2008] EWHC 1186 (Comm) at [573].

[80] FCA Handbook COBS 3.5.3R; see para 8.45 above.

[81] [2008] EWHC 1186 (Comm) at [235].

[82] [2010] EWCA Civ 1221 at [186].

11.87 The Court of Appeal held that even if the statements were counter-factual, they were still sufficient to prevent Springwell from suing for misrepresentation or negligent advice. Lord Justice Aikens held that the effect of the terms was twofold:

> First and foremost they mean that Springwell is contractually estopped from contending that there were any actionable representations made by Chase on which Springwell could base its current claims either under the Misrepresentation Act or for negligent misstatement. Secondly, they point strongly against any statements of JA from being actionable, either as misrepresentations under the 1967 Act or as negligent misstatements.[83]

11.88 The Court of Appeal accepted that the terms and conditions were effectively exclusion clauses. Therefore, to be valid, they had to be reasonable within the terms of the Unfair Contract Terms Act 1977 and section 3 of the Misrepresentation Act 1967. However, the trial judge had found that the terms were reasonable, and the Court of Appeal saw no reason to overturn that finding.[84]

Other cases

11.89 The courts have reached similar conclusions in other cases.[85] For example in *Titan Steel Wheels Ltd v Royal Bank of Scotland plc,*[86] the claimants bought two "currency swap" products from the defendant bank. These swaps were not simply hedges but involved considerable risk. When they resulted in substantial losses, Titan sued the bank for selling an unsuitable product. Looking at the contractual documents, the judge followed *Springwell* in finding that the bank had no duty to advise on whether a product was suitable.

11.90 These cases suggest that if a pension fund were to be sold an unsuitable product by a bank or broker via an investment manager, the court would be unlikely to impose any duties on the bank or broker which went beyond the terms of the contract with the investment manager.

CONCLUSION

11.91 There are substantial differences between the approach currently taken by the courts and the aspiration set out in Recommendation 7 of the Kay Review.

11.92 Firstly, Professor Kay saw fiduciary standards as raising regulatory requirements, rather than simply mirroring them. He thought that these standards should be independent of the classification of the client and should apply whenever participants gave advice on investment decisions. This is also reflected in the Government's principle for participants in equity investment markets.

---

[83] [2010] EWCA Civ 1221 at [171].

[84] Above, at [183]-[184].

[85] See *Winnetka Trading Corp v Julius Baer International Ltd* [2011] EWHC 2030 (Ch).

[86] [2010] EWHC 211 (Comm).

11.93 By contrast, the courts have been heavily influenced by the client classifications set out in the regulatory regime. Where an IFA, for example, is required to consider the suitability of an investment for a retail client, the courts will incorporate the suitability requirement into the IFA's duty of care towards the client.[87] But where the regulations permit a participant to sell investments to a professional client or eligible counterparty on an "execution only" basis, they have held that there is no duty to consider suitability.[88]

11.94 Secondly, Professor Kay thought that fiduciary duties should not be capable of being contractually overridden. He saw fiduciary duties as arising from the factual relationship, such as the advice given. Again, the Government's principle states that the obligation to act in the best interests of clients may not be contractually overridden. By contrast, the courts start with contract, and what the contract says about the duties each party owes to the other. They then interpret whether what was said was really "advice" in the light of the contractual relationship.[89]

11.95 Thirdly, Professor Kay argued that the legal responsibilities should be directed not only to the immediate professional client but also to the ultimate saver. The courts have been extremely cautious in holding that parties in the chain owe duties to others, beyond their immediate client. As we say in Chapter 6, in *Caparo Industries plc v Dickman*[90] the House of Lords held that auditors owe duties only to the shareholders of the company which employs them, and only for certain purposes: they have no duty of care to future investors. In *Seymour*, the court also confined duties of care between the immediate parties. There a consultant had given negligent advice to an IFA, who had passed on that advice to the ultimate saver. The court found that although the IFA could sue the consultant, the saver could not. We believe a court would adopt a similar approach to fiduciary duties.

11.96 Finally, both Professor Kay and the Government's response argued that the direct and indirect costs of services should be reasonable and disclosed.[91] The courts will require participants to disclose their charges, but there is no common law rule permitting the courts to assess whether charges are reasonable. Courts have a limited power under the Unfair Terms in Consumer Contracts Regulations 1999 to assess the fairness of price terms in consumer contracts which are not in plain, intelligible language – but even this power has been interpreted restrictively.

---

[87] See *Loosemore v Financial Concepts* [2001] Lloyd's Rep PN 235; *Rubenstein v HSBC Bank* [2011] EWHC 2304.

[88] See *JP Morgan Bank v Springwell Navigation Corp* [2008] EWHC 1186 (Comm); *Titan Steel Wheels Ltd v Royal Bank of Scotland plc* [2010] EWHC 211 (Comm).

[89] For a statement of the contract first approach, see *Kelly v Cooper* [1993] AC 205; for priority given to contract terms, see *JP Morgan Bank v Springwell Navigation Corp* [2008] EWHC 1186 (Comm).

[90] [1990] 2 AC 605.

[91] For discussion see paras 1.6 and 1.10 above.

11.97 To summarise, therefore, the courts are more likely to impose fiduciary duties to the first links in the investment chain, to protect unsophisticated and vulnerable individuals. It is clearly established that pension trustees owe fiduciary duties to prospective pensioners, and IFAs would appear to owe duties of care to consider the suitability of investments for retail clients. However, fiduciary duties and duties of care are less likely to play a significant role at the top of the chain, when apparently sophisticated parties trade with each other on a professional client or eligible counterparty basis and their relationship is governed by a contract they have bargained for. Further, the law concerned with fiduciary duties or duties of care does not permit courts to consider whether prices are reasonable.

CHAPTER 12
DUTIES ON OTHERS IN THE INVESTMENT CHAIN: SPECIFIC EXAMPLES

12.1 The last chapter looked at the courts' overall approach to imposing duties on those in the investment chain. Here we look at specific examples.

12.2 We start with contract-based pensions. We have seen that pension trustees are under duties to act in the best interests of the beneficiaries. However, there is much less clarity over the duties owed by those involved in providing contract-based pensions. We look at the possible liabilities of employers, financial advisers and pension providers.

12.3 Even within a trust-based pension chain, there is uncertainty over the duties owed by non-trustees. In Chapter 3 we described the various intermediaries and advisers in typical investment chains, including investment consultant, brokers, investment managers and custodians. Here we report some of the concerns raised about these parties and consider how far the law of fiduciary duties might be used to address these concerns. We do so highly tentatively. Any court decision will depend on the detailed facts of the case brought. The law is flexible and uncertain and involves multiple stages.

A THREE STAGE PROCESS

12.4 The first question is whether the relationship is capable, in theory, of having a fiduciary character. This is a wide test: many relationships will fall within it. Fiduciary relationships may arise whenever there is a trust or agency arrangement, or where one party is vulnerable to another's misuse of discretion. Slaughter and May state that in the financial services sector:

> Persons who are generally assumed to be fiduciaries include agency brokers, advisers, fund managers and custodians (but not pure deposit takers, or market makers and dealers who do not purport to act in the interests of their counterparties).[1]

12.5 But this is only the start of the process. The courts will then look carefully at the contract to see how far the relationship is modified by the express or implied terms of the contract.

12.6 Thirdly, the nature of the duty owed will depend on the facts of the case. A relationship may be fiduciary for some purposes but not others. As we have seen, the courts are often reluctant to intervene out of respect for commercial relationships, regulatory rules and contractual bargains. Nevertheless, faced with the right facts they may step in to do justice in the case.

---

[1] Slaughter and May, *Conflicts of interest: a potential pressure point in the regulatory reform project* (2010) p 2.

CONTRACT-BASED PENSION SCHEMES

12.7 As we saw in Chapter 2, defined contribution pensions may either be trust-based or contract-based. Increasingly, workplace contracts are organised through a "group personal pension". Here the employee enters into a contract with the pension provider, though the employer chooses the scheme and makes arrangements to collect and pay contributions.[2] As one textbook notes:

> From an employee relations point of view, the arrangements will have the appearance of being a scheme run by the employer, although legally this is a series of individual schemes taken out by each employee.[3]

12.8 In discussions, consultees consistently said that while trustees were subject to fiduciary duties, contract-based providers were not subject to these duties. We think this is an over-simplification. As we saw in Chapter 11, fiduciary duties are not incompatible with contractual relationships. On the other hand, contractual parties are not subject to the same duties to exercise their powers for the purpose for which they were given. Nor are they subject to the duties placed on trustees by the pensions legislation. Furthermore, any fiduciary duties or duties of care are likely to be interpreted in line with the terms of the contract and regulatory rules. Litigation in this area is inherently uncertain.

12.9 In Chapter 13 we consider some of the problems with contract-based pensions, including low levels of engagement by buyers, high (and non-transparent) charges and the lack of independent review. If a consumer found that their pension was much less than expected because the charges were too high or the investment strategy had been unsuitable, would they be entitled to redress? Below we consider the potential liabilities of employers, financial advisers and pension providers.

Employers

12.10 It was suggested that employers may be blamed for failing to exercise sufficient care in their choice of pension provider. We think this would be a difficult case to make in law.

12.11 In Chapter 6 we discuss the courts' caution when imposing duties of care in respect of pure economic loss.[4] The courts look not only at the proximity of the relationship but also consider questions of public policy. We anticipate that the courts would be reluctant to impose liabilities on employers in areas which are outside their areas of expertise. The courts would be conscious that, where auto-enrolment is concerned, employers are obliged to enrol their staff and have not voluntarily assumed responsibility.

---

[2] *Tolley's Pensions Law* (Issue 79 2013) para A3.21.

[3] Above, para A3.21.

[4] See para 6.42 above.

12.12 Furthermore, in making a choice, over half of employers rely on a financial adviser, who is subject to Financial Conduct Authority (FCA) regulation.[5] Where this is the case, the courts are likely to reach the conclusion that employers are entitled to rely on the professional, regulated advice they are given.

Financial advisers

12.13 In Chapter 3 we describe the range of advisers used by employers to select pension schemes. Often advisers will also give advice to employees. These advisers must be regulated by the FCA and are subject to the FCA's "suitability" requirements.[6] In particular, when a financial adviser gives advice to an individual employee about a pension scheme, the adviser must obtain information from the client and have a reasonable basis for believing that the recommended transaction meets the client's investment objectives.[7] As we saw in Chapter 11, the courts have held that advisers who breach the suitability rules are liable to compensate their clients for the loss caused.[8]

12.14 The problem is that advisers may only be employed on a one-off basis, when the scheme is set up. They are much less likely to be employed to monitor the scheme over time, to assess whether a scheme which was suitable initially continues to be suitable many years later. Pension schemes are long-term products and many aspects can change. An investment strategy initially thought to be low to medium risk may become high risk; charges may become uncompetitive; and as people grow older, their risk appetite may decrease. In low cost schemes, it is unlikely that people will be given advice about these issues.

Pension providers

12.15 In Chapter 13 we outline the main criticisms made of contract-based pension providers. These concern non-transparent charges and the lack of ongoing monitoring and governance.

---

[5] Spence Johnson, *Defined Contribution Market Intelligence* (2013) p 25.

[6] See FCA Handbook COBS 9.

[7] FCA Handbook COBS 9.2.2R.

[8] See *Loosemore v Financial Concepts* [2001] Lloyd's Rep PN 235 and *Gorham v British Telecommunications plc* [2000] 1 WLR 2129. See paras 11.65 and 11.68 above.

Non-transparent charges

12.16 As we discussed in Chapter 11, the courts will not consider the reasonableness of prices which have been freely agreed.[9] However, if a price term is not in plain and intelligible language, it may be assessed for fairness under the Unfair Terms in Consumer Contracts Regulations 1999.[10] The Law Commission and Scottish Law Commission have recommended that the law should be clarified to state that the courts may assess non-transparent charges which are not presented in such a way that an average consumer would be aware of the term.[11] This change is now included in the Draft Consumer Rights Bill, presented to Parliament in June 2013.[12]

12.17 The courts have no jurisdiction to look at unreasonably high annual management charges which are clearly presented to members. However, under the Draft Consumer Rights Bill, the courts would have power to assess the fairness of additional charges which are hidden in small print.

Lack of ongoing monitoring

12.18 Contract-based pension providers are subject to FCA rules. Under COBS 2.1.1R "a firm must act honestly, fairly and professionally in accordance with the best interests of its client". The FCA Handbook makes clear that this duty applies to those operating personal or stakeholder pension schemes.[13] More specifically, under COBS 9.2.1R, a pension provider must "take reasonable steps to ensure that ... a decision to trade ... is suitable for its client". Under COBS 9.2.2R, the provider must obtain enough information "to understand the essential facts" about the client.

12.19 It is clear that the provider must consider the suitability of its products when the member enters the scheme. We think that if a pension provider sells pension plans which are unsuitable for its members, it would be liable for economic loss caused by a lack of care and skill (in the same way as financial advisers have been held liable).

12.20 What is less clear is how often the provider must review the suitability of a scheme over time. COBS 9.2.5R states that a firm is entitled to rely on the information provided by its clients "unless it is aware that the information is manifestly out of date, inaccurate or incomplete". This would appear to be a fairly high hurdle.

---

[9] See para 11.53 and following above.

[10] SI 1999 No 2083.

[11] Law Commission and Scottish Law Commission, Unfair Terms in Consumer Contracts: Advice to the Department for Business, Innovation and Skills (2013). See para 11.55 above.

[12] Draft Consumer Rights Bill (June 2013) Cm 8657, cl 67.

[13] FCA Handbook COBS 2.1.1R applies to "designated investment business" which includes establishing, operating or winding up a personal or stakeholder pension scheme (Financial Services and Markets Act 2000 (Regulated Activities) Order 2001 SI 2001 No 544, reg 52).

12.21 In response to Office of Fair Trading concerns, providers said that they have to consistently demonstrate to the FCA that their products are suitable and that they undertake annual reviews.[14] However, the obligation is not clearly defined. It is unclear how far the review is aimed at existing members as well as new members and how far the providers must seek new information from clients.

12.22 As far as the courts are concerned, we think that they will be highly influenced by FCA rules and by the terms of the contract. Even if a court found that a pension provider owed a fiduciary duty based on the "vulnerability" of the saver, that duty is unlikely to go further than the terms of the contract and the FCA rules.

OTHER INTERMEDIARIES IN THE INVESTMENT CHAIN

12.23 Below we look at the duties owed by other intermediaries involved in the investment chain, including investment consultants, brokers, investment managers, collective investment schemes and custodians. As we saw in Chapter 3, investment consultants play a particularly important role in defined benefit pension schemes. Others, such as brokers and custodians, are involved in almost all investment chains.

INVESTMENT CONSULTANTS

12.24 Pension funds are often highly dependent on investment consultants. In their research study, Anna Tilba and Terry McNulty found:

> While consultants perceive their role purely as advisory, the trustees for the most part regard consultant's advice to be *"telling"* or directing the trustee as to what investment strategy to pursue.[15]

12.25 In our meetings with stakeholders, concern was expressed about the apparent lack of regulation of investment consultants. We discuss this issue in Chapter 8 and conclude that investment consultants will not fall within the FCA regulatory regime so long as they only give "generic advice".[16]

Duties of care

12.26 Investment consultants owe a duty to their clients to use reasonable care and skill in carrying out this work. They may seek to exclude or limit their liability, but section 2(2) of the Unfair Contract Terms Act 1977 requires that any restriction is reasonable. In our initial discussions we were told that it is common for investment consultants to exclude or place a low cap on their liability to pension funds.

---

[14] Office of Fair Trading, *Defined contribution workplace pension market study* (2013) para 7.41.

[15] A Tilba and T McNulty, "Engaged versus disengaged ownership: the case of pension funds in the UK" (2013) 21(2) *Corporate Governance: An International Review* 165 at 173.

[16] See paras 8.20-8.21 above.

Conflicts of interest

12.27 Tilba and McNulty highlight the mutual dependence of investment consultants and investment managers:

> Investment consultants rely on investment fund managers and their investment strategies, to provide a "value added" service to their pension fund clients. Significantly, and at the same time, the fund managers depend on consultants for their recommendations and access to prospective pension fund clients.[17]

12.28 The significance of this dependence was consistently raised in our initial meetings with stakeholders. In their response to our short paper, the Network for Sustainable Financial Markets told us that this reliance combined with common exclusion of responsibilities:

> has resulted in the creation of loopholes that dilute fiduciary responsibilities and introduce inequality in application of the fundamental principles on which fiduciary duty is grounded.[18]

12.29 In discussion, concerns were raised that investment consultants may be subject to potential conflicts of interest. What would happen if an investment consultant were to have a particularly close relationship with an investment manager? There was also concern where consultants combine independent advice with in-house services, such as fiduciary management or investment management. In their response to our short paper, ShareAction commented that:

> there is significant scope for conflicts of interest to arise in the giving of investment advice. For example, consultants may have incentives to advise pension funds towards complexity, since this necessitates more advice, but the costs associated with these more complex strategies may not be justified by better outcomes for beneficiaries.[19]

---

[17] A Tilba and T McNulty, "Engaged versus disengaged ownership: the case of pension funds in the UK" (2013) 21(2) *Corporate Governance: An International Review* 165 at 174.

[18] Network for Sustainable Financial Markets, Response to "Fiduciary Duties of Investment Intermediaries: Initial Questions" (July 2013).

[19] ShareAction, Response to "Fiduciary Duties of Investment Intermediaries: Initial Questions" (July 2013).

Fiduciary duties

12.30   Would a court find that an investment consultant who gave advice in the face of a conflict of interest had breached a duty of loyalty? This is clearly a possibility. As one commentator puts it, when an adviser gives "a specialist skilled personal service to a client with the expectation that the client will rely on that advice", there will normally be a fiduciary relationship.[20] Under US law, the investment advisory relationship is generally regarded as fiduciary.[21] In contrast, we were told that it is not generally accepted in practice in the UK that investment consultants owe fiduciary duties.

12.31   The outcome of any litigation is uncertain. The court will look at all the aspects of the relationship, including the terms of the contract, to see how far it was reasonable to expect the pension scheme to rely on the advice, and how far the pension scheme was vulnerable to poor advice. Where the client exercises independent judgment and represents their own interests, advice may be no more than providing information such that fiduciary duties do not arise.[22] This is particularly so in commercial, sales-based relationships. For example, in *Sinclair Investment Holdings SA v Versailles Trade Finance Ltd (In Adminstrative Receivership)*[23] a "sales pitch" did not impose a fiduciary relationship.

12.32   A court will also look at the regulatory regime. The court may be reluctant to intervene if it thinks that the investment consultant has complied with the relevant regulations. As we note, investment consultants are often not caught by the FCA Handbook. If the court thinks that investment consultants have fallen through the regulatory net, it may be more inclined to intervene to provide the necessary protection. In the end, the outcome will depend on the facts of the case.

BROKERS

12.33   A broker entering a market to execute an order on behalf of a client may retain an element of discretion to decide who to trade with and at what price to trade. This is a classic agency relationship which may import fiduciary obligations. For example, in *Hancock v Smith*,[24] delivering share certificates to a broker with instructions to sell was held to give rise to a fiduciary relationship.

---

[20]   D Frase, "Conflicts of interest" (2012) 97(Jun) *Compliance Officer Bulletin* 1 at 5.

[21]   Investment Advisers Act 1940; *Santa Fe Industries, Inc v Green* (1977) 430 US 462, interpreting *SEC v Capital Gains Research Bureau* (1963) 375 US 180; *Transamerica v Lewis* (1979) 444 US 11 at 17; *Financial Planning Association v SEC* (2007) 482 F 3d 481 (DC) at 490; FXC Investors Corp, SEC Release No 218, 2002 WL 31741561 (ALJ Dec 9, 2002); D Busch and D DeMott, *Liability of Asset Managers* (1st ed 2012) para 13.43. See generally A Laby, "SEC v. Capital Gains Research Bureau and the Investment Advisers Act of 1940" (2011) 91 *Boston University Law Review* 1051.

[22]   *James v Australia and New Zealand Banking Group Ltd* (1986) 64 ALR 347 at 366-368.

[23]   [2007] EWHC 915 (Ch) at [76]-[87].

[24]   (1889) 41 Ch D 456.

12.34   In some circumstances, the courts have found that brokers acting as agents should not make a secret profit from the deal. In *Glynwill Investments NV v Thompson McKinnon Futures Limited*[25] a foreign exchange dealer filled orders by entering the market and dealing with other market makers. It then applied a mark-up to the price which it charged to customers. A customer argued that the dealer was acting as its agent and ought to rebate the mark-up. Conversely, the dealer pointed to the terms of its contract which stated that it was dealing as principal throughout.

12.35   The court looked at the substance of the relationship and concluded the relationship was substantively one of principal and agent. The customer was therefore entitled to recover the mark-up.[26] As we said in our 1995 Report, the courts would not apply contract terms where they are "a mere sham".[27] Some brokers, however, may also trade for their own account and may provide both broking and dealing services to the same client. In these arrangements, fiduciary duties are less clear and the circumstances of the individual transaction need to be considered.[28]

12.36   The courts require that brokers have contractual authority for their charges. However, the courts do not require that the charges are transparent or easy to compare. In practice, therefore, fiduciary duties may have only a limited role to play in dealing with the problem of hidden charges.

Concern over charges disclosure

12.37   Professor Kay expressed concern about the way that investment manager's fees are disclosed. He was especially critical of the way that investment managers accounted for broking charges. He commented that the existing obligations make "investment strategies appear more costly relative to trading strategies, and this impression is misleading".[29] He expressed hope that the current Investment Management Association (IMA) consultation would arrive at an appropriate disclosure regime.[30] If not, he thought that the issue should be addressed through regulation.

---

[25]   13 February 1992 (unreported, Tuckey QC).

[26]   See also *Brandeis Brokers v Black* [2001] 2 All ER (Comm) 980 for an example of a firm held not to be dealing as an arm's length counterparty but on behalf of its client, incurring fiduciary obligations.

[27]   Fiduciary Duties and Regulatory Rules (1995) Law Com No 236 para 3.42. See para 11.37 above.

[28]   D Frase, "Conflicts of interest" (2012) 97(Jun) *Compliance Officer Bulletin* 1 at 4.

[29]   J Kay, *The Kay Review of UK Equity Markets and Long-Term Decision Making: Final Report* (2012) para 9.15.

[30]   Above, para 9.15. For the IMA consultation, see Investment Management Association, *Fund Management Charges, Investment Costs and Performance* (2012).

12.38   In its response, the Government noted that the issue has been the subject of increasing public debate, and welcomed new initiatives on cost transparency from the IMA. The response commented that a collaborative, industry-led approach is likely to be best placed to resolve technical questions on disclosure.[31] It said that the Government's progress report in summer 2014 would assess to what extent further action might be appropriate.[32]

12.39   In September 2012 the IMA published voluntary industry guidance on enhanced disclosure of charges and costs incurred by UK-authorised funds.[33] It has been suggested that the IMA guidance does not go far enough. Gina Miller, on behalf of The True and Fair Campaign comments:

> We still do not have fair and open pricing for investment products. Without this information, how can investors make suitable informed choices? Our analysis suggests that investors pay £18.5bn each year in hidden costs and fees.[34]

12.40   We understand that the FCA has launched a thematic review into the issue.[35] We think that is a matter which is best addressed by the FCA rather than by law reform.

INVESTMENT MANAGERS

12.41   In Chapter 10 we explained that where pension trustees delegate investment decisions to an investment manager, the investment manager must invest scheme assets in the best interests of the beneficiaries.[36]

12.42   For other investment managers the position is less clear. The main factors of discretion, power and vulnerability are usually present. Investment managers often have power to exercise discretion over their clients' assets, and clients depend on the investment manager acting in their best interests. Therefore, it is argued that there is "a particularly clear basis" for the existence of fiduciary duties in this type of relationship.[37] Whilst there is no authority directly on point, in *Ata v American Express Bank Limited*[38] Mr Justice Rix reasoned that an investment manager with a discretionary right to trade on a client's behalf was in a fiduciary position.

---

[31]   Department for Business, Innovation and Skills, *Ensuring equity markets support long-term growth: The Government Response to the Kay Review* (2012) para 3.39.

[32]   Above, para 3.40.

[33]   Investment Management Association, *Enhanced disclosure of fund charges and costs* (2012).

[34]   G Miller, "Transparency over the true cost of investment is more vital than ever" (27 August 2013) *City AM*.

[35]   See N Reeve, "FCA kicks off fund management fee review", *FT Adviser* (15 August 2013).

[36]   See para 10.123 above.

[37]   D Frase, "Conflicts of interest" (2012) 97(Jun) *Compliance Officer Bulletin* 1 at 6. See also J Penner, "Exemptions" in P Birks and A Pretto, *Breach of Trust* (1st ed 2002) p 245.

[38]   7 October 1996 (unreported, Rix J). This part of Rix J's judgment was not disturbed by the Court of Appeal in its judgment reported in *The Times*, 26 June 1998.

12.43 We would stress, however, that a court is likely to give weight both to contract terms and the regulatory regimes in reaching a decision on the facts.

Advice compared with "execution only" sales

12.44 As we saw in Chapter 8, the FCA rules distinguish between personal recommendations about particular investments and "execution only" business. For personal recommendations, the adviser must take reasonable steps to ensure that the advice they give and investment management decisions they take are suitable for their client.[39] For "execution only" business, however, no such duty arises.

12.45 In *JP Morgan Bank v Springwell Navigation Corp*,[40] the court looked to the contract terms to decide whether a trade involved advice or was "execution only". Where the contract said that no advice had been relied on, the court found that there was no duty on a salesperson to consider suitability, irrespective of whether the customer had in fact been guided by the advice. This suggests that where an apparently sophisticated party buys investments on an "execution only" basis, neither duties of care nor fiduciary duties arise.

An example: selling unsuitable derivatives to a pension scheme

12.46 We have speculated on what this might mean for a pension scheme. An example might be where a pension scheme's investment manager contracts with a bank on an eligible counterparty basis to buy some extremely risky derivatives, which are unsuitable for the pension scheme. The scheme suffers loss as a result.

THE INVESTMENT MANAGER'S LIABILITY

12.47 We think the investment manager is liable in these circumstances. In this example there has been a direct contravention of the Occupational Pension Schemes (Investment) Regulations 2005, which state that derivative instruments may only be made in so far as they contribute to a reduction of risks or facilitate efficient portfolio management.[41] We think that the investment manager's duty of care will incorporate this requirement. As we have seen, when pension trustees delegate their functions to a investment manager, the investment manager cannot exclude or limit their liability for breach of their duty of care.[42] It appears, therefore, that the investment manager would be required to compensate the fund for the loss.

---

[39] FCA Handbook COBS 9.21R(1). See para 8.55 and following above.

[40] [2010] EWCA Civ 1221. See para 11.78 and following above.

[41] SI 2005 No 3378, reg 4(8).

[42] See para 7.12 above.

12.48 The more difficult question is whether the bank would be liable. Borrowing from the facts of *Springwell*, what would happen if the bank employed a smooth and persuasive salesperson, who telephoned the investment manager regularly, reading out the bank's research reports and using words like "conservative" and "liquid"? Would the courts find that the bank had a responsibility to the prospective pensioners to ensure that the investment manager was warned against buying an unsuitable product?

12.49 Recent cases suggest that the UK courts would not hold the bank liable in these circumstances. Instead the court is likely to be swayed by the contract terms stating that the bank cannot be taken to have given advice. Given the flexibility of the law, it is difficult to be certain: it is possible that the fact that the bank knew the investment manager acted on behalf of a pension fund would make a difference. Our tentative conclusion, however, is that the bank would not be held to have breached either a duty of care or a fiduciary duty.

PROCURING A BREACH OF TRUST?

12.50 The courts may not be entirely without sanctions against the bank if they thought that it had behaved in a particularly egregious way. In Chapter 5 we discussed the case of *Wilson v Hurstanger Ltd*,[43] where a mortgage lender was found to have procured the broker's breach of fiduciary duty by paying the broker an undisclosed commission.[44] If the bank had been aware of the investment manager's breach of trust, and behaved in an unconscionable way, it is possible this may amount to procuring a breach of trust.

COLLECTIVE INVESTMENT SCHEMES

12.51 Where an individual invests in a collective investment scheme the situation is complex. In a unit trust scheme there will typically be both trustees and trust managers who make day-to-day investment decisions. Therefore:

> it is possible to view the trustee and the unit trust manager as sharing trust or trust-like duties, with the manager agreeing to manage the assets in accordance with the trust deed for the benefit of the unitholders… It is the combination of the vulnerability of the investor, the control over assets and the manager's wide power to affect the value of the investor's property which brings the fiduciary relationship into existence.[45]

12.52 For unit trusts, it is possible that both the trustees and managers would be subject to fiduciary obligations, though these would be read subject to the relevant documentation. Where a duty did arise, it would be owed to the class of unit holders as a whole.

---

[43] [2007] EWCA Civ 299.

[44] [2007] EWCA Civ 299 at [43]. See para 5.36 above.

[45] D Frase, "Conflicts of interest" (2012) 97(Jun) *Compliance Officer Bulletin* 1 at 6. See also K Sin, *The Legal Nature of the Unit Trust* (1st ed 1997) p 171-173.

12.53   In contrast, investments in an open-ended investment company are unlikely to give rise to fiduciary duties to investors. They are not set up under trust. Essentially the individual is buying units in the profits of the scheme as opposed to instructing another to invest on their behalf. It is therefore difficult to find a fiduciary relationship, as the obligations to investors are essentially arm's length and are governed by contract and company law. The duties of company directors are generally owed to the company as a whole, not to shareholders.[46] Moreover, the duty imposed by regulation 35 of the Open-Ended Investment Companies Regulations 2001 to have regard to the interests of an OEIC's employees and shareholders is owed only to the company.[47]

Voting

12.54   ShareAction suggested that conflicts of interest may arise when collective investment schemes hold shares in their own parent companies and exercise voting rights. They noted issues which arose during the "Shareholder Spring" when some investment managers were required to vote on client shares in relation to controversial pay packages at their own companies. Some managers, such as Aviva Investors, had a published policy of not casting votes for shares in Aviva plc unless explicitly instructed by a client. In contrast, another scheme did vote in favour of the controversial remuneration policies of its parent company.[48]

12.55   When voting on matters affecting a parent company, the UK Stewardship Code states that:

> Institutional investors should put in place, maintain and publicly disclose a policy for identifying and managing conflicts of interest with the aim of taking all reasonable steps to put the interest of their client or beneficiary first.[49]

This is not mandatory. Authorised funds need only explain whether or not they comply with the Code. Where funds do sign up to the Code, they may explain that they do not comply with a specific principle.[50]

12.56   It is difficult to know how a court would rule on this issue. Our tentative conclusion is that a unit trust scheme is unlikely to have a positive duty to vote, but when it does exercise a vote it should do so for the benefit of the unitholders as a whole. However, an open-ended investment company may not be constrained to use votes for the benefit of its investors.

---

[46]   *Snell's Equity* (32nd ed 2010) para 7-004.

[47]   Open-Ended Investment Companies Regulations 2001 SI 2001 No 1228, reg 35(2).

[48]   ShareAction, Response to "Fiduciary Duties of Investment Intermediaries: Initial Questions" (July 2013).

[49]   Financial Reporting Council, *The UK Stewardship Code* (2012) p 6.

[50]   Above, p 4.

CUSTODIANS

12.57 We think that when custodians hold assets for others they do so on trust. The custodian holds the legal title for the client who retains a beneficial interest.[51] Generally, custodians will not be entitled to exercise any discretion and so will act as "bare trustees", who may only deal with the property in accordance with their client's instructions. In a trust-based pension scheme, the client will be the trustees, who will either give instructions themselves or will authorise their investment manager to do so.

Stock lending

12.58 The main controversy affecting custodians relates to stock lending. This is where custodians "lend" the client's investment to a third party, typically to enable the borrower to sell short. The borrower is obliged to return the securities to the lender, either on demand or at the end of any agreed term. Stock lending introduces a risk that the borrower may default, though the custodian may obtain collateral to guard against this. It also introduces a conflict of interest. The borrower, who is selling short, wishes the share value to decline, though the original client wishes it to increase. A further problem is that in some cases, the custodian retains the fee rather than rebating it to the client.

12.59 Professor Kay recommended that "all income from stock lending should be disclosed and rebated to investors".[52] He argued that:

> The risks associated with stock lending ... remain with the fund whose stock is lent (and hence with the saver). There is therefore a divergence between the recipient of the income and the bearer of the risk for which the income is compensation. Such a divergence may distort competition and give an artificial, and inappropriate, incentive to engage in stock lending. More broadly, such divergence is inconsistent with fiduciary principles.[53]

12.60 By contrast, Blackrock has argued that income from such lending should not be passed to investors. In its evidence to the BIS Select Committee, it said that stock lending was "a well-established and low risk activity" which "has wider benefits for financial markets as it provides liquidity that helps to improve settlement efficiency and contributes to tighter trading spreads for investors".[54]

---

[51] For the Law Commission's analysis of the law in this area, see Law Commission, *The UNIDROIT Convention on Substantive Rules regarding Intermediated Securities: Further Updated Advice to HM Treasury* (2008). For the position in Scots law, under which the custodian who requires title to be transferred is seen as indistinguishable from a nominee and so probably a trustee, see Supplementary and Miscellaneous Issues in the Law of Trusts (2011) Scottish Law Commission Discussion Paper No 148 para 5.13.

[52] J Kay, *The Kay Review of UK Equity Markets and Long-Term Decision Making: Final Report* (2012) Recommendation 10.

[53] Above, para 9.25.

[54] The Kay Review of UK Equity Markets and Long-Term Decision Making, Third Report of the Select Committee on Business, Innovation and Skills (2013-14) HC 603 at Ev 131.

The European Securities and Markets Authority (ESMA) guidelines

12.61   ESMA is an independent EU authority whose role is to enhance investor protection and contribute to safeguarding the stability of the EU's financial system. In July 2012 it issued guidelines that UCITS[55] asset managers should return all securities lending revenues to investors, "net of direct and indirect operational costs".[56] The guidelines came into force across Europe in early 2013.

12.62   The guidelines go some way to addressing the issue, but suffer from weaknesses. Firstly, they only apply to asset managers of collective investment schemes which are authorised under the UCITS Directive. In summary, these are schemes which may be marketed to members of the general public across Europe. The guidelines do not apply, for example, to custodians holding the assets of pension trustees.

12.63   Secondly, the guidelines have been criticised for failing to define "an indirect operational cost". This allows asset managers to interpret the guidelines creatively, retaining fees to offset against a range of costs. It has been suggested that "asset managers have been reluctant to overhaul their current securities lending practices since the new rules were announced".[57]

What would a court decide?

12.64   We think that if a custodian were to lend stock without any contractual authority, this would amount to a breach of trust. The custodian's role is to look after the investment – not to lend it to others. Furthermore, retaining the fee would breach the prohibition on making a secret profit.

12.65   In practice, however, the issue is governed by the contractual terms in the agreement with the custodian. A court would almost certainly uphold practices which were in line with the agreed terms. Trustees would be liable for agreeing contract terms which were not in the interests of the beneficiaries. However, what is in the interests of beneficiaries is for the trustees to decide, weighing up the risks associated with stock lending against the reduction in fees which stock lending allows.

---

[55] UCITS stands for Undertakings for Collective Investment in Transferable Securities. A UCITS is an open-ended collective investment vehicle which complies with the requirements of the UCITS IV Directive (2009/65/EC).

[56] European Securities and Markets Authority, *Guidelines for competent authorities and UCITS management companies* (2012), available at http://www.esma.europa.eu/system/files/2012-832en_guidelines_on_etfs_and_other_ucits_issues.pdf.

[57] D Ricketts, "ESMA adds guidance, but not clarity, on securities lending" (21 March 2013) *Financial Times/Ignites Europe*.

12.66 If there is to be any change in stock lending practices by custodians holding the assets of pension funds, we think this would need to be introduced through a change in the FCA rules. We are aware that the FCA is currently looking into this issue in relation to the life insurance business.[58]

CONCLUSION

12.67 In this chapter we have considered how the courts would apply fiduciary duties to some specific controversial practices in financial markets. The examples we have given illustrate the uncertainties associated with this area of law.

12.68 There are major difficulties in relying on "judge-made" law to control complex and fast-moving financial markets. Judges can only decide the cases brought before them. Very few cases are brought – and those most vulnerable to poor practice may be those least able to mount legal challenges. Further, rules are developed only after the event – often long after the event. As we saw in *JP Morgan Bank v Springwell Navigation Corp*,[59] the securities were bought from 1996, the loss occurred in 1998 and the Court of Appeal ruling was in 2010. When cases reach court it is too late to prevent the practice: the courts can only provide financial redress. Large compensation payments can introduce further disruptions to the market, adding to cost and risk.

12.69 Professor Kay summarised the standards which he associated with fiduciary duties:

> Fiduciary standards require that the client's interests are put first, that conflict of interest should be avoided, and that the direct and indirect costs of services provided should be reasonable and disclosed.[60]

12.70 The law on fiduciary duties does not set specific controls on prices or charges. The rest is broadly true: fiduciary duties require that clients' interests are put first and that conflicts of interest should be avoided. However, as explained above, the existence and extent of a fiduciary duty depends on the particular facts of each case and is influenced by the terms of any contract and the relevant regulatory regime. It is difficult to say how the courts would apply these principles to any particular example. Court based rules do not provide an easy answer to the concerns raised. If further controls are needed, for example, to control investment consultants' conflicts of interest or to rebate stock lending fees, this will require detailed discussion of changes to regulations.

---

[58] T Jefferies, "Watchdogs to probe pension funds over hidden investing practices that boost their profits but put savers' cash at risk" (11 July 2013) *This is Money*, available at http://www.thisismoney.co.uk/money/investing/article-2360118/FCA-looks-life-insurance-holders-miss-stock-lending-profits.html.

[59] For the Court of Appeal decision, see [2010] EWCA Civ 1221. The case is discussed at para 11.78 and following above.

[60] J Kay, *The Kay Review of UK Equity Markets and Long-Term Decision Making: Final Report* (2012) Principle 5. See also the principle set out in the Government response. Department for Business, Innovation and Skills, *Ensuring equity markets support long-term growth: The Government Response to the Kay Review* (2012) para 2.8. For the full principle see para 1.10 above.

CHAPTER 13
WORKPLACE DEFINED CONTRIBUTION PENSIONS: PROBLEMS IN PRACTICE

13.1 Under our terms of reference we have been asked "to consider whether fiduciary duties, as established in law or as applied in practice, are conducive to investment strategies that are in the best interests of the ultimate beneficiaries". As we saw in Chapter 2, workplace defined contribution (DC) pensions may be trust-based or organised on the basis of contracts with individual employees. It is well established in law that pension trustees are under legal duties to act in the beneficiaries' interests. For contract-based pensions, however, the legal duties on providers are much less certain.

13.2 In this chapter we consider how well the governance of workplace DC pension schemes works in practice. We concentrate on this form of investment because of its social importance. It is estimated that there are currently 7.9 million members of DC schemes.[1] This figure is projected to rise to 17.4 million by 2022.[2] These individuals are dependent on intermediaries' investment strategies to provide them with an income in old age – and, if these strategies fail, there will be consequences for society as a whole. Yet concerns have been raised about the way that these schemes operate. In September 2013, a market study by the Office of Fair Trading (OFT) recommended changes.[3]

13.3 Here, we briefly consider the current regulation of workplace DC pensions and then list the criticisms that are made of this market and of the regulatory regime.

13.4 We then contrast the UK approach with pension regulation in Australia. Drawing on the paper by the Australian law firm Clayton Utz in Appendix C, we describe the Australian single regulatory regime, which is based on trust law standards.

THE CURRENT WORKPLACE PENSION MARKET

13.5 In Chapter 2 we described the changing nature of workplace pensions, as defined benefit (DB) schemes close to new members and DC schemes grow. The nature of DC schemes has also changed over the last 20 years. During the early 1990s, many employers established their own trust-based DC schemes. From the late 1990s onwards, however, employers increasingly turned to "group personal pension" schemes run by insurers.[4]

---

[1] Spence Johnson, *Defined Contribution Market Intelligence* (2013) p 14. Some people may be members of more than one scheme.

[2] Above, p 17.

[3] Office of Fair Trading, *Defined contribution workplace pension market study* (2013) ch 9..

[4] The research consultancy, Spence Johnson, reports that the average trust-based DC scheme was established in 1993, while the average workplace contract-based DC scheme was established in 2001: Spence Johnson, *Defined Contribution Market Intelligence* (2013) p 11.

Figure 13.1: Summary of the various forms of pension provision.[5]

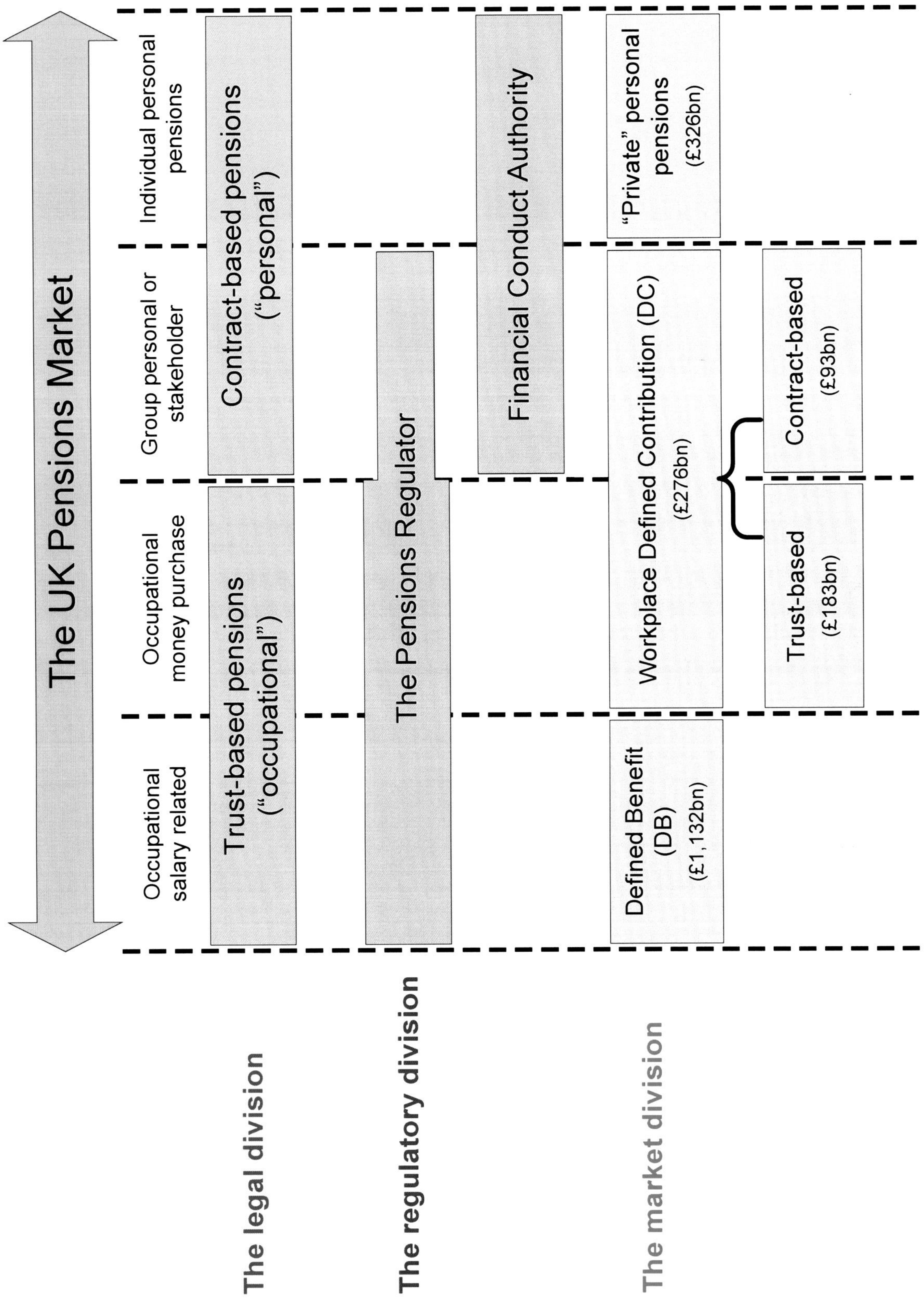

[5] Produced by reference to Spence Johnson, *Defined Contribution Market Intelligence* (2013) p 8. We are grateful to Spence Johnson for allowing the data to be reproduced.

13.6 The various forms of pension provision are summarised in Figure 13.1 (and further explanation is given in Chapter 2). The division between trust-based and contract-based schemes is important from a legal and regulatory perspective, but it is less important to the market. When setting up a DC scheme, employers have a choice between contract-based and trust-based schemes. There are many similarities between contract-based schemes and so called "bundled" trust schemes, where a single provider provides both administrative and fund management services to the scheme.

13.7 The introduction of auto-enrolment from October 2012 to October 2018 will bring further changes to the market. It is estimated that the value of assets in workplace DC pension schemes is currently around £276 billion. This is projected to increase to £829 billion by 2022.[6]

13.8 Much of this growth is expected to be in contract-based pensions, but not exclusively. Many new entrants to the pension market have been set up as "master trusts". Master trusts are multi-employer trust-based pension schemes, which a pension provider manages under a single account. The most important master trust is the Government sponsored National Employment Savings Trust, but there are others. The OFT reported that there were 44 master trusts established in the UK in 2012, and that the market was growing quickly. It identified more than 10 master trusts established since September 2011.[7]

13.9 Some master trusts have roots in the occupational pension market. For example, The People's Pension is set up by a not-for-profit organisation with a background in supplying employee benefits to the construction industry. Others have been established by insurance companies.[8] The OFT comments that the reason why so many new entrants to the pension market are master trusts is that "master trusts are subject to less regulation on entry and on an ongoing basis".[9]

THE REGULATION OF DC PENSIONS

13.10 In Chapter 2 we highlighted the complexities of the workplace pension market. The regulatory system divides pensions into "occupational" and "personal" pensions, but these terms have the potential to confuse.

13.11 "Personal schemes" were first introduced by the Social Security Act 1986 as an option for those who were self-employed or had opted out of their employer's occupational pension scheme. However, from the late 1990s, "group personal pensions" were increasingly used by employers as an alternative to trust-based occupational pension schemes. Personal pensions may now be arranged by an employer as a "group personal pension" or taken out privately as a "self-invested personal pension" (known as a SIPP).

---

[6] Spence Johnson, *Defined Contribution Market Intelligence* (2013) p 18.

[7] Office of Fair Trading, *Defined contribution workplace pension market study* (2013) para 4.27.

[8] Above, para 4.9.

[9] Above, para 4.28.

Different regulators

13.12   The Pensions Regulator (TPR) is the primary regulator for trust-based schemes, while the Financial Conduct Authority (FCA) is the primary regulator of contract-based pensions.

13.13   Contract-based pensions are generally provided by insurance companies, who must be registered with the FCA and who are subject to ongoing FCA monitoring. Detailed rules are contained in the FCA's Conduct of Business Sourcebook. Insurers are also monitored by the Prudential Regulatory Authority, which considers issues of financial safety and capital liquidity. Further, all workplace schemes (both contract-based and trust-based) must register with TPR, which oversees payments by employers into the scheme.[10] Therefore, in Figure 13.1 TPR is shown as having a more limited regulatory role for contract-based pensions than for trust-based pensions.

13.14   Complaints about selling or investment are heard by the Financial Ombudsman Service, while the Pensions Ombudsman has jurisdiction to hear complaints concerning maladministration.[11]

Different regulations

13.15   To add further complexity to the issue, "stakeholder" pensions are subject to different regulations than non-stakeholder pensions. Stakeholder pensions offer greater protection, with stronger controls over the extent to which the member is expected to make a choice and the fees which the provider is entitled to charge. In Figure 13.2 we illustrate the key differences.

---

[10]   See Pension Schemes Act 1993, s 111A and the Personal Pension Schemes (Payments by Employers) Regulations 2000 SI 2000 No 2692.

[11]   Pension Schemes Act 1993, s 146.

Figure 13.2: Differences between stakeholder and non-stakeholder pensions.

	Stakeholder pensions	Non-stakeholder pensions
"Defined contribution"	✓	✓
May be "trust-based"	✓	✓
May be "contract-based"	✓	✓
The employer may collect contributions	✓	✓
The employer may pay into the scheme	✓	✓
The provider must offer a default investment option	✓	If used for auto-enrolment
The provider must apply "life-styling" to the default investment option	✓	✗
Regulatory limit on the fees the provider may charge	✓	✗
Regulatory minimum rate of return	✓	✗
The provider must prepare a "Statement of Investment Principles"	✓	If trust-based

Stakeholder pensions

13.16   Stakeholder pensions were introduced in 2001. They were established under the Welfare Reform and Pensions Act 1999 as a new way for low earners who were not making any pension provision to save for retirement.[12] They may be set up under trust or on a contractual basis by a manager who has permission by the FCA to establish a stakeholder pension scheme.[13] They are available to both the employed and the self-employed.

[12]   For the Government's consultation document and Green Paper, see Department of Social Security, *Stakeholder Pensions: A Consultation Document* (1997); A new contract for welfare: Partnership in pensions (1998) Cm 4179.

[13]   Stakeholder Pension Schemes Regulations 2000 SI 2000 No 1403, reg 2(2).

13.17 Stakeholder pensions are primarily governed by the Stakeholder Pension Schemes Regulations 2000 (the Stakeholder Regulations).[14] Where a scheme is trust-based, many of the Pensions Act 1995 provisions also apply.[15] The FCA rules will apply to contract-based schemes.

Fees and return rates

13.18 Under the Stakeholder Regulations, administration charges are capped by law at 1.5% of the fund value per year for the first 10 years and thereafter at 1%.[16] There is also limited statutory protection ensuring at least a minimal rate of return: returns on funds held on deposit must accrue on a daily basis, net of fees or charges, at not less than the base rate minus two per cent a year.[17] On 1 October 2000, when the relevant provisions of the Stakeholder Regulations came into force, the base rate was 6%, giving a guaranteed rate of 4%. With the current base rate at 0.5%, this provides relatively little protection – savers are seemingly guaranteed a return of not less than minus 1.5%.

Default funds

13.19 All stakeholder schemes must include a default investment option and members may not be compelled to make an investment choice.[18] Where the member makes no choice, the manager of a scheme is required to adjust the investment strategy as the member nears retirement. This is known as "lifestyling", and is designed to reduce the impact of market volatility on the member's "pot".[19]

---

[14] SI 2000 No 1403.

[15] As set out in the Welfare Reform and Pensions Act 1999, sch 1, para 1.

[16] Stakeholder Pension Schemes Regulations 2000 SI 2000 No 1403, reg 14. Historically most contracts lapse in the first five-to-seven years making the effective cap 1.5%: see The Pensions Institute, *Caveat Venditor: The brave new world of auto-enrolment should be governed by the principle of seller not buyer beware* (2012) p 18.

[17] Stakeholder Pension Schemes Regulations 2000 SI 2000 No 1403, reg 8(2).

[18] Stakeholder Pension Schemes Regulations 2000 SI 2000 No 1403, reg 3(3).

[19] Stakeholder Pension Schemes Regulations 2000 SI 2000 No 1403, reg 10A(2).

Statement of Investment Principles (SIP)

13.20 The manager of a stakeholder scheme must prepare a SIP. This applies to both trust-based and contract-based stakeholder schemes, although the requirement comes from different pieces of legislation.[20] For trust-based schemes, the SIP requirement is the same as for other occupational pension schemes, as set out in the Occupational Pension Schemes (Investment) Regulations 2005 (Investment Regulations).[21] For contract-based schemes, the provisions are similar, with two notable differences:

(1) The trustees of a trust-based stakeholder scheme must review their SIP at least every three years and "without delay after any significant change in investment policy".[22] By contrast, managers of contract-based stakeholder schemes are only required to revise their SIP "from time to time".[23]

(2) Unlike the trustees of a trust-based stakeholder pension scheme, the managers of a contract-based stakeholder pension scheme are not required to state their policy on securing compliance with the Investment Regulations.[24] These regulations, among other things, require investment of the scheme assets in the best interests of the beneficiaries.[25]

Suitability and diversification

13.21 Managers of stakeholder pensions are subject to some of the same duties as trustees are under the Pensions Acts and associated regulations, with respect to the matters they must consider when making investments. For example, they must have regard to:

(1) the need for diversification of investments, in so far as appropriate to the circumstances of the scheme; and

---

[20] For contract-based stakeholder schemes, see Stakeholder Pension Schemes Regulations 2000 SI 2000 No 1403, reg 9. For trust-based stakeholder schemes, see Welfare Reform and Pensions Act 1999, sch 1, para 1(2)(b)(iii); Pensions Act 1995, s 35; Occupational Pension Schemes (Investment) Regulations 2005 SI 2005 No 3378, reg 2.

[21] Occupational Pension Schemes (Investment) Regulations 2005 SI 2005 No 3378, reg 2(3); see para 7.14 and following above.

[22] Welfare Reform and Pensions Act 1999, sch 1, para 1(2)(b)(iii); Pensions Act 1995, s 35; Occupational Pension Schemes (Investment) Regulations 2005 SI 2005 No 3378, reg 2(1).

[23] Stakeholder Pension Schemes Regulations 2000 SI 2000 No 1403, reg 9(3).

[24] Stakeholder Pension Schemes Regulations 2000 SI 2000 No 1403, reg 9. Compare Welfare Reform and Pensions Act 1999, sch 1, para 1(2)(b)(iii); Pensions Act 1995, s 35; Occupational Pension Schemes (Investment) Regulations 2005 SI 2005 No 3378, reg 2(3). The combined effect of these provisions is that the SIP of a trust-based stakeholder scheme must state the trustees' policy for securing compliance with section 36 of the Pensions Act 1995. In particular, s 36(1) requires trustees (and any investment manager to whom discretion has been delegated) to exercise their powers of investment in accordance with regulations.

[25] Occupational Pension Scheme (Investment) Regulations 2005 SI 2005 No 3378, reg 4(2).

(2)   the suitability for the purposes of the scheme of any investment or investment option proposed.[26]

13.22   Further, the manager of the scheme and anyone managing the funds of the scheme must obtain and consider proper advice as to whether an investment is satisfactory, unless they themselves would be suitably qualified to provide that advice.[27]

Loyalty

13.23   The Stakeholder Regulations provide some protection by compelling the scheme provider to act in the interests of the members. For example, payments into a scheme and income or capital gain on those payments or investments may not be used in any way which does not result in the provision of benefits for or in respect of members.[28] However, this provision is qualified: there is a list of circumstances in which the provider may make a deduction from the funds, including for administrative charges.[29]

13.24   Where a stakeholder pension is set up under contract, there is no one like a trustee in place to look after members or to monitor the investments made on their behalf. Nor is there an explicit duty that the provider should act in the best interests of the scheme members.

Non-stakeholder pension schemes

13.25   Not all DC pensions must comply with the Stakeholder Regulations. However, where a scheme is used for the purposes of automatic enrolment, it must not require members to express a choice: a default fund must be offered.[30]

13.26   In this context there is no statutory requirement that the default fund is "lifestyled". However, guidance published by DWP in May 2011 states that "the investment strategy should take into account, on reasonable grounds, the retirement profile of members (ie number of years from retirement age). The guidance also states that the default option should "take account of the likely characteristics and needs of employees" and should be reviewed at least every three years.[31]

[26]   Stakeholder Pension Schemes Regulations 2000 SI 2000 No 1403, reg 10(3).

[27]   Stakeholder Pension Schemes Regulations 2000 SI 2000 No 1403, reg 10(4)-(7).

[28]   Stakeholder Pension Schemes Regulations 2000 SI 2000 No 1403, reg 3(4) and 13(1).

[29]   Stakeholder Pension Schemes Regulations 2000 SI 2000 No 1403, reg 14 and 14B.

[30]   Pensions Act 2008, s 17(2).

[31]   Department for Work and Pensions, *Guidance for offering a default option for defined contribution automatic enrolment pension schemes* (2011).

13.27　For contract-based "group personal pensions", there are no statutory maximum fees or minimum return rates. Instead, the rules aim to ensure adequate disclosure. Currently, under the Personal Pension Schemes (Disclosure of Information) Regulations 1987,[32] members must be provided with basic information about the scheme at the time of joining (or within three months of joining). This includes conditions of membership, how rights under the scheme may be transferred and the charging structure.[33] Further, the provider must annually send the member information,[34] such as the accumulated total of contributions for the year, the value of the member's rights in the scheme and an illustration of the amount of pension that could be available on retirement.[35]

13.28　The Government has recently announced that it intends to reform these disclosure obligations, to align the personal pension disclosure requirements with occupational pensions.[36] The Government has said that it will continue to work closely with the FCA to ensure that the obligations are consistent and straightforward.[37] The new regulations are also likely to include obligations to inform members whether their funds are being invested on a lifestyled basis.[38]

PROBLEMS WITH WORKPLACE DC PENSIONS

13.29　In recent years, DC pensions have come under the spotlight. Many groups have produced reports into the governance and regulation of such schemes. These include the Fabian Society, the Work and Pensions Select Committee, the National Audit Office, the Pensions Institute and ShareAction. Notably, in September 2013 the OFT published a detailed market study of DC workplace pensions. The Department for Work and Pensions (DWP) is also consulting on the core standards that DC schemes ought to offer.[39]

13.30　These reviews reflect the views presented to us in initial discussions with stakeholders. Here we discuss problems with charges, member choice and governance. We then consider the problems with dual regulation.

---

[32]　SI 1987 No 1110. These are modelled on the disclosure obligations of other forms of occupational pension: see the Occupational Pension Schemes (Disclosure of Information) Regulations 1996 SI 1996 No 1655.

[33]　Personal Pension Schemes (Disclosure of Information) Regulations 1987 SI 1987 No 1110, reg 4 and sch 1.

[34]　Personal Pension Schemes (Disclosure of Information) Regulations 1987 SI 1987 No 1110, reg 5 and sch 2. However, there are exemptions from these requirements in respect of persons who are in receipt of pension benefits under the scheme, who are within two years of their expected retirement date or whose accrued rights to money purchase benefits under the scheme were less than £5,000 when the information was last provided.

[35]　Personal Pension Schemes (Disclosure of Information) Regulations 1987 SI 1987 No 1110, sch 2, para 2A.

[36]　Department for Work and Pensions, *The Occupational and Personal Pension Schemes (Disclosure of Information) Regulations 2013: Government response to the consultation* (2013).

[37]　Above, p 15.

[38]　Above, p 16; The Occupational and Personal Pension Schemes (Disclosure of Information) Regulations 2013 (draft), reg 18 and sch 2, para 30.

[39]　Department for Work and Pensions, *Quality standards in workplace defined contribution pension schemes: Call for evidence* (2013).

Charges

13.31 Charges make a significant difference to the benefits a member receives on retirement. Figure 13.3 sets out data published by the Organisation for Economic Cooperation and Development (OECD) that illustrates the impact of different levels of asset management charges in terms of reductions in benefits, assuming a 40-year contribution period.

Figure 13.3: Impact of charges on pension size.

Charge as % of assets	Reduction of pension
0.05%	1.2%
0.15%	3.6%
0.25%	5.9%
0.50%	11.4%
0.75%	16.5%
1.00%	21.3%
1.50%	29.9%

Source: OECD, *Pensions Outlook* (2012) p 175.

Criticisms of charges

13.32 Many organisations have criticised the fee structure of DC pensions. A report by the Pensions Institute at Cass Business School (the Cass Report) highlighted high and complicated fee structures in contract-based pensions and found "disingenuous practices" in respect of charge and cost disclosure.[40] Similarly, the Fabian Society has criticised the lack of transparency, noting some schemes "are excessively priced" and "absorb too high a share of the individual's pension savings".[41] For a minority of cases they found that "as much as half of a person's savings can be absorbed in costs and charges".[42]

[40] The Pensions Institute, *Caveat Venditor: The brave new world of auto-enrolment should be governed by the principle of seller not buyer beware* (2012) pp 9 and 17-19.

[41] Fabian Society, *Pensions at Work, that Work: Completing the unfinished pensions revolution* (2013) p 6.

[42] Above, p 6.

13.33 The OFT has investigated the issue in depth, looking at both contract-based and bundled trust schemes. They comment that, before the introduction of stakeholder pensions in 2001, the industry levied a wide variety of charges: annual percentage charges were supplemented by initial charges, ongoing fixed charges, early surrender penalties and other one off charges. In 2001, the industry moved toward levying a single percentage charge, known as the Annual Management Charge (AMC). There is now more competition based on this visible AMC. The majority of the market now charges on this basis.

13.34 However, problems remain:

(1) Many pre-2001 schemes continue to charge more – and continue to be open to new members, including new auto-enrolled members. The OFT estimates that over 1.3 million members of these "legacy" schemes continue to pay well over the odds in charges.[43]

(2) Even in post-2001 schemes, AMCs are not calculated on a consistent basis. Some providers charge additional fees for administration and fund management. Furthermore, out of 13 schemes, only 5 included legal and audit fees within the AMC. The others passed them on in the form of a Total Expenses Ratio at the end of the year.[44]

(3) Many schemes increase the AMC when the member stops contributing to the pension scheme. This is referred to as providing "active member discounts", and may reflect the fact that employers wish to focus on costs incurred by their current staff. When staff leave their employment, they may be unaware that their pension costs have increased. Where costs did increase for deferred members, it was by an average of 0.47 percentage points.[45]

(4) None of the providers include investment transaction costs within the AMC. These costs are taken directly from the fund and are implicitly reflected in the performance of the investments. They include:

(a) brokers' commissions.

(b) bid-offer spreads – that is, the difference between the price paid when an investment is bought and the price received when an investment is sold. This is the profit paid to the market maker.

(c) foreign exchange fees associated with transactions.

---

[43] The OFT calculates that 1.377 million members of legacy schemes will together pay an additional £1.9 billion in AMCs over the remaining lifetime of their pensions – as well as further amounts in additional charges: Office of Fair Trading, *Defined contribution workplace pension market study* (2013) paras 6.45-6.46.

[44] Office of Fair Trading, *Defined contribution workplace pension market study* (2013) para 6.21.

[45] Above, para 6.16.

(d)   local taxes (including UK stamp duty).[46]

The OFT recommendations on charges

13.35   The OFT recommended that charges should be disclosed in a single framework which would allow employers to compare a commonly defined single charge. However, this single charge should not include investment management transaction costs. The OFT commented that "their inclusion could potentially create incentives for investment managers to avoid carrying out transactions in order to keep costs down, even where this is contrary to the members' interest".[47] Instead, transaction costs could be scrutinised by Independent Governance Committees.

13.36   It is true that including transaction costs would decrease incentives to trade. The danger, however, is that continuing to allow these costs to be taken out of profits may create inappropriate incentives to trade. This occurs when investment managers and brokers have close relationships of mutual dependency. In Chapter 8 we set out the FCA rules which prohibit investment managers from accepting goods or services from brokers. However, managers may still accept research. We also noted recent concern about the way that some managers had used broking commissions to pay for corporate access. This is prohibited under the rules, but the Investment Managers Association feared that additional services of this type could be included within "bundled content services".[48] We return to this issue in Chapter 14.

13.37   In response to the OFT's concerns regarding legacy schemes, members of the Association of British Insurers agreed to carry out an audit of schemes which charged more than the equivalent of a 1% AMC, under the supervision of an Independent Project Board. The OFT did not recommend a cap on charges, but would not rule out a cap following the audit.[49] For trust-based schemes, the OFT recommended that TPR should require trustees to carry out value for money exercises and report the results to TPR.[50]

---

[46]   Office of Fair Trading, *Defined contribution workplace pension market study* (2013) para 6.28.

[47]   Above, para 9.19.

[48]   See paras 8.66 to 8.68 above.

[49]   Office of Fair Trading, *Defined contribution workplace pension market study* (2013) paras 9.23-9.24. DWP has announced that it will consult on introducing a charge cap: see Department for Work and Pensions, *Quality standards in workplace defined contribution pension schemes: Call for evidence* (2013) p 5.

[50]   Above, para 9.26.

Member investment choices

13.38 As we have seen, stakeholder schemes and schemes used for automatic enrolment must offer a default option. In other DC schemes, members may be expected to make investment choices. And even with auto-enrolment, choices may be available. The Cass Report criticised the drive towards member driven investment, arguing that members made potentially "ill-informed decisions that they do not revisit and which can cost three or more times the charge of the default fund".[51] As one interviewee stated:

> I have always thought this drive to self-selection total cobblers – as a wise head of a US investment company put it, "We can't all be our own [Chief Investment Officer]".[52]

13.39 As ShareAction explains, care needs to be taken as to "the role in which the saver is cast". They query:

> Should they be seen as a consumer actively making informed decisions about their money, or as a vulnerable beneficiary with little influence and still less understanding of the decisions being made on their behalf?[53]

13.40 The OFT summarised studies which showed that most people find decisions about pensions to be complex, hard, unpleasant and time-consuming. In a 2011 DWP study, 63% of people agreed that "sometimes ... pensions seem so complicated that I cannot really understand the best thing to do". Similarly, in 2012 only 45% of active DC members had looked at their fund value in the last year.[54] The OFT concluded that:

> Given the complexity of the pensions sector and the long-term commitment required to properly monitor the value of savings, most employees are not sufficiently knowledgeable or engaged in their work based pension to achieve good outcomes.[55]

13.41 The OFT concluded that "the buyer side of the DC workplace pensions market is one of the weakest that the OFT has analysed in recent years".[56] Employees fail to engage with pensions while employers do not have the capability or incentive to drive competition.

---

[51] The Pensions Institute, *Caveat Venditor: The brave new world of auto-enrolment should be governed by the principle of seller not buyer beware* (2012) p 22.

[52] Above, p 22.

[53] FairPensions (later known as ShareAction), *Whose duty? Ensuring effective stewardship in contract-based pensions* (2012) p 7.

[54] Office of Fair Trading, *Defined contribution workplace pension market study* (2013) paras 5.8-5.10.

[55] Above, para 5.7.

[56] Above, para 1.9.

Governance

13.42 In Chapter 1 we looked briefly at long-term trends in equity markets, noting the successive cycles of growth and volatility. It is not necessarily unreasonable for a 30 year old employee to put money into an equities pension now, to provide a return for their retirement around 2050 – but no-one can predict what the markets will do in thirty to forty years time. One should expect the unexpected.[57] It is vital that both investment strategies and charges are reviewed over time and adjusted accordingly.

13.43 The OFT commented that:

> All pension providers, advisers, and industry experts that we consulted … told us that good governance is crucial to achieving good member outcomes.[58]

13.44 The OFT argued that "the performance of financial markets, the cost of pension provision and investment philosophies can all evolve significantly over time". Given the lack of oversight from most scheme members and many employers, effective governance is "crucial for ensuring that the scheme continues to offer value for money".[59]

13.45 Unfortunately, there is a lack of clear governance structures in contract-based pensions, and many trust-based schemes are too small[60] (or too tied to a single provider[61]) for governance to be effective.

Governance in contract-based schemes

13.46 In contract-based schemes, responsibility for reviewing investment strategies may be "spread across a complex and potentially-conflicted range of entities".[62] This applies to both default schemes and chosen schemes.

---

[57] For an analysis of the effect of unexpected events (or "black swans") see N Taleb, *Fooled by Randomness: The Hidden Role of Chance in Life and in the Markets* (2001) and *The Black Swan* (2007).

[58] Office of Fair Trading, *Defined contribution workplace pension market study* (2013) para 7.18.

[59] Above, para 7.18.

[60] Above, paras 7.26 to 7.27. See also Department for Work and Pensions, *Quality standards in workplace defined contribution pension schemes: Call for evidence* (2013) paras 57 and 59.

[61] Above, para 7.30.

[62] The Pensions Institute, *Caveat Venditor: The brave new world of auto-enrolment should be governed by the principle of seller not buyer beware* (2012) p 23.

13.47 As far as default schemes are concerned, DWP guidance states:

> The ongoing responsibility for the default option may vary between provider, adviser, fund manager, employer and governance committee in different situations and for different aspects of a scheme.[63]

13.48 There are also problems with the options available for selection. As one stakeholder queried in our initial discussions, "who has the obligation to remove an under-performing fund from the options available to members? And what should happen to those members sitting in the under-performing fund?"

13.49 DWP is currently consulting on governance issues, stating:

> There may not be any body with an identified ongoing responsibility for considering whether the scheme is being run in members' interests. Without any body with this overall responsibility, including beyond the point of sale, it is not clear whether and how conflicts of interest are identified and addressed and who is ensuring that decisions are taken in the interest of members of the scheme.[64]

13.50 This leaves a gap in the way that schemes are monitored over time. This has been recognised by TPR and the FCA, who have issued guidance that employers "may wish to put in place some form of ongoing monitoring on a voluntary basis".[65] The OFT reports that a few larger employers have set up governance committees to monitor costs and investment performance. However, small and medium employers did not have the resources to do this.[66]

THE OFT'S FINDINGS

13.51 The OFT noted that contract-based providers "do not have a recognised equivalent of the trustee board that is ultimately accountable for representing the needs of scheme members".[67] Without strong governance, "providers may not have the incentive and ability to address high charges, poor administration, poor performance and outdated or unsuitable investment strategies".[68] There were particular problems where funds were managed in-house.

---

[63] Department for Work and Pensions, *Guidance for offering a default option for defined contribution automatic enrolment pension schemes* (2011) para 16.

[64] Above, pp 8-9.

[65] Financial Services Authority and The Pensions Regulator, *A guide on the regulation of work place contract-based pensions* (2007), available at http://www.fsa.gov.uk/static/pubs/pensions/regulation_workplace.pdf. See also The Pensions Regulator, *Monitoring your pension scheme: Management committees for employers* (2013), available at http://www.thepensionsregulator.gov.uk/docs/employer-management-committees.pdf.

[66] Office of Fair Trading, *Defined contribution workplace pension market study* (2013) paras 5.25-5.26.

[67] Above, para 7.33.

[68] Above, para 7.34.

13.52 In their defence, providers argued that, even though they did not have a fiduciary duty to act in members' best interests, they were still required to treat customers fairly under FCA rules. They said that they must demonstrate to the FCA that their product is suitable for consumers and, therefore, they review their products frequently.[69]

13.53 In reply, the OFT noted that providers had not addressed high charges in legacy schemes. Furthermore, the providers may be constrained by contract terms. In some cases they cannot make changes to the investment strategy without the members' agreement, making it difficult to respond to changes in the global economy.[70]

Governance in trust-based schemes

13.54 The OFT noted that there were also problems with trust-based schemes. Fiduciary duties are not an easy answer – and may work better in theory than in practice. The OFT found that:

(1) Large, single employer trust-based schemes tended to deliver good governance. However, even here some trustee boards in hybrid schemes focused too heavily on the DB scheme, to the detriment of the DC scheme.[71]

(2) In small and medium sized single employer trusts, trustees often lacked the necessary expertise. The OFT quoted a review by TPR which showed that 52% of small schemes and 38% of medium schemes had failed to review their SIPs in the last three years, even though this was a legal obligation.[72]

(3) Master trust schemes may suffer from conflicts of interest. Trustees who are appointed and paid by the provider may lack the motivation to challenge the provider's actions. Furthermore, in some cases, the trust deed may prevent trustees from changing the investment manager of underperforming funds.[73]

---

[69] Office of Fair Trading, *Defined contribution workplace pension market study* (2013) para 7.41.

[70] Above, para 7.44.

[71] Above, para 7.24-7.25.

[72] Above, para 7.26; see para 7.14 above.

[73] Above, para 7.30.

The Association of British Insurers (ABI) agreement

13.55 In light of these concerns, the OFT and DWP held discussions with the ABI. The ABI has now agreed to introduce Independent Governance Committees, which will be embedded within pension providers. This will apply to both contract-based pensions and bundled trust-based schemes. The new committees will have independent chairs and a majority of independent members – and the ABI has undertaken that they will have the expertise and resources needed to carry out their duties.[74]

13.56 The committees will consider whether the schemes offer value for money. Where a committee identifies a problem, it will report on proposed action to the pension provider's board. The board must then implement the action, or explain why it has not done so. Where the board fails to act, the committee may inform employers and employees, make the matter public or contact the regulator.

13.57 The OFT commented that:

> The implementation of these Committees will need careful consideration, given the potential for conflicts of interest with the providers' duty to shareholders, and given the information asymmetry that the Committee may face in monitoring the provider.[75]

13.58 The OFT recommended that the key elements of this scheme should be set out in minimum governance standards to apply to all pension schemes, including all trust-based schemes. It highlighted that the standards must ensure that trustees are genuinely able to carry out their fiduciary duties, "including by moving scheme assets to alternative fund managers and administrators where that is in the members' interest".[76] It recommends that TPR should require trust-based schemes to report the results of their value for money assessments, and should use this data as part of their risk framework to target any further regulatory activity.[77]

A long-term solution?

13.59 The OFT considered that these various solutions would address risks of consumer detriment in the short to medium term – but that "a longer term challenge remains".[78] It set out a series of principles which need to inform future policy, including robust independent governance and better alignment of incentives.

---

[74] Office of Fair Trading, *Defined contribution workplace pension market study* (2013) para 9.12.

[75] Above, para 9.13.

[76] Above, para 9.14.

[77] Above, para 9.26.

[78] Above, para 9.35.

13.60   The OFT also stressed the need for economies of scale.[79] It recommended that TPR should investigate the possibility of closing trust-based schemes that offer poor value for money. It also recommended that, following this investigation, the Government should consider whether TPR's powers are sufficient and whether trustees should be required to do more to prove that they have considered value for money.[80]

DUAL REGULATION

Concerns

13.61   The stakeholders we met expressed concern about the dual regulation of pensions by TPR and the FCA. We were told that it may allow some behaviour to "slip through the net". Recent reviews have raised similar issues.

13.62   For example, the Work and Pensions Select Committee expressed concern that, although the FCA is responsible for enforcing standards in contract-based schemes, it did not devote sufficient resources to the issue. The Committee queried whether the FCA was the appropriate body to regulate contract-based pensions.[81] If the FCA is to remain responsible, the Committee urged it:

> To adopt a pensions-specific regulatory strategy and to set up a well-resourced team dedicated solely to proactively regulating contract-based pension schemes.[82]

13.63   The National Audit Office (NAO) has also criticised the lack of a joined-up approach to DC pension regulation. In a review of TPR's role in relation to DC schemes it noted that:

> There is no single public body leading on the regulation of defined contribution schemes and ultimately accountable for the delivery of regulatory objectives.[83]

13.64   Further, the NAO found that TPR may not have the powers necessary to intervene in areas which were within its regulatory sphere:

> It has no powers regarding the providers of contract-based schemes, but it has the statutory objective to protect members' benefits in these schemes.[84]

---

[79]   Office of Fair Trading, *Defined contribution workplace pension market study* (2013) para 9.37.

[80]   Above, para 9.27.

[81]   Improving governance and best practice in workplace pensions, Sixth Report of the Select Committee on Work and Pensions (2012-13) HC 768-I para 104.

[82]   Above, para 104.

[83]   The Pensions Regulator: Regulating defined contribution pension schemes, Report by the Comptroller and Auditor General (2012-13) HC 466 p 8.

[84]   Above, p 9.

13.65 In January 2013, TPR launched a consultation and analysis of the regulation of workplace DC schemes and the alignment of the two regulatory systems.[85] This did, however, identify some gaps in protection. For example, it found that the FCA "has no specific requirements for individual pension charges to be disclosed to the employer at the point of sale or at any other time".[86] It also found that there is no requirement for providers of work-based personal pensions to encourage members to review the fund they are invested in.[87]

13.66 In its response to the Work and Pensions Select Committee, DWP have confirmed that the Government believes the overall regulatory architecture is sound.[88] However, TPR has indicated that they will jointly publish a document with the FCA in autumn 2013 setting out in more detail how the regulation of work-based personal pensions operates.[89]

"Regulator shopping"

13.67 Whenever providers are given a choice of regulator there is a risk that providers may choose the scheme which meets their short-term goals. In other words, the scheme with less capital may choose the regulator with less prudential supervision, while the scheme offering the harsher terms may choose the regulator with lower conduct of business requirements. The OFT highlights an example of "regulator shopping": new entrants to the market have tended to choose master trust structures because the regulatory burden is lower.[90]

---

[85] The Pensions Regulator, *Regulating work-based defined contribution pension schemes* (2013), available at http://www.thepensionsregulator.gov.uk/docs/regulating-dc-pension-schemes-consultation.pdf.

[86] The Pensions Regulator, *Principles and features for good quality pension schemes: Initial analysis of the presence of the regulator's defined contribution quality features in FSA regulation of work-based personal pensions* (2013) p 6, available at http://www.thepensionsregulator.gov.uk/docs/principles-and-features-for-good-quality-pension-schemes.pdf.

[87] Above, p 23.

[88] Improving governance and best practice in workplace pensions: Government Response to the Committee's Sixth Report of Session 2012-13, First Special Report of Session 2013-14 (2013-14) HC 485 p 8.

[89] The Pensions Regulator, *DC consultation response: Regulating work-based defined contribution pension schemes* (2013) p 8, available at http://www.thepensionsregulator.gov.uk/docs/regulating-work-based-dc-pension-schemes-consultation-response.PDF.

[90] Office of Fair Trading, *Defined contribution workplace pension market study* (2013) para 4.24.

13.68   Master trusts are not subject to prudential or capital requirements and (unlike DB schemes and insurance companies) their funds are not necessarily protected on the provider's insolvency – though employers are unlikely to understand the different levels of protection involved.[91] The OFT reports that new pension providers tend to make losses in the early years until they achieve sufficient scale to break even.[92] It noted concerns that some new providers may fail to achieve this scale,[93] so the risk of insolvency is not simply theoretical. The OFT recommended that "Government and regulators should aim to ensure an equivalent level of protection" between the master trusts and contract-based pensions.[94]

A COMPARISON WITH AUSTRALIA

13.69   To understand what an alternative regulatory system might look like, we commissioned a paper from a leading Australian law firm, Clayton Utz, on the Australian system. This is set out in Appendix C.

Similarities and differences

13.70   Australia is a useful point of comparison because Australian pensions have much in common with the UK. Their pension funds have a trust structure which derives from English law. Indeed, the relevant legislation refers specifically to English concepts, such as the duty of trustees to exercise their powers "in the best interests of the beneficiaries".[95] Like the UK, Australian pensions have moved from DB to DC schemes. In Australia, this change appears to have taken place earlier: Clayton Utz comment that the vast majority of assets are now in DC funds. There has also been a similar shift from industry or employer specific funds to retail funds, which offer membership to anyone who wishes to join. Retail funds now account for over a quarter of all funds under management.

13.71   Against this common background, however, there are some marked differences:

(1)   Australian pensions are more generously funded. Employers are required to make pension contributions of 9.25% of "ordinary time earnings" and this will rise to 12% by 2019.

(2)   All schemes must be trust-based. Trustees must review their investment strategy regularly.

---

[91]   Office of Fair Trading, *Defined contribution workplace pension market study* (2013) paras 8.26-8.31.

[92]   Above, para 4.19.

[93]   Above, para 8.25.

[94]   Above, para 9.33.

[95]   See General Covenant under Superannuation Industry (Supervision) Act 1993, s 52 (Australia); see Appendix C section 5.3 below.

(3)   The market is much more consolidated. Under pressure from Government, the number of funds fell from 3,810 in 2000 to 336 in 2012. Over half of all funds under management are now held by the largest twenty funds. This provides economies of scale and also gives funds access to a wider range of assets. Clayton Utz comment that many large funds invest in property or infrastructure projects. Often a consortium of funds will pool assets into special purpose vehicles to do this.

(4)   There is one dominant regulator, the Australian Prudential Regulation Authority (APRA). Although trustees also require a license from the Australian Securities and Investment Commission (responsible for consumer protection in financial markets), the APRA takes the lead. All schemes are subject to licensing and prudential supervision by the APRA.

13.72   Employers must make superannuation contributions to the fund nominated by the employee. As in the UK, around 80% of employees do not make a choice, and in this case the employer nominates a default fund. From 2017, all default funds must be a "MySuper" product with controlled fees and standardised information (similar to stakeholder pensions).

13.73   Australia also has a vibrant sector for self-managed pensions. A "self-managed super fund" has fewer than five members and each member is also a trustee (or director of the corporate trustee). The number of self-managed funds increased from 469,102 in March 2012 to 503,320 in March 2013. These schemes appeal to the well off, and now account for almost a third of funds under management.

A single regulatory structure based on trust law

13.74   For present purposes, it is interesting to note that in Australia all pensions fall within the same regulatory structure, which is explicitly based on trust law concepts. To bring greater clarity, the legislation restates principles of equity and trust law, including fiduciary duties. This includes requirements to:

(1)   Formulate, review regularly and give effect to an investment strategy, having regard to:

(a)   risk and likely return;

(b)   the composition of investments, including the extent to which the investments expose the fund to risks from inadequate diversification;

(c)   the liquidity of the investments; and

(d)   the costs that might be incurred.

(2)   Exercise due diligence in developing, offering and regularly reviewing each investment option.

(3)   Ensure the investment options offered to each beneficiary allow adequate diversification.

13.75 In addition, trustees are subject to the general covenants, which include the need to:

(1) act honestly;

(2) exercise the same degree of care, skill and diligence as a prudent superannuation trustee would exercise;

(3) perform their duties and exercise their powers in the best interests of the beneficiaries;

(4) where there is a conflict of interest, give priority to the needs of the beneficiaries and to ensure their interests are not adversely affected by the conflict; and

(5) act fairly in dealing with classes of beneficiaries within the entity.[96]

13.76 Other standards require trustees to have an "investment governance framework", which is broadly similar to a SIP in the UK. Similarly, trustees must have a risk management framework and outsourcing policy.

Explicit regulatory pressures towards consolidation

13.77 The reduction in the number of funds (from 3,810 to 336 over 12 years) reflects an explicit Government objective. Regulatory pressure towards economies of scale continues. For example, in relation to MySuper products, trustees are required to consider the need for scale. Under the Superannuation Act they must "determine on an annual basis" whether the beneficiaries are "disadvantaged, in comparison to the beneficiaries of other funds", due to insufficient numbers of beneficiaries or pooled assets.[97] In July 2013, DWP consulted on whether a similar approach should be introduced in the UK.[98]

CONCLUSION

13.78 We have been asked to consider whether fiduciary duties, as established in law or as applied in practice, are conducive to investment strategies that are in the best interests of the ultimate beneficiaries.

13.79 For contract-based pensions, there are problems with the way that fiduciary duties are established in law. The duties appear unduly uncertain. As discussed in Chapter 12, contract-based pension providers must consider the suitability of a scheme for the member when the member first joins, but there are no clear obligations to review the suitability of the scheme or the SIP at specified intervals thereafter. Nor is there an explicit statement that decisions on charging or trading must be made in the best interests of the scheme member. Another problem is where the investment principles are set out in the contract and become outdated. The provider may not have power to change them without each members' consent, which may be difficult to obtain.

---

[96] Superannuation Act, s 52 (Australia).

[97] Superannuation Act, s 29VN (Australia).

[98] Department for Work and Pensions, *Quality standards in workplace defined contribution pension schemes: Call for evidence* (2013) p 19.

13.80   For trust-based schemes, fiduciary duties are clearly established in law. However, there are some problems in the way that the duties are applied in practice. Small trust-based schemes may lack the resources to supervise investment managers. It is a matter of concern that a review by TPR showed that 52% of small schemes and 38% of medium schemes had failed to review their SIPs in the last three years, even though this was a legal obligation.[99] Furthermore, in some master trust schemes, the trustees may lack the ability or motivation to move funds from an underperforming fund run by the pension provider.

13.81   We are aware that DWP is carrying out a programme of work to address these issues. In Chapter 14 we ask for views about these issues in a way designed to assist DWP in this work.

---

[99] Office of Fair Trading, *Defined contribution workplace pension market study* (2013) para 7.26.

PART 5

CONCLUSIONS AND QUESTIONS

CHAPTER 14
CONCLUSIONS AND QUESTIONS

14.1 In this chapter we summarise the conclusions we have reached and ask consultees for their views.

14.2 Under our terms of reference we are asked whether fiduciary duties, as established in law or as applied in practice, are conducive to investment strategies that are in the best interests of the ultimate beneficiary. We address this question in four parts:

   (1) In Chapter 10 we set out the legal duties placed on pension trustees to act in the best interests of beneficiaries. Our tentative view is that, as established in law, these duties are satisfactory. We ask consultees if they agree.

   (2) In Chapter 12 we concluded that the fiduciary-type duties placed on the providers of workplace contract-based pensions are unduly uncertain. We note recent initiatives to address this issue and ask for views.

   (3) In Chapter 13 we summarised problems with the way that fiduciary duties apply in practice in workplace defined contribution (DC) pension schemes. We understand that the Department for Work and Pensions (DWP) are carrying out a major programme of work to consider these issues, and urge consultees to engage in this process.

   (4) As regards other intermediaries in the investment chain, the law is extremely flexible but also uncertain. As we noted in Chapters 11 and 12, the courts are heavily influenced by the terms of the contract and by the regulatory regime. We think that any statutory reform of the law of fiduciary duties would result in new uncertainties and could have unintended consequences. We ask if there should be stronger rights to sue for breach of Financial Conduct Authority (FCA) rules and whether the rules need to be strengthened in some areas.

PENSION TRUSTEES' DUTIES TO ACT IN THE BEST INTERESTS OF BENEFICIARIES

14.3 In Chapter 10 we consider the duties on pension trustees when devising an investment strategy in the best interests of the ultimate beneficiaries. We were asked how far fiduciaries may, or must, consider:

   (1) factors relevant to long-term investment performance which might not have an immediate financial impact, including questions of sustainability or environmental and social impact;

   (2) interests beyond the maximisation of financial return; and

   (3) generally prevailing ethical standards, and/or the ethical views of their beneficiaries, even where this may not be in the immediate financial interest of those beneficiaries.

Conclusions on the current law

14.4 The primary duty is that trustees must use their powers for the purpose for which they are given. In the case of a pension scheme, investment powers are granted to trustees so that they can earn returns to provide a pension. The pension legislation requires that investment powers are be exercised "to ensure the security, quality, liquidity and profitability of the portfolio as a whole",[1] without "excessive reliance on any particular asset, issuer or group of undertakings".[2] The trust instrument may, however, require the trustees to do or refrain from particular things.

14.5 Within these broad parameters, trustees are given considerable discretion, so long as trustees reach their decision in the right way. In particular pension trustees:

(1) must not "fetter their discretion" by, for example, applying a pre-existing moral or political judgment;

(2) must consider the relevant circumstances; and

(3) must obtain proper advice.

14.6 Stakeholders raised five possible factors which trustees may wish to take account of in making investment decisions. Our conclusions are set out below.

(1) Wider factors relevant to long-term investment performance may be taken into account where they would further the purpose of the power of investment. This includes environmental, social and governance factors relevant to financial returns. Trustees should consider, in general terms, whether they will take account of such factors. However, they are free not to use an approach based on these factors if they consider that another strategy would better serve the interests of their beneficiaries.

(2) Wider systemic considerations (or "macroeconomic factors") may be taken into account. The anticipated benefits of an investment decision based on such factors must, however, outweigh the likely costs. Again, trustees should consider, in general terms, whether to take account of such factors, but remain free to use a different approach if this would better serve their beneficiaries.

(3) "Quality of life factors" (that is, factors relating to beneficiaries' quality of life now and in the future)[3] may only be taken into account when choosing between two equally beneficial investments. They may not be taken into account when this would result in a lower return.

---

[1] Occupational Pension Scheme (Investment) Regulations 2005 SI 2005 No 3378, reg 4(3).

[2] Occupational Pension Scheme (Investment) Regulations 2005 SI 2005 No 3378, reg 4(7).

[3] See para 10.79 and following above.

(4)   General ethical issues, unrelated to risks, returns or the interests of beneficiaries, may only be taken into account in limited circumstances. They may be used in a defined benefit (DB) pension fund set up by a religious group, other charity or political organisation. Where DC schemes allow individual members a choice of investment strategies, ethical issues can be taken into account with the members' consent. In other cases they should only be used where trustees have good reason to think that scheme members share the moral viewpoint and where they anticipate that the decision will not result in lower returns to the fund.

(5)   Trustees may consider the views of their beneficiaries when making investment decisions, but there is no need for them to do so. Trustees must make the ultimate decision.

> Q1: Do consultees agree that this is a correct statement of the current law?

Evaluating the law

14.7   Our terms of reference ask us to evaluate the current law against certain criteria. In particular, we have been asked to consider whether the duties:

(1)   reflect an appropriate understanding of the scope of beneficiaries' best interests;

(2)   give sufficient certainty to market participants;

(3)   permit sufficient diversity of strategy;

(4)   encourage long-term investment strategies;

(5)   allow fiduciaries to invest in line with generally prevailing ethical standards, even where this may not be in the immediate financial interest of beneficiaries; and

(6)   require a sufficient balance of risk and benefit.

14.8   We consider each of these issues below.

An appropriate understanding of beneficiaries' best interests?

14.9   We think the law is right to focus on the purpose for which trustees have been given their investment powers. Pension trustees should focus on providing pensions. As we say in Chapter 10, this is not an easy task. For some DC schemes, with low contributions and low returns, the chances of providing employees with adequate incomes in old age may be low. Without a sustained focus on the objective, the chances of success reduce further.

14.10 Pension trustees may come under outside pressure to use their investment powers to further other objectives. In Chapter 10 we mentioned potential government pressure to invest in infrastructure. As one commentator put it, schemes may be regarded as "the magic porridge pot" out of which the money for roads and railways can be found.[4] External pressure groups may also campaign for pension trustees to use their investment powers to combat a wide range of social ills, from tax avoidance to smoking. We think it may be helpful for trustees to be able to quote the law of fiduciary duties to resist pressures to act in ways which would reduce the benefits available to members.

14.11 Our provisional conclusion is that the law reflects an appropriate understanding of beneficiaries' best interests. We ask if consultees agree.

> Q2: Do consultees agree that the law reflects an appropriate understanding of beneficiaries' best interests?

Sufficient certainty?

14.12 The law is flexible and allows trustees wide discretion to invest as they see fit. We see advantages to this flexibility, as it allows trustees to respond to new challenges over time. Our tentative view is that it is worth preserving this flexibility, even if the result is some uncertainty.

14.13 The main substance of how pension trustees should exercise their powers is set out in the Occupational Pension Scheme (Investment) Regulations 2005.[5] As we noted in Chapter 7, these do not apply to schemes with fewer than 100 active, deferred or pension members. We ask if the Regulations should be extended to all schemes.

14.14 In their paper on Australian pensions in Appendix C, Clayton Utz describe how fiduciary duties are set out in statutory "covenants" under section 52 of the Superannuation Industry (Supervision) Act 1993. These have recently been amended, clarified and expanded. The authors comment that many of the reforms simply made explicit matters which were previously implicit:

> For example, it has probably never been appropriate for a superannuation trustee to fail to have regard to the availability of accurate valuation information when selecting investments, to ignore the tax consequences of investment decisions or to fail to understand, monitor and manage the fees and costs incurred in the investment of the fund's assets. Explicit reference to these and other matters in the amended section 52 covenants is intended to address perceived shortcomings in investment behaviour by participants in the superannuation industry.[6]

---

[4] R Ellison, "Pointing the finger" (July 2013) *Pensions World* 14 at 14. See para 10.92 above.

[5] SI 2005 No 3378.

[6] See, for example, Australian Government, *Super System Review – Final Report – Part Two* (2012) ch 3.6.

14.15 We are interested in whether consultees think that there are specific issues in the UK which would benefit from similar types of statutory clarification.

> Q3: Do consultees think that the law is sufficiently certain?
>
> Q4: Should the Occupational Pension Scheme (Investment) Regulations 2005 be extended to all trust-based pension schemes?
>
> Q5: Are there any specific areas which would benefit from statutory clarification?

A diversity of strategy?

14.16 Some stakeholders argue that the law on investment duties encourages "herding behaviour". Where individuals seek to protect themselves against criticism by doing what everyone else is doing, legal duties may become a "lemming standard".[7] As Lord Myners said in 2010, "in this world, it is fine to be wrong or even lose money, as long as you do so in the company of others".[8]

14.17 The Network for Sustainable Financial Markets told us:

> The fiduciary duty of prudence has been understood as a mandate to favor the status quo, which has artificially suppressed demand for investment advisors and consultants to update their business models to address conceptual shortcomings and has discouraged fiduciaries from leaving the safety of the "investor herd".[9]

14.18 An investment manager or trustee may not be rewarded for acting contrary to the herd. ShareAction gave the example of investment managers who lost contracts in the 1990s because they foresaw the dot com bubble and refused to invest in technology equities. Herding may lead to an unhealthy focus on benchmark-relative performance, which encourages short-term investment. It may also increase systemic risk.

14.19 We think that where herding does occur it is mainly caused by the nature of human behaviour. This is exacerbated by an industry structure in which pension schemes rely on the advice of a small number of investment consultants and where investment managers are judged in relation to other investment managers. We do not think that herding is caused by trustees' legal duties, or that a change in the law would make a practical difference.

---

[7] See K Johnson, *Back to the Future of Pension Trust Fiduciary Duties* (2010), available at http://www.fairpensions.org.uk/sites/default/files/uploaded_files/KeithJohnsonFiduciaryDuty.pdf.

[8] Lord Myners, Speech to the International Corporate Governance Network (March 2010), quoted in FairPensions (later known as ShareAction), *Protecting our Best Interests: Rediscovering Fiduciary Obligation* (2011) p 23.

[9] Network for Sustainable Financial Markets, Response to "Fiduciary Duties of Investment Intermediaries: Initial Questions" (July 2013).

14.20 It is true that duties of care measure behaviour against that of others performing similar services. For example, professional trustees are judged against what "it is reasonable to expect of a person acting in the course of that kind of business or profession".[10] In this sense trustees may be wise to look at general market practice. However, this should be tempered with a healthy dose of common sense; the standard does not measure behaviour simply against what others are doing but what a *reasonable* trustee would do.

14.21 Our provisional conclusion is that the law gives trustees considerable discretion to make their own decisions. So long as they keep the purpose of the power of investment in mind, consider relevant factors and follow the procedural requirements we have outlined, the courts will not second guess their decisions.

> Q6: Do consultees agree that the law permits a sufficient diversity of strategies?

Encouraging long-term investment strategies?

14.22 The Occupational Pension Scheme (Investment) Regulations 2005 set out the general legal principle: assets should be invested in a manner "appropriate to the nature and duration of the expected future retirement benefits payable under the scheme".[11] Trustees are entitled to consider any factor which might impact on investment performance over this time frame.

14.23 As we noted in Chapter 2 there are many pressures on trustees which discourage long-term investment strategies. For DB schemes, these include the statutory funding objective and the need to show any deficit in the employer's company accounts based on accounting standards FRS17 or IAS19.

14.24 Furthermore, both DB and DC pension trusts are often small. They lack internal resources and are highly dependent on their investment consultants and investment managers. As Professor Kay put it, investment consultants are a source of short-termist behaviour "because they are typically making recommendations to trustees based on recent performance histories, rather than the future approach and strategy of the manager".[12] They may also recommend complex arrangements which require further professional advice but make it difficult for trustees to oversee the strategy. Our provisional conclusion is that these sorts of pressures are the cause of short-term investment strategies – not the law of fiduciary duties.

> Q7: Do consultees agree that the main pressures towards short-termism are not caused by the duty to invest in beneficiaries' best interests?

---

[10] Trustee Act 2000, s 1. This is discussed in Chapter 6.

[11] SI 2005 No 3378, reg 4(4).

[12] The Kay Review of Equity Markets and Long-Term Decision Making, Third Report of the Select Committee on Business, Innovation and Skills (2013-14) HC 603 at Ev 4.

Allow investments in line with generally prevailing ethical standards?

14.25   As we have seen, trustees should consider ethical issues in only very limited circumstances. Trustees should not invest in activities which are illegal. Nor do we think that trustees should invest in activities which contravene international conventions. For example, trustees should not invest in firms manufacturing cluster bombs, banned by the Convention on Cluster Munitions.

14.26   Outside these narrow areas, however, ethical issues are highly contested. To take a recently debated example, some people think that payday lending at high interest rates is wrong, while others think that the ability to borrow money quickly for short periods provides a useful service. Moral condemnation of payday lending is not necessarily "generally prevailing".

14.27   As explained in Chapter 10, the current law permits trustees to disinvest from payday lending if they think that public condemnation of the practice will lead to a risk that the business model is unsustainable. But trustees should only disinvest for purely ethical reasons if two conditions are satisfied. Firstly, the trustees must have good reason to think that scheme members would share their outlook. Secondly, they should anticipate that the decision will not result in financial detriment to the scheme. In practice it is unlikely that trustees will be aware of members' views or that members will have common views unless the scheme is small and has members from a common source, such as a religious group.

14.28   The law requires trustees to focus on providing pensions to their members, setting aside their own political, moral or religious views. As Lord Murray observed in *Martin v City of Edinburgh District Council*,[13] it is not reasonable or practicable for fiduciaries to divest themselves "of all personal preferences, of all political beliefs, of all moral, religious or other conscientiously held principles". Nevertheless, they must do their "best to exercise fair and impartial judgment" on the merits of the issue before them.[14] We see advantages to legal rules which remind trustees that their duty is to provide pensions and not to improve the world in some general sense, possibly at the expense of their beneficiaries. We ask consultees whether they agree.

> Q8: Do consultees agree that the law is right to allow trustees to consider ethical issues only in limited circumstances?

---

[13]   [1989] Pens LR 9, 1988 SLT 329.

[14]   [1989] Pens LR 9 at [33], 1988 SLT 329 at 334.

A balance of risk and benefit?

14.29 Trustees are required to balance risk and returns. The Occupational Pension Scheme (Investment) Regulations 2005 set out the general principle: the power of investment should be exercised in a manner "calculated to ensure the security, quality, liquidity and profitability of the portfolio as a whole".[15] The assets should be properly diversified to "avoid excessive reliance on any particular asset, issuer or group of undertakings and so as to avoid accumulations of risk in the portfolio as a whole".[16]

14.30 Some stakeholders argued that the Regulations require too much diversification. The Kay Review identified fragmented shareholding as a major factor in discouraging the effective engagement between shareholders and companies.[17] As UNISON stated in their response to our short paper, "fiduciaries are legally bound to diversify assets, so that even the largest collective funds in the world must collaborate to exercise influence over corporate practice in any one company or sector".[18] Similarly, ShareAction told us that "prevailing interpretations of fiduciary duty may encourage excessive diversification".[19]

14.31 Diversification duties may also have pushed funds to diversify across managers and mandates. For example, at the turn of the century, the average externally managed pension fund had around three mandates whilst by 2010 they had nine.[20] Inevitably, this creates greater potential for conflicts of interest throughout the chain and the need for greater oversight of those fulfilling delegated duties.

14.32 We welcome views on whether the current rules encourage excessive diversification. We also ask if the law provides the right balance of risk and return. We would be interested to know whether pension funds may be incurring hidden risks, for example in the recent move towards investments in swaps and derivatives, as part of liability driven investment strategies.

> Q9: Does the law encourage excessive diversification?
>
> Q10: Does the law encourage trustees to achieve the right balance of risk and return?
>
> Q11: Are there any systemic areas of trustees' investment strategies which pose undue risks?

---

[15] SI 2005 No 3378, reg 4(3).

[16] Occupational Pension Scheme (Investment) Regulations 2005, reg 4(7). See also *Nestle v National Westminster Bank plc* [1993] 1 WLR 1260; Trustee Act 2000 ss 4(3)(a) and (b).

[17] J Kay, *The Kay Review of UK Equity Markets and Long-Term Decision Making: Final Report* (2012) para 5.34.

[18] UNISON, Response to "Fiduciary Duties of Investment Intermediaries: Initial Questions" (July 2013).

[19] ShareAction, Response to "Fiduciary Duties of Investment Intermediaries: Initial Questions" (July 2013).

[20] Lane Clark and Peacock LLP, *Investment Management Fees Survey* (2011) p 13, citing a 2010 survey by The WM Company.

Is the law satisfactory?

14.33 Finally we ask whether the law works in the best interests of beneficiaries or whether it requires reform. We welcome views on this overarching question.

> Q12: Overall, do consultees think that the legal obligations on trustees are conducive to investment strategies in the best interests of the ultimate beneficiaries?
>
> Q13: If not, what specifically needs to be changed?

Consolidation of pension funds

14.34 Finally, many stakeholders told us that the best means of encouraging long-term investment strategies would be to move towards greater consolidation within trust-based pension funds, both DB and DC funds. Consolidation was supported by, among others, the National Association of Pension Funds (NAPF), UNISON and the Fabian Society. We also note the major consolidation of the Australian pension market.

14.35 It was suggested that larger funds would provide economies of scale. Stakeholders drew our attention to the study by APG, the Dutch investment manager, into the investment performance of the Local Government Pension Scheme (LGPS) which suggested that "substantial improvement in investment performance could be realised by increasing the size of funds".[21] Furthermore, larger funds would lead to more expert, better resourced trustees with the capacity to act as engaged shareholders.

14.36 We note that DWP consulted on this issue in July 2013.[22] If consultees have further views on this issue we will pass those views to the relevant government departments.

FIDUCIARY-TYPE DUTIES IN CONTRACT-BASED PENSION SCHEMES

Duties to review suitability

14.37 Pension trustees are under clear duties to consider and review their statement of investment principles. In Chapter 12 we highlighted that the duties on contract-based pension providers are much less certain.

---

[21] APG, *Performance analysis of LGPS funds*, p 2. See para 2.55 above.

[22] Department for Work and Pensions, *Quality standards in workplace defined contribution pension schemes: Call for evidence* (2013) p 19

14.38   As we saw in Chapter 13, stakeholder pensions and pensions used for the purposes of auto-enrolment must offer a default investment option. In stakeholder pensions this must be "lifestyled". In other words, the investment strategy must be adjusted over time to reduce the risk of market volatility as the member nears retirement. For non-stakeholder pensions used for auto-enrolment, lifestyling is not a legal obligation, though it is good practice. Although trustees should review their statement of investment principles at least every three years, there is no equivalent requirement on contract-based providers to review the investment strategy applying to default funds. In July 2013, DWP consulted on whether reviews should take place regularly, at least every three years.[23]

14.39   When a member makes an initial choice of investment strategy, the regulations appear to place the onus on the individual to review and update that choice, even though most people find decisions about pensions to be "complex, hard, unpleasant and time-consuming".[24] There is no clear responsibility on either the employer or the pension provider to tell the member that they have chosen an overly expensive or under-performing fund, which is no longer operating in their interest. The FCA rules impose some duties on providers to consider the suitability of decisions to trade for the end investor, but it is not clear how often investment strategies must be reassessed or when providers should seek new information about their scheme members.[25]

14.40   Our provisional view is that the rules requiring contract-based pension providers to reassess the suitability of investment strategies over time should be clarified and strengthened, both for default schemes and for chosen schemes. This is to meet the principle in the Government's response to the Kay Review that pension providers should act in the best long-term interests of their clients. We ask consultees for views.

Independent Governance Committees

14.41   In Chapter 13 we noted that following discussions with OFT and DWP, the Association of British Insurers (ABI) has agreed to introduce Independent Governance Committees embedded within insurance pension providers.

14.42   There are many difficult questions about how these committees will work, including how they will be appointed, resourced and supported in their work. Unlike trustees, the committees will not have the power to change investment strategies or fund managers. Instead they will make proposals to the pension provider's board, who may act on the proposal or may explain why they do not propose to act. It remains to be seen how far the threat that committees will make their proposals public will influence pension providers.

14.43   Furthermore, it is not clear from the published material whether members of the committees will be under explicit legal duties to act in the interests of members – and if so, whether they can exclude liability for breaches of these duties.

---

[23]   Department for Work and Pensions, *Quality standards in workplace defined contribution pension schemes: Call for evidence* (2013) p 15.

[24]   Office of Fair Trading, *Defined contribution workplace pension market study* (2013) para 5.10. See para 13.40 above.

[25]   See para 8.55 and following above.

14.44 Our tentative view is that members of the committees should be subject to clear legal duties to act in the interests of members. We appreciate, however, that if members carry unlimited personal liability for breaches of those duties it may be difficult to find individuals willing to carry out the task. We think that pension providers should provide a full indemnity to the members of their committees for any liabilities they incur. Pension providers are best placed to control the quality of the committees' work. After all, they will appoint and resource the committees. An indemnity will give pension providers a clear interest in ensuring that the committees carry out their tasks correctly.

> Q14: Do consultees agree that the duties on contract-based pension providers to act in the interests of scheme members should be clarified and strengthened?
>
> Q15: Should specific duties be placed on pension providers to review the suitability of investment strategies over time? If so, how often should these reviews take place?
>
> Q16: Should members of Independent Governance Committees be subject to explicit legal duties to act in the interests of scheme members?
>
> Q17: Should pension providers be obliged to indemnify members of Independent Governance Committees for liabilities incurred in the course of their duties?

WORKPLACE DC PENSION SCHEMES: DO FIDUCIARY DUTIES WORK IN PRACTICE?

14.45 Whatever the merits of fiduciary duties established in law, there is evidence of problems in the way they are applied in practice in workplace DC schemes. We described these problems in Chapter 13. In both trust-based and contract-based schemes, there may be insufficient review of high charges or unsuitable or out-dated investment strategies.

Governance

14.46 It appears that on their own, legal duties are insufficient to ensure that pension schemes work in the interests of their members. Legal duties need to be embedded in an industry structure which provides the expertise and resources for good governance; and duties must be enforced by efficient regulation. The main concerns were that:

(1) Many single employer trust-based schemes are too small: trustees often lacked the necessary expertise and support to exercise their duties.

(2) Master trust schemes may suffer from conflicts of interest. Trustees who are appointed and paid by the pension provider may not be able to challenge the provider's actions. In particular, trustees may lack the power to change investment managers when in-house funds are underperforming.

(3) The dual regulatory system allows possibilities for "regulator shopping", enabling providers with less capital to choose a scheme with lower prudential requirements.

Charges: should investment transaction costs be included in the overall charge?

14.47 In Chapter 13 we noted initiatives to make charges in DC schemes much more transparent. One issue is of particular relevance to the concerns raised in the Kay Review that investment managers favour short-term trading over long-term investment. This is whether charging structures should be aimed at encouraging trading or at encouraging long-term investment. In its response to the review, the Government set out the following principle:

> Market incentives should enable and encourage companies, savers and intermediaries to adopt investment approaches which achieve long-term returns by supporting and challenging corporate decisions in pursuit of long-term value.[26]

In its directions for Government and regulators, the response said that "regulatory practice should favour investing over trading, not the other way round".[27]

14.48 This raises the question whether investment transaction costs (such as brokers' commissions and bid-offer spreads) should be accounted for within an overall charge. Alternatively, should they be taken straight from the fund as an additional expense?

14.49 In Chapter 13 we noted the OFT view that the single "framework" charge should not include investment transaction costs, as "their inclusion could potentially create incentives for investment managers to avoid carrying out transactions in order to keep costs down", even where trading is in members' interests.[28] By contrast, allowing transaction costs to be deducted from funds may create inappropriate incentives to trade.

14.50 As we discussed in Chapter 12, the Investment Management Association has recently consulted on the introduction of a new Statement of Recommended Practice for the financial statements of UK authorised funds. They recommend more comprehensive disclosure of fund performance and charges, and in particular transaction costs. The question is whether transaction costs should be within the single framework charge or whether they should be levied in addition, and subject to scrutiny by trustees and Independent Governance Committees.

---

[26] Department for Business, Innovation and Skills, *Ensuring equity markets support long-term growth: The Government Response to the Kay Review* (2012) Principle 9.

[27] Above, para 2.25.

[28] Office of Fair Trading, *Defined contribution workplace pension market study* (2013) para 9.19.

14.51   DWP is planning to launch a consultation on charges in pension schemes in the autumn of 2013. The Minister for Pensions confirmed in May that he wished to consult on charges, including on whether a cap should be placed on charges in workplace schemes. We hope that DWP will be asking questions about investment transaction costs. We would urge consultees to respond to DWP with comments on where the balance of advantage lies. Is it better to incentivise investment managers in a way which encourages beneficial trading of investment? Or should the incentives be aimed at discouraging unnecessary trading?

14.52   There are no ideal answers. The question is whether it is better to stay with the existing system (which may favour too many short-term trades) or to take steps to reduce incentives to trade (with the possibility that this may lead to too few trades).

Conclusion

14.53   We have been asked whether fiduciary duties as applied in practice are conducive to investment strategies in the best interests of the ultimate beneficiaries. In the case of workplace DC pension schemes we think legal duties alone are insufficient to ensure good outcomes for members. The duties need to be embedded in an industry structure and regulatory framework which reinforce and encourage independent review of investment strategies.

14.54   Issues about industry structure and regulatory enforcement are outside our terms of reference. DWP is carrying out a programme of work in this area. We have already included details of the consultation on charges. As part of this project, DWP provided us with the following outline of their other work:

> The Department for Work and Pensions (DWP) has a significant programme of work underway to ensure that members of workplace pension schemes are subject to appropriate protection. This ongoing policy development is based on extensive stakeholder consultation and is reflected in legislation that forms part of the current Pensions Bill. It is undertaken in conjunction with the Pensions Regulator and the Financial Conduct Authority.
>
> On 4 July 2013 the DWP launched a Call for Evidence on quality standards in workplace DC schemes. This exercise asked stakeholders, including industry and consumer bodies, for evidence and views on pension scheme governance, default investment options, administration and record keeping, and the scale of schemes. This exercise closed on 9 September 2013 and the DWP is currently examining the evidence ahead of bringing forward proposals in due course.
>
> By their work on both scheme quality and scheme charges, the DWP intends to respond in a comprehensive manner to the report of the Office of Fair Trading into the workplace pensions market, which was published in September 2013. The DWP is already working with the OFT and the pensions industry on an audit of legacy workplace schemes, as a result of a recommendation by the OFT in their report.

14.55 We urge consultees to engage with this work programme and respond to the consultation opportunities which are offered. If consultees have concerns which are not addressed in the consultation, we are happy to receive comments which we will pass to the relevant government agencies.

FIDUCIARY DUTIES IN THE REST OF THE INVESTMENT CHAIN

The debate

14.56 One of the key recommendations underpinning Professor Kay's ideas for reform was that non-excludable fiduciary standards should apply to all relationships in the investment chain which involve discretion over the investments of others or advice on investment decisions.[29] This view was shared by Lord Myners who conducted a similarly comprehensive review of investment problems. In his evidence to the BIS Select Committee, Lord Myners felt that intermediaries should have fiduciary responsibilities to the end client:

> We need to place great clarity around the concept of the intermediary – the adviser – acting wholly and unquestionably in the best interest of the client. At the moment, we know that is not the case. The test is one of fairness and disclosure, and Kay himself makes the point that in, for instance, the area of what he calls "stock lending", disclosure is inadequate... There needs to be clarity about fiduciary responsibility, backed up by a tough regulatory regime that says: if you misbehave, you are out – and out for good.[30]

---

[29] J Kay, *The Kay Review of UK Equity Markets and Long-Term Decision Making: Final Report* (2012) Recommendation 7.

[30] The Kay Review of Equity Markets and Long-Term Decision Making, Third Report of the Select Committee on Business, Innovation and Skills (2013-14) HC 603 at Ev 19.

14.57 Other stakeholders shared this view. In their response to our short paper, EIRIS[31] commented that "there is a mutual dependence along the chain of mediation and prudence and loyalty apply to most, if not all stages of the chain".[32] In her evidence to the BIS Select Committee, Anita Skipper of Aviva Investors stated that "the whole chain has to have the same sort of basis of duty, right through from the ultimate owner to the company".[33] Equally, Chris Hitchen, Chief Executive of the Railways Pension Trustee Company, felt that Government intervention was needed to apply fiduciary duty throughout the investment chain, noting:

> At the moment it applies at my end of the chain but it does not apply at the transactional end, and Government intervention may be required to prevent it being stopped from going down the chain by contractual arrangements.[34]

14.58 Others accepted that fiduciary duties should apply but thought that the duties should be subject to contractual modification. The IMA, in their written evidence to the BIS Select Committee, was clear that:

> As an agent, an asset manager has a fiduciary responsibility to its clients, as well as responsibilities derived both from contractual agreement and regulation. Combined with fee structures, these elements help to ensure that the manager acts in the client's best interest.[35]

14.59 However, they felt that parties should be free to limit the scope of their obligations in contract. They stated:

> We do not consider it would be sensible from the viewpoint of the UK's competitiveness to prohibit contractual modification of a range of, sometimes disputed, statements of fiduciary responsibility, developed through case law in many areas of business. It is essential that services can be tailored to the needs of global investors services from the UK, especially where the investor concerned has no interest in UK equity investment.[36]

---

[31] EIRIS is an international not-for-profit provider of research into corporate environmental, social and governance performance.

[32] EIRIS, Response to "Fiduciary Duties of Investment Intermediaries: Initial Questions" (July 2013).

[33] The Kay Review of Equity Markets and Long-Term Decision Making, Third Report of the Select Committee on Business, Innovation and Skills (2013-14) HC 603 at Ev 59.

[34] Above, at Ev 65.

[35] Above, at Ev 146.

[36] Above, at Ev 149.

14.60 Others also felt that there were difficulties in requiring other intermediaries in the investment chain to fulfil fiduciary obligations. In their response to our short paper, the Chartered Financial Analyst Society of the United Kingdom (CFA UK) felt that agents providing investment services were not subject to the same level of duty to the end investor as fiduciaries. They commented that "it would not be possible" for agents providing investment services to meet fiduciary duties because:

> Investment firms face conflicts on a daily basis. They are paid by their clients so profit from their position and act on behalf of more than one client so cannot meet an undivided loyalty rule.... It is only those that represent a single beneficiary that can and should meet the fiduciary standard.[37]

The current law

14.61 As we discuss in Chapter 11, the current law is very different from the position advocated by Professor Kay and Lord Myners. We reached four conclusions:

(1) The law is far from clear: the law of fiduciary duties is extremely flexible but also inherently uncertain.

(2) The courts look at the contract first, and interpret the parties' duties to each other in line with the contract. For example, if a contract between two apparently sophisticated parties states that a sale is made on an "execution only" basis, the courts will not go behind the contract to imply duties that the seller should act in the interests of the buyer.

(3) The courts are highly influenced by the regulatory regime. They are reluctant to go beyond the rules set out by Parliament and regulators.

(4) The courts are cautious in finding that those in the investment chain owe duties to others outside the immediate contractual or trust-based relationship. The classic case is *Caparo Industries v Dickman*,[38] where the House of Lords held that auditors owe duties only to the shareholders of the company which employs them as a body, and only for certain purposes: they have no duty of care to future investors.

Should the law of fiduciary duties be reformed generally?

14.62 We have considered whether there should be a general reform of the law of fiduciary duties to introduce more certain duties which cannot be excluded by contract. Our provisional view is that the law of fiduciary duties as such should not be reformed by statute. As we have seen, fiduciary duties are difficult to define and inherently flexible. We think that this is one of their essential characteristics: they form the background to other more definite duties, allowing the courts to intervene where the interests of justice require it.

---

[37] CFA UK, Response to "Fiduciary Duties of Investment Intermediaries: Initial Questions" (July 2013).

[38] [1990] 2 AC 605.

14.63   As we saw in Chapter 1, the uncertainty surrounding the definition of fiduciary duties led the Government to avoid using the word "fiduciary" to provide clarity to the debate.[39]   The difficulties of using the word fiduciary would multiply if one were to attempt statutory reform. Any attempt to change fiduciary duties through legislation would result in new uncertainties and could have unintended consequences, especially for trusts.

14.64   If there is a need for greater clarity in some areas, we think it would be better to enact specific duties rather than attempt to codify an area of law which has always depended on the facts of the case. We ask if consultees agree.

> Q18: Do consultees agree that the general law of fiduciary duties should not be reformed by statute?

An alternative right to sue?

14.65   There is an argument that where investors suffer loss as a result of the wrongful actions of others, they should be compensated for their loss. This, it is said, would introduce a new ethos into financial markets and deter poor behaviour.

14.66   We have considered whether there are any ways in which such a reform might be introduced, other than through the reform of fiduciary duties. We think that the simplest way would be to extend rights to sue for breach of statutory duty under section 138D of the Financial Markets and Services Act 2000. At present, rights are limited: only a private person can bring an action, and only for breach of certain rules.[40] The right could be extended to enable businesses to sue. It could also be extended to enable actions on the basis of the FCA Principles for Business. For example, Principle 6 states that:

> A firm must pay due regard to the interests of its customers and treat them fairly.

Market participants could be given the right to sue any firm which had caused them loss by breaching this principle.

14.67   On the other hand, there are strong arguments against such a change. In practice trustees are allowed considerable discretion and are rarely liable unless they have acted unreasonably or dishonestly. It is unclear what would be achieved in practice by applying a similar approach along the investment chain.

14.68   Nor would increased rights to sue necessarily prevent misbehaviour. Civil litigation is inherently uncertain, costly and slow. As we have seen, some cases may take a decade or more to resolve. There is a danger that litigation would introduce greater costs, risks and instability after the event. It may also encourage defensive rather than good behaviour.

---

[39]   Department for Business, Innovation and Skills, *Ensuring equity markets support long-term growth, The Government Response to the Kay Review* (2012) para 2.8.

[40]   See para 8.72 and following above.

14.69　The courts are particularly concerned about extending duties to others outside the immediate contractual or trust-based relationship. In *Caparo*, Lord Bridge counselled against the creation of "liability in an indeterminate amount for an indeterminate time to an indeterminate class".[41] Similarly, Lord Oliver was concerned about "a limitless vista of uninsurable risk".[42]

14.70　Our provisional conclusion is that there should be no statutory extension of rights to sue within financial markets. The effect of any such change would be uncertain and potentially disruptive. It would add substantially to costs in the chain, including insurance and legal costs. However, we would welcome views on this issue.

> Q19: Should rights to sue for breach of statutory duty under section 138D of the Financial Markets and Services Act 2000 be extended?

Strengthening FCA rules

14.71　We have not been asked to review the FCA Handbook. That is a mammoth undertaking, which lies outside our expertise and resources. Our project sits alongside Recommendation 7 of the Kay Review that:

> Regulatory authorities at EU and domestic level should apply fiduciary standards to all relationships in the investment chain which involve discretion over the investments of others, or advice on investment decisions.[43]

14.72　Nevertheless, our discussions with stakeholders emphasised the centrality of FCA regulation. Financial markets cannot function without good regulation. For example, the long term nature of pension funding means that it is impossible for scheme members or trustees to choose between products in the same way that they could choose between consumer durables. There were many areas in which stakeholders thought that current regulations were inadequate. As we discuss in Chapter 11, where the FCA rules impose clear duties, it is likely that the courts will interpret duties of care in line with these rules.

---

[41]　[1990] 2 AC 605 at 621, quoting Cardozo CJ in *Ultramares Corporation v Touche* (1931) 174 NE 441 (NY) at 444.

[42]　Above, at 643.

[43]　J Kay, *The Kay Review of UK Equity Markets and Long-Term Decision Making: Final Report* (2012) Recommendation 7.

14.73   There are two issues where we seek views: the regulation of investment consultants and custodians. It is not our responsibility to recommend changes to FCA rules, but we will pass the responses we receive to BIS and the FCA for their consideration. We have not asked about investment managers' fees as the FCA is already conducting a thematic review.[44] Nor do we ask about the Stewardship Code, as the Financial Reporting Council is currently reviewing the implementation of the Code.[45]

Investment consultants

14.74   As we discuss in Chapter 12, stakeholders expressed concern about the apparent lack of regulation of investment consultants. Investment consultants appear not to fall within the FCA regulatory regime so long as they only give "generic advice".[46] Questions were raised about potential conflicts of interest, so that an investment consultant's advice may not be independent. Instead, there is the possibility that the advice might be coloured by a particularly close relationship with an investment manager or the presence of an in-house offering. We conclude that the law on this issue is unclear.

> Q20: Is there a need to review the regulation of investment consultants?

Custodians

14.75   Today securities are often held electronically and indirectly. Shares are held through a chain of intermediaries. Instead of "owning" a share certificate, the investor is registered on the computer system of an intermediary, who in turn is registered on the computer system of a higher level custodian. The job of a custodian is simple: to hold the asset safely and to account for its ownership correctly. The world's financial markets depend on custodians carrying out this function honestly and efficiently. Two questions were raised about the role of custodians.

---

[44]   See para 12.40 above.

[45]   Financial Reporting Council, *Additional information on the Stewardship Code*, available at http://www.frc.org.uk/Our-Work/Codes-Standards/Corporate-governance/UK-Stewardship-Code/Background.aspx.

[46]   See paras 8.20-8.21 above.

THE LEGAL FRAMEWORK

14.76 The first question concerns the legal framework under which intermediated shares are held. In the past there has been some debate over the legal relationship that governs this ownership structure. It can be viewed as either a back-to-back chain of creditor debtor relationships, or as a series of trusts, where each tier holds an interest for the benefit of those in the tier below.[47] It now seems settled that the arrangement is trust-based, which protects the investor's interest if one party in the chain becomes insolvent. However, some areas of uncertainty remain.[48]

14.77 In October 2009, UNIDROIT produced a convention on the underlying law of intermediated securities.[49] From 2006 to 2008, the Law Commission analysed successive drafts of the convention. We advised the UK Government to sign and ratify the convention to bring legal clarity at an international level.[50] However, the UNIDROIT Convention has not been ratified by any country. Similarly, whilst the European Commission has also been looking at the issue, no legislative proposals have yet been published. We are interested to know whether the law in this area needs to be reviewed to ensure that it is fit for purpose.

> Q21: Is there a need to review the law of intermediated shareholdings?

STOCK LENDING

14.78 The main controversy affecting custodians relates to stock lending. This is where custodians lend the client's investment to a third party, typically to enable the borrower to sell short. This introduces a risk that the borrower may default, though the custodian may obtain collateral to guard against this. Where there is an appropriate term in the contract, the custodian is entitled to retain the fee rather than rebating it to the client. Professor Kay recommended that "all income from stock lending should be disclosed and rebated to investors".[51]

> Q22: Should the FCA review the regulation of stock lending by custodians?

---

[47] See R McCormick, *Legal Risk in the Financial Markets* (1st ed 2006) paras 7.17-7.40; M Yates and G Montagu, *The Law of Global Custody* (4th ed 2013) paras 5.62-5.67.

[48] For the Law Commission's analysis of the law in this area, see Law Commission, *The UNIDROIT Convention on Substantive Rules regarding Intermediated Securities: Further Updated Advice to HM Treasury* (2008).

[49] See UNIDROIT Convention on Substantive Rules for Intermediated Securities 2009.

[50] Law Commission, *The UNIDROIT Convention on Substantive Rules regarding Intermediated Securities: Further Updated Advice to HM Treasury* (2008).

[51] J Kay, *The Kay Review of UK Equity Markets and Long-Term Decision Making: Final Report* (2012) Recommendation 10.

CHAPTER 15
LIST OF QUESTIONS

We would like comments and responses on the following.

PENSION TRUSTEES' DUTIES TO ACT IN THE BEST INTERESTS OF BENEFICIARIES

Question 1 Do consultees agree that Chapter 10 represents a correct statement of the current law? (14.6)

Question 2 Do consultees agree that the law reflects an appropriate understanding of beneficiaries' best interests? (14.11)

Question 3 Do consultees think that the law is sufficiently certain? (14.15)

Question 4 Should the Occupational Pension Scheme (Investment) Regulations 2005 be extended to all trust-based pension schemes? (14.15)

Question 5 Are there any specific areas where the law would benefit from statutory clarification? (14.15)

Question 6 Do consultees agree that the law permits a sufficient diversity of strategies? (14.21)

Question 7 Do consultees agree that the main pressures towards short-termism are not caused by the duty to invest in beneficiaries' best interests? (14.24)

Question 8 Do consultees agree that the law is right to allow trustees to consider ethical issues only in limited circumstances? (14.28)

Question 9 Does the law encourage excessive diversification? (14.32)

Question 10 Does the law encourage trustees to achieve the right balance of risk and return? (14.32)

Question 11 Are there any systemic areas of trustees' investment strategies which pose undue risks? (14.32)

Question 12 Overall, do consultees think that the legal obligations on trustees are conducive to investment strategies in the best interests of the ultimate beneficiaries? (14.33)

Question 13 If not, what specifically needs to be changed? (14.33)

FIDUCIARY-TYPE DUTIES IN CONTRACT-BASED PENSION SCHEMES

Question 14 Do consultees agree that the duties on contract-based pension providers to act in the interests of scheme members should be clarified and strengthened? (14.42)

Question 15 Should specific duties be placed on pension providers to review the suitability of investment strategies over time? If so, how often should these reviews take place? (14.42)

Question 16 Should members of Independent Governance Committees be subject to explicit legal duties to act in the interests of scheme members? (14.42)

Question 17 Should pension providers be obliged to indemnify members of Independent Governance Committees for liabilities incurred in the course of their duties? (14.42)

FIDUCIARY DUTIES IN THE REST OF THE INVESTMENT CHAIN

Question 18 Do consultees agree that the general law of fiduciary duties should not be reformed by statute? (14.61)

Question 19 Should rights to sue for breach of statutory duty under section 138D of the Financial Markets and Services Act 2000 be extended? (14.67)

Question 20 Is there a need to review the regulation of investment consultants? (14.71)

Question 21 Is there a need to review the law of intermediated shareholdings? (14.74)

Question 22 Should the FCA review the regulation of stock lending by custodians? (14.75)

APPENDIX A
TERMS OF REFERENCE

A.1 On 26 March 2013 the Law Commission received a reference from the Secretary of State for Business, Innovation and Skills in the following terms:

(1) To investigate the extent to which, under existing law, fiduciary duties apply to:

(a) Intermediaries (including investment managers and pension scheme trustees) investing on behalf of others;

(b) those providing advice or other services to those undertaking investment activity.

(2) To evaluate what fiduciary duties permit or require such persons to consider when developing or discharging an investment strategy in the best interests of the ultimate beneficiaries: in particular, the extent to which fiduciaries may, or must, consider:

(a) factors relevant to long-term investment performance which might not have an immediate financial impact, including questions of sustainability or environmental and social impact;

(b) interests beyond the maximisation of financial return;

(c) generally prevailing ethical standards, and / or the ethical views of their beneficiaries, even where this may not be in the immediate financial interest of those beneficiaries;

(3) To consult relevant stakeholders in the equity investment chain on their understanding of what the content and application of fiduciary duties in this context is, or should be, and to consider their responses;

(4) To consider whether fiduciary duties, as established in law or as applied in practice, are conducive to investment strategies that are in the best interests of the ultimate beneficiaries. In particular, to consider whether the duties:

(a) reflect an appropriate understanding of the scope of beneficiaries' best interests;

(b) are sufficiently certain in content and application to market participants;

(c) permit sufficient diversity of strategy;

(d) sufficiently encourage long-term investment strategy and consideration of factors which might impact on long-term investment performance;

(e)   allow fiduciaries to invest in line with generally prevailing ethical standards, and / or the ethical views of their beneficiaries, even where this may not be in the immediate financial interest of those beneficiaries;

(f)   require a sufficient balance of risk and benefit; and

(g)   are sufficiently balanced against each other.

(5)   To identify any areas where changes to fiduciary duties are needed in relation to these criteria and to make recommendations.

APPENDIX B
CONSUMER REDRESS

B.1   In this Appendix we describe three avenues of redress for individuals who have a problem with their pension: the Financial Ombudsman Scheme, the Pensions Ombudsman and the Financial Conduct Authority's consumer redress schemes.

FINANCIAL OMBUDSMAN SERVICE (FOS)

B.2   The FOS is a statutory dispute resolution scheme set up under the Financial Services and Markets Act 2000 (FSMA).[1] It aims to resolve disputes between businesses providing financial services and consumers, quickly and informally. It is funded in part from an industry levy and in part from recovery of standard and special case fees payable by firms where a complaint is referred to it.[2]

Who can bring a complaint?

B.3   The FOS exists to protect consumers and very small businesses, together with small charities and other trusts. The following can bring complaints to the FOS:

(1)   a consumer;

(2)   a micro-enterprise which employs fewer than 10 persons and which has a turnover or annual balance sheet that does not exceed €2 million;

(3)   a charity with an annual income of less than £1 million; and

(4)   a trustee of a trust which has a net asset value of less than £1 million.[3]

B.4   Generally parties classified as "professional clients" by their broker cannot bring a complaint to the FOS by the terms of their brokerage agreement. Faced with such a classification, the FOS will consider whether the consumer was appropriately classified.[4]

---

[1]   Financial Services and Markets Act 2000, s 225(1).

[2]   *McMeel and Virgo on Financial Advice and Financial Products: Law and Liability* (Release 10 2012) para X.2.22.

[3]   FCA Handbook DISP 2.7.3R.

[4]   Financial Ombudsman Service, *Online technical resource: stocks and shares,* http://www.financial-ombudsman.org.uk/publications/technical_notes/stocks-and-shares.htm (last visited 30 September 2013).

Who may complaints be brought against?

B.5 The Ombudsman can consider a complaint under its compulsory jurisdiction if it relates to an act or omission by a firm in carrying on one or more specified activities.[5] For pension matters, there is a clear potential for overlap with the Pensions Ombudsman. In a Memorandum of Understanding, the FOS has said that it deals with matters which predominantly concern advice in respect of the sale or marketing of individual pension arrangements.[6] Meanwhile, the Pensions Ombudsman deals with complaints of maladministration against those responsible for managing occupational or personal pension schemes.

How are complaints decided?

B.6 The FOS is not bound by strict law. Instead, the complaint is determined "by reference to what is, in the opinion of the ombudsman, fair and reasonable in all the circumstances of the case".[7] Further, the award against the respondent may be of "such amount as the ombudsman considers fair compensation for loss or damage… suffered by the complainant.[8]

B.7 In determining what is fair and reasonable in all the circumstances, the Ombudsman is required to take into account the following:

(1)   the relevant law;

(2)   regulations;

(3)   regulators' rules, guidance and standards;

(4)   relevant codes of practice; and

(5)   where appropriate, what the Ombudsman considers to have been good industry practice at the relevant times.[9]

---

[5]   FCA Handbook DISP 2.3.1R. The list of specified activities includes regulated activities (other than auction regulation bidding), as defined in the Financial Services and Markets Act 2000 (Regulated Activities) Order 2001 SI 2001 No 544.

[6]   Memorandum of Understanding between the Pensions Ombudsman and the Financial Ombudsman Service (21 May 2013), available at http://www.financialombudsman.org.uk/publications/pdf/memorandum-of-understanding.pdf.

[7]   Financial Services and Markets Act 2000, s 228(2).

[8]   Financial Services and Markets Act 2000, s 229.

[9]   FCA Handbook DISP 3.6.4R.

The monetary limit

B.8 The FOS may require firms to pay awards of up to £150,000.[10] For larger sums, it may recommend higher awards, but may not require payment of any sum in excess of the limit.[11] The FOS has recently expressed concern that £150,000 is too low for some pensions disputes:

> The amount of money at stake in pension disputes is also often substantial. Although we can now tell a business to pay a maximum of £150,000 compensation to an individual consumer – for new complaints we received from 1 January 2012 – some complaints involve substantially more money than this. Businesses may agree to settle any *recommendation* we make above this level – but the recommendation itself is not legally binding on them.[12]

The FOS in practice

B.9 The FOS deals with a large and growing caseload. In the year up to March 2012, there were 264,375 new cases;[13] in the year to March 2013, this rose to 508,881.[14] Of these, 4% of complaints were about investments and pensions, amounting to 19,834 complaints - an increase of a third from the previous year.[15] The breakdown of these cases is shown below.

Figure B.1: Complaints to the FOS relating to investments and pensions (2012/13).

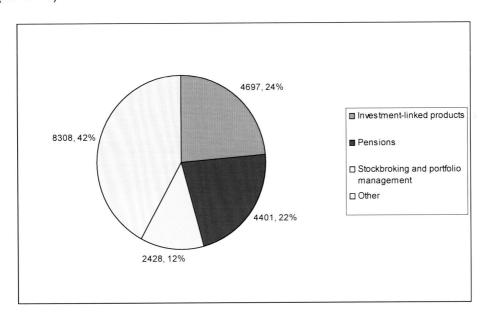

Source: FOS, Annual review of consumer complaints about insurance, credit, banking, savings, investment (financial year 2012/2013).

[10] FCA Handbook DISP 3.7.4R.

[11] FSMA 2000, s 229(5).

[12] Financial Ombudsman Service, *Annual review of consumer complaints about: insurance, credit, banking, savings and investment* (financial year 2012/2013) p 71.

[13] Above, p 33.

[14] Above, p 33.

[15] Above, p 68.

B.10 In their 2012/13 Annual review, the FOS noted that disputes were becoming "more entrenched" and "legalistic".[16] Many involved customers who had invested in products carrying greater levels of risk than described:

> During the year we continued to see a significant number of complaints where an investment product was recommended that carried a level of risk that did not suit the consumer concerned. These disputes often involved disagreement between the business and the consumer about how the consumer's attitude to investment risk had been categorised at the point of sale.[17]

B.11 Of the complaints that concerned pensions, 55% of complaints were brought against life insurance and investment product providers, 21% were brought against IFAs and 9% were brought against banks.[18] The FOS noted that pension disputes were difficult to resolve: they are more likely to require an ombudsman's final decision, the last stage of the complaints process, than complaints about any other financial product.[19]

THE PENSIONS OMBUDSMAN (TPO)

B.12 The Pension Ombudsman's role is to investigate and determine disputes of fact or law or complaints of sustained injustice in consequence of maladministration by those responsible for managing occupational or personal pension schemes.[20] There is no statutory definition of maladministration; TPO notes that the term has been said to involve "bias, neglect, inattention, delay, incompetence, ineptitude, perversity, turpitude, arbitrariness and so on".[21]

B.13 TPO deals with fewer cases than the FOS. In 2012/13, it received 2,766 new enquiries, of which 1,074 were accepted for investigation.[22] Complaints about entitlement to an ill health pension benefit were the highest single cause of complaint, amounting to 11% of completed complaints.[23]

---

[16] Financial Ombudsman Service, *Annual review of consumer complaints about: insurance, credit, banking, savings and investment* (financial year 2012/2013) p 75.

[17] Above, p 69.

[18] Above, p 135.

[19] Above, p 71.

[20] Pension Schemes Act 1993, s 146.

[21] Pensions Ombudsman and Pension Protection Fund Ombudsman, *How he can help you* (2007) p 5.

[22] Pensions Ombudsman and Pension Protection Fund Ombudsman, *Annual Report and Accounts 2012/13* (2013) p 9.

[23] Above, p 16.

B.14 Complaints may be made by, amongst others, actual or potential beneficiaries of occupational or personal pension schemes.[24] These include members of the scheme; the widow, widower, surviving civil partner or any surviving dependant of a deceased member of the scheme; and a person who is entitled to a pension credit as against the trustees or managers of the scheme.[25]

B.15 TPO has noted that automatic enrolment has not affected its workload. However, it expects that it will do so over time as more people become members of pension schemes.[26]

B.16 A Memorandum of Understanding exists between the FOS and TPO.[27] TPO deals predominantly with matters concerning the administration and/or management of personal and occupational pensions. On the other hand, the FOS deals primarily with matters concerning the advice and marketing of individual pension arrangements.

B.17 Where a complaint or dispute is received by one of these bodies and appears better suited to the other, the receiving ombudsman will seek the consent of the complainant before transferring it to the other body. Where it is unclear which of the two bodies is the appropriate one to handle the complaint, the FSO and TPO will consult and liaise on how best to handle the complaint. In 2012/13, 3% of enquiries to TPO were referred to the Financial Conduct Authority (FCA) or FOS.[28]

FCA CONSUMER REDRESS SCHEMES

B.18 In 1994 the industry regulator ordered a review of sales of personal pension policies. This review has been described as a "prototype" for section 404 of FSMA, which authorised the FCA to establish a scheme directing firms to review past business.[29] These provisions have been replaced by the Financial Services Act 2010, which now allows the FCA to establish "consumer redress schemes".[30]

B.19 The FCA may establish a consumer redress scheme if:

(1) It appears to the FCA that there may have been a widespread or regular failure by relevant firms to comply with requirements applicable to the carrying on by them of any activity.

---

[24] Pension Schemes Act 1993, s 146(1).

[25] Pension Schemes Act 1993, s 146(7).

[26] Pensions Ombudsman and Pension Protection Fund Ombudsman, *Annual Report and Accounts 2012/13* (2013) p 11.

[27] Memorandum of Understanding between the Pensions Ombudsman and the Financial Ombudsman Service (21 May 2013), http://www.financialombudsman.org.uk/publications/pdf/memorandum-of-understanding.pdf.

[28] Pensions Ombudsman and Pension Protection Fund Ombudsman, *Annual Report and Accounts 2012/13* (2013) p 11.

[29] *McMeel and Virgo on Financial Advice and Financial Products: Law and Liability* (Release 10 2012) para X.2.123.

[30] Financial Services and Markets Act 2000, s 404, as inserted by the Financial Services Act 2010, s 14.

(2)   It appears to the FCA that, as a result of this failure to comply, consumers have suffered (or may suffer) loss or damage in respect of which, if they brought legal proceedings, a remedy or relief would be available in the proceedings.

(3)   The FCA considers that it is desirable to make rules for the purpose of securing that redress is made to the consumers in respect of the failure (having regard to other ways in which consumers may obtain redress).[31]

B.20   Under a consumer redress scheme a firm is required to take one or more of the following steps in relation to the relevant activity:

(1)   The firm must investigate whether, on or after a specified date, it has failed to comply with the requirements that are applicable to the carrying on by it of the relevant activity.

(2)   The firm must determine whether the failure has caused (or may cause) loss or damage to consumers.

(3)   If the firm determines that the failure has caused (or may cause) loss or damage to consumers, it must then determine what the redress should be in respect of the failure and make the redress to the consumers.[32]

B.21   Consumer redress schemes are also binding on the FOS in an important respect. If a consumer makes a complaint to the FOS in respect of an act or omission of a firm and, at the time the complaint is made, the subject-matter of the complaint falls to be dealt with (or has been dealt with) under a consumer redress scheme, then the FOS must determine the complaint by reference to what, in its opinion, the consumer redress scheme would have provided.[33]

---

[31] Financial Services and Markets Act 2000, ss 404(1)(a)-(c), as inserted by the Financial Services Act 2010, s 14.

[32] Financial Services and Markets Act 2000, ss 404(4)-(7), as inserted by the Financial Services Act 2010, s 14.

[33] Financial Services and Markets Act 2000, s 404B(4), as inserted by the Financial Services Act 2010, s 14.

APPENDIX C
FIDUCIARY LAW IN AUSTRALIA: A PAPER BY CLAYTON UTZ

This paper was commissioned by the Law Commission from Clayton Utz, a leading Australian law firm. It provides a background to the Australian occupational pensions (or "superannuation") market and explains the role of fiduciary duties. We have drawn on this throughout our Paper, particularly in relation to the problems with contract-based pensions in England and Wales.

GLOSSARY

Australian Prudential Regulation Authority (APRA)

Supervises superannuation funds and issues RSE Licences.

Australian Securities and Investments Commission (ASIC)

Responsible for consumer protection and market integrity, including in the area of superannuation. Also issues Australian Financial Services Licenses (AFSLs).

Complying superannuation fund

A superannuation fund which complies with the SIS Act and SIS Regulations.

Financial Services Council (FSC)

Publishes Standards and Guidance Notes for investment funds.

Funds under management (FUM)

This may refer to the total value of all superannuation funds or to the assets being managed under a single superannuation fund.

Investment management agreement (IMA)

An agreement governing the relationship between superannuation trustees and any investment managers.

MySuper product

A complying superannuation fund which meets certain further legislative criteria.

Regulated Superannuation Entity (RSE)

A superannuation entity regulated by APRA.

Self-managed super fund (SMSF)

One of five types of superannuation fund, with fewer than five members.

Superannuation guarantee charge (SGC)

A special tax levied on employers who fail to make superannuation contributions to a complying superannuation fund.

Stronger Super reforms

Reform of the superannuation industry, given effect on 1 July 2013.

Superannuation Industry (Supervision) Act 1993 (SIS Act) and **Superannuation Industry (Supervision) Regulations 1994 (SIS Regulations)**

Collectively, this is the key legislation governing the superannuation industry.

Superannuation Prudential Standards (SPS)

Legally binding prudential standards issued by APRA under the SIS Act.

1. Introduction

Australia's system of superannuation effectively requires employers to pay a specified proportion of employees' earnings into a "complying" superannuation fund. A complying superannuation fund, among other characteristics, has a trust structure, is maintained solely for the purpose of providing retirement or death benefits and is bound by the *Superannuation Industry (Supervision) Act* 1993 (**SIS Act**) and *Superannuation Industry (Supervision) Regulations* 1994 (**SIS Regulations**), the key legislation governing the superannuation industry.

Superannuation funds that are "public offer" funds can offer membership to anyone who may wish to join. Employees are entitled to choose the superannuation fund which receives contributions made on their behalf and may transfer their entitlements from one fund to another. Employers must choose a default fund in the event that an employee does not make an election.

Employers who fail to make contributions to complying superannuation funds on behalf of their employees are subject to a special tax known as the superannuation guarantee charge (**SGC**). This effectively makes employer contributions compulsory. The required contribution as of 1 July 2013 is 9.25% of "ordinary time earnings". This figure is scheduled to rise gradually to 12% by 2019.

Prior to introduction of the SGC twenty years ago, defined-benefit schemes were the prevalent form of superannuation fund in Australia. However, the vast majority of assets accumulated since the introduction of the SGC are held in defined-contribution funds (generally referred to in Australia as "accumulation" funds). Most former defined-benefit funds have become "hybrid" funds, only accepting contributions to the accumulation section of the fund. A dwindling proportion of superannuation funds in Australia is held in pure defined-benefit schemes.

There is thus a comprehensive system of private retirement accounts in Australia, underpinned by a system of compulsory contributions and with virtually all of the $1.6 trillion of funds under management (**FUM**) held in trust.

Regulation of the superannuation industry in Australia has recently been the subject of substantial reform. Legislative changes and other rules effecting the reforms, collectively known as Stronger Super, took effect on 1 July 2013. They were preceded by a major federal government review of the superannuation system which issued its final report in June 2010 (widely known as the "Cooper report", after Jeremy Cooper, former Deputy Chairman of the Australian Securities and Investments Commission (**ASIC**), who headed the review).[1] Many of the Cooper report's recommendations were incorporated into Stronger Super.

2. Composition of the superannuation industry

The superannuation industry in Australia is divided into five main segments, which together account for over 97% of FUM.[2]

Retail funds operate on a commercial basis. They offer superannuation products to the general public and usually form part of a larger banking or wealth management conglomerate. Retail funds account for 26.3% of FUM.

Industry funds operate for the benefit of employees working in a particular industry, although increasingly these funds open themselves to the general public as well. Industry funds are generally not-for-profit. They account for 19.8% of FUM.

---

[1] Australian Government, "Super System Review – Final Report" (June 2012).

[2] APRA Statistics, *Quarterly Superannuation Performance*, March 2013.

Corporate funds are set up to service employees of a single employer entity or corporate group. Corporate funds account for 3.8% of FUM.

Public sector funds operate pursuant to Commonwealth, State or Territory Acts which set up the funds for the benefit of public sector employees. Public sector funds account for 15.7% of FUM.

Self-managed super funds (SMSFs) have fewer than five members, and each member is also a trustee of the fund or a director of the corporate trustee. SMSFs account for 31.5% of FUM.

The composition of the Australian superannuation industry is in a state of rapid evolution. Excluding SMSFs, the number of non-public offer funds decreased by 95 per cent from 3,329 to 160 funds over the twelve years to June 2012.[3] The majority of these funds were corporate funds that exited the industry. During the same period, the number of public offer funds decreased by 63 per cent from 481 to 176.[4] Industry observer Rice Warner predicts a further 50% reduction in the number of funds by 2017.[5]

Continued consolidation of superannuation funds is driven, in part, by legislative changes taking effect on 1 July 2013 that implement the federal government's Stronger Super reforms of the superannuation industry. One intended consequence of the changes is to drive consolidation among superannuation funds. The government expects that fund members will benefit from the increased economies of scale that flow from consolidation.

As at June 2012, the largest twenty superannuation funds by assets comprised ten retail, six industry, one corporate and three public sector funds, accounting for 57.3% of total FUM.[6]

At the same time as consolidation among funds with more than four members, there has been a very substantial increase in the number of SMSFs. The proportion of total FUM held in SMSFs increased from 30.9% in March 2012 to 31.5% in March 2013.[7] During the same period the total number of SMSFs in operation increased from 469,102 to 503,320.[8] This continued the trend of the preceding decade.

SMSFs are regulated by the Taxation Commissioner but are not subject to prudential supervision. Many SIS Act and SIS Regulations rules apply differently to SMSFs. In considering the application of fiduciary law within the superannuation industry, this paper limits itself to consideration of retail, industry, corporate and public sector funds. The following sections do not take account of the law relating to SMSFs.

3.   Regulation of superannuation funds

Under the *Income Tax Assessment Act 1997* concessional tax treatment is available to a "complying" superannuation fund. The SIS Act and SIS Regulations set out the requirements applicable to a complying superannuation fund. Significantly, a complying superannuation fund is required to have a trust structure and to make an irrevocable election to be bound by the SIS Act.

---

[3] APRA Statistics, *Annual Superannuation Bulletin*, June 2012.

[4] Ibid.

[5] Rice Warner Actuaries, *Superannuation Market Projections Report 2012*, December 2012.

[6] APRA, "Superannuation industry overview", *APRA Insight*, No 1 of 2013.

[7] APRA Statistics, *Quarterly Superannuation Performance*, March 2013.

[8] Ibid.

Non-complying superannuation funds are taxed on a non-concessional basis and therefore subject to substantially higher rates of tax.

In this way, and including the SGC levied on employers who do not make contribution on behalf of their employees to complying superannuation funds, taxation laws underpin the existence of a large, compulsory superannuation industry consisting of funds that comply with the requirements of the SIS Act and SIS Regulations.[9]

With the exception of certain public sector funds, superannuation funds are subject to licensing and prudential supervision by the Australian Prudential Regulation Authority (**APRA**). All trustees operating an APRA-regulated superannuation entity (**RSE**) must hold an RSE Licence issued by APRA (with the exception of trustees operating public sector superannuation schemes). An RSE licensee must register any RSE of which it is trustee. RSE licensing requirements are prudentially focused.

Although the SIS Act, SIS Regulations and Prudential Standards use the terminology "RSE licensee" and "RSE", this paper uses the more familiar terms "trustee" and "superannuation fund".

The Australian Securities and Investments Commission (**ASIC**) is responsible for consumer protection and market integrity across the financial system, including in the area of superannuation, and administers the *Corporations Act 2001* (**Corporations Act**) rules relating to disclosure by superannuation funds. ASIC also administers the system of Australian Financial Services Licenses (**AFSLs**). Most superannuation trustees are thus required to be licensed by both APRA and ASIC.

From 1 July 2013, superannuation funds subject to the prudential supervision of APRA are required to comply with the Superannuation Prudential Standards made by APRA under the SIS Act.

Prudential standards are intended to improve the clarity and certainty of prudential regulation by providing legally binding additional detail on the prudential matters set out in the SIS Act. Under the enabling provisions of the SIS Act, the prudential standards may be drafted to grant APRA powers and discretions to, among other things, approve, impose, adjust or exclude specific prudential requirements in relation to specific licensees or their subsidiaries.[10]

The prudential standards issued by APRA create rules and reporting obligations relating, among other things, to outsourcing, fitness and propriety, conflicts of interest and investment governance.[11] An entity licensed by APRA as a superannuation trustee must comply with the prudential standards as a condition of the licence.[12] APRA has enforcement powers relating to licence conditions.[13]

APRA also issues Prudential Practice Guides that provide greater detail as to how APRA expects industry participants to comply with the prudential requirements that are placed on them.

4. Overarching rules relating to investment of superannuation assets

The context of investment governance in the superannuation industry is limited by a number of SIS Act rules that limit the activities of superannuation funds. Key rules include the following.

---

[9] Certain public sector funds may also be complying superannuation funds even if not bound by the SIS Act.

[10] Section 34C(5) of the SIS Act.

[11] Prudential Standards SPS 231, 520, 521 and 530, respectively.

[12] Sections 10(1) and 29E(1)(a) of the SIS Act.

[13] See Part 2A of the SIS Act.

4.1   Sole purpose test

Section 62 of the SIS Act requires the trustee of a superannuation fund to ensure that the fund is maintained solely for one or more "core purposes". If the trustee wishes, the fund can also be administered for one or more "ancillary purposes".

Core purposes include the provision of benefits upon retirement; attainment of age 65 (this age is specified in SIS Regulation 13.18); or death prior to retirement or attainment of age 65.

Ancillary purposes include the provision of benefits upon termination of employment; cessation of employment due to ill health; death after retirement or attainment of age 65; or other benefits approved by APRA.

4.2   Concept of "investment"

"Investment" has a wide meaning in the SIS Act. An "asset" means any form of property and, to avoid doubt, includes money in any currency.[14] To "invest" means to apply assets in any way, or make a contract, for the purpose of gaining interest, income, profit or gain.[15]

4.3   Borrowing

Section 67 of the SIS Act provides that the trustee of a superannuation fund must not borrow money except in limited circumstances. One such circumstance is a temporary borrowing to cover settlement of securities transactions. Here the duration of the borrowing cannot exceed seven days and the total amount borrowed must not exceed 10% of the value of the assets of the fund.

The most important exception to the borrowing prohibition permits some limited recourse borrowing arrangements.[16] Such an arrangement must fit within the precise terms of the exception, including the requirement that the borrowed money is applied to a "single acquirable asset".

A related prohibition is SIS Regulation 13.14 which provides that the trustee of a superannuation fund must not give a charge over, or in relation to, an asset of the fund. SIS Regulation 13.11 defines "charge" to include "a mortgage, lien or other encumbrance."

These prohibitions do not prevent superannuation funds from investing in geared unit trusts or companies. Many large superannuation funds invest in property or infrastructure assets via special purpose companies or trusts that acquire assets with the assistance of borrowed funds. It is also common practice for a consortium of superannuation funds to pool funds into a special purpose company or trust for this purpose.

5.   General trust law and the trust deed

General trust law and the provisions of the applicable trust deed, in addition to the legislation and prudential standards governing superannuation funds, provide the rules governing the operation of a superannuation fund, including investment.

---

[14] Section 10(1) of the SIS Act.

[15] Ibid.

[16] Section 67A of the SIS Act.

5.1   Investment covenants

Section 52 of the SIS Act sets out certain covenants that the trustee of a superannuation fund must comply with in administering the trust. These covenants are binding and if the governing rules of the fund do not contain them, then they are deemed to be contained in the fund's rules (that is, in the trust deed).[17] There are general covenants, investment covenants, insurance covenants and covenants related to risk.

In many instances, the covenants restate principles of equity and trust law, including certain fiduciary duties applicable to trustees. To the extent that they do so, the section 52 covenants ensure that superannuation trustees are subject to ordinary trustees' duties irrespective of anything else in the trust deed, and that they are accountable in this respect both to the beneficiaries of the fund and to APRA.

The investment covenants are as follows:[18]

(a)   to formulate, review regularly and give effect to an investment strategy for the whole of the entity, and for each investment option offered by the trustee in the entity, having regard to:

(i)   the risk involved in making, holding and realising, and the likely return from, the investments covered by the strategy, having regard to the trustee's objectives in relation to the strategy and to the expected cash flow requirements in relation to the entity; and

(ii)   to the composition of the investments covered by the strategy, including the extent to which the investments are diverse or involve the entity in being exposed to risks from inadequate diversification; and

(iii)   the liquidity of the investments covered by the strategy having regard to the expected cash flow requirement in relation to the entity;

(iv)   whether reliable valuation information is available in relation to the investments covered by the strategy;

(v)   the ability of the entity to discharge its existing and prospective liabilities;

(vi)   the expected tax consequences for the entity in relation to the investments covered by the strategy;

(vii)   the costs that might be incurred by the entity in relation to the investments covered by the strategy; and

(viii)   any other relevant matters;

(b)   to exercise due diligence in developing, offering and regularly reviewing each investment option;

---

[17] Section 52(1) of the SIS Act

[18] Section 52(6) of the SIS Act.

(c)   to ensure the investment options offered to each beneficiary allow adequate diversification.

The Stronger Super reforms expanded and added detail to these investment covenants. The covenant to formulate an investment strategy for each investment option – not just for the entity – is new. Sub-paragraphs (iv), (vi), (vii) and (viii) of covenant (a) are also new, as are covenants (b) and (c).

In many instances, the investment management and custodial functions in relation to a superannuation fund are outsourced to separate entities. These entities generally do not owe fiduciary obligations directly to the members of the fund (see section 8 below). The policy of the expanded and enhanced investment covenants appears to be to ensure that trustees themselves take an interest and satisfy themselves in relation to the enumerated matters, which include the need to regularly review investment options and to ensure adequate diversification is available to members. APRA's Prudential Standards require the board of directors of an incorporated superannuation trustee to be actively involved in consideration of the fund's investment strategies.[19]

Certain of the investment covenants address specific matters bearing on investment decision-making. For example, under sub-paragraph (iv) of investment covenant (a) trustees would need to consider the risk associated with holding unlisted assets that may become illiquid and difficult to value. Under sub-paragraph (vi), trustees must consider after-tax returns and require their investment managers to manage superannuation fund mandates in a tax-aware manner. Shortcomings of industry practice in relation to these matters, or the risks of such, were identified in the report of the Cooper review.[20]

5.2   Investment covenants, the duty of caution and the defence under section 55(5) of the SIS Act

In addition to the investment covenants set out in the SIS Act, a trustee investing trust funds is under a duty to exercise "such care as an ordinary prudent man would take if he were minded to make an investment for the benefit of other people for whom he felt morally bound to provide."[21] This "prudent person rule" incorporates a duty that is often referred to as the duty of caution or the duty not to speculate. This duty, or a version of it, is arguably reflected in the second of the "general covenants" set out in the SIS Act:

> to exercise, in relation to all matters affecting the entity, the same degree of care, skill and diligence as a prudent superannuation trustee would exercise in relation to an entity of which it is trustee and on behalf of the beneficiaries of which it makes investments.[22]

---

[19] Prudential Standard SPS 530.

[20] Australian Government, "Super System Review – Final Report – Part Two" (June 2012) Chapters 3.5 and 3.6.

[21] *Re Whiteley* (1886) 33 Ch D 347 at 355 per Lindley LJ.

[22] Section 52(2)(b) of the SIS Act. A "prudent superannuation trustee" is a person whose profession, business or employment is or includes acting as a trustee of a superannuation entity and investing money on behalf of beneficiaries of the superannuation entity: section 52(3). Prior to 1 July 2013, this covenant referred only to "an ordinary prudent person ... dealing with property of another for whom the person felt morally bound to provide." As such, it is based more directly on the duty of caution as expressed by Lindley LJ in *Re Whiteley*. The current test, importing the standard to be expected of a "prudent superannuation trustee", applies to all matters affecting the trustee entity a higher standard previously applicable to the exercise of trustees' investment powers by virtue of State and Territory trustee legislation (e.g. *Trustee Act 1925* (NSW) s 14A), and subject to contrary provision in the trust deed. This higher statutory test reflects the development of the general law duty of care applicable to professional trustees: *Bartlett v Barclays Bank Trust Co Ltd (No 1)* [1980] Ch 515 at 534; *Australian Securities Commission v AS Nominees Ltd* (1995) 133 ALR 1 at

Prior to Stronger Super, section 55(5) of the SIS Act provided that, in an action for loss or damage suffered by a person as a result of the making of an investment by or on behalf of a trustee, the defendant had a defence if it could demonstrate compliance with the investment covenants. This left unclear the role of the general law duty of caution and its corresponding general covenant in relation to investment of superannuation assets. From 1 July 2013, section 55(5) was amended to provide that the statutory defence requires demonstrated compliance with *all* of the SIS Act covenants that have relevance to the claim.

This amendment to section 55(5) appears to re-establish, in the context of an action for loss on an investment, a clear role for the duty of caution in relation to the investment of superannuation assets. Few such actions have been run since the introduction of the SIS Act regime. It remains to be seen whether this changes as a result of the amendment to the conditions of the statutory defence.

5.3 General covenants

General covenants under section 52 of the SIS Act that impact on the investment process include the following:

(a) to act honestly in all matters concerning the entity;

(b) to exercise, in relation to all matters affecting the entity, the same degree of care, skill and diligence as a prudent superannuation trustee would exercise in relation to an entity of which it is trustee and on behalf of the beneficiaries of which it makes investments;

(c) to perform the trustee's duties and exercise the trustee's powers in the best interests of the beneficiaries;

(d) where there is a conflict between the duties of the trustee to the beneficiaries, or the interests of the beneficiaries, and the duties of the trustee to any other person or the interests of the trustee or an associate of the trustee:

    (i) to give priority to the duties to and interests of the beneficiaries over the duties to and interests of other persons; and

    (ii) to ensure that the duties to the beneficiaries are met despite the conflict; and

    (iii) to ensure that the interests of the beneficiaries are not adversely affected by the conflict; and

    (iv) to comply with the prudential standards in relation to conflicts;

(e) to act fairly in dealing with classes of beneficiaries within the entity;

(f) to act fairly in dealing with beneficiaries within a class;

…

(i) if there are any reserves of the entity – to formulate, review regularly and give effect to a strategy for their prudential management, consistent with the entity's

---

14. For further discussion see P Turner, "Back to the future? Does the care, skill and diligence covenant proposed in Stronger Super heighten existing requirements?" (2012) 23(7) *Australian Superannuation Law Bulletin* 126.

investment strategies and its capacity to discharge its liabilities (whether actual or contingent) as and when they fall due[.]

Covenant (d) overrides the Corporations Act duties owed to a company by its directors, other officers and employees.[23]

Covenants (d), (e) and (f) were inserted effective 1 July 2013 as part of the Stronger Super reforms. They might be understood as articulating certain elements of the duty to act in the best interests of the beneficiaries of the fund.[24]

In terms, covenant (d) appears to fundamentally cut across the fiduciary standard at general law, under which a person must not allow him or herself to be placed in a position of conflict except with the informed consent of the beneficiary or where permitted under the rules of the trust.[25] However, the covenant may have been drafted with the intention, not expressly stated, that it applies in cases where a conflict arises and, under the general law, the trustee is nonetheless permitted to proceed.[26]

5.4   Covenants by the directors of a corporate trustee

Section 52A of the SIS Act sets out covenants by each director of a corporate superannuation trustee. Like the section 52 covenants made by the trustee, these covenants are deemed to be incorporated into the governing rules of the trust. The covenants create duties owed directly to the beneficiaries of the trust. Their terms reflect certain of the section 52 covenants.

Two of the directors' covenants set out a relevant standard of care, skill and diligence. Both refer to the standard expected of a prudent "superannuation entity director ". Section 29VO(3) of the SIS Act defines these words to mean:

> a person whose profession, business or employment is or includes acting as director of a corporate trustee of a superannuation entity and investing money on behalf of beneficiaries of the superannuation entity.

Under section 52A(2)(b), a director of a corporate superannuation trustee covenants to exercise, in relation to all matters affecting the entity, the same degree of care, skill and diligence as a prudent superannuation entity director would exercise in relation to an entity where he or she is a director of the trustee of the entity and that trustee makes investments on behalf of the entity's beneficiaries.

Under section 52A(2)(f) and (5), the same director covenants to exercise the degree of care and diligence that a superannuation entity director would exercise in the circumstances of the corporate trustee for the purposes of ensuring that the corporate trustee carries out the covenants referred to in section 52.

---

[23] Section 52(4) of the SIS Act.

[24] Australian Government, "Super System Review – Final Report – Part Two" (June 2012) Chapter 2.2.1.

[25] Chief Justice of New South Wales Thomas Bathurst, "Super powers: Changes make trustee duties unclear" (2013) 51(4) *Law Society Journal* 53.

[26] Explanatory Memorandum, Superannuation Legislation Amendment (Trustee Obligations and Prudential Standards) Bill 2012 (Cth) at 1.51.

Section 52A was inserted into the SIS Act effective from 1 July 2013. It was intended to clarify the duties of directors of corporate superannuation trustees and the persons to whom those duties are owed.[27]

Previously, the SIS Act provided that each director of a corporate superannuation trustee covenanted, in respect of each section 52 covenant, to exercise the degree of care and skill of a reasonable person in the position of director of the trustee to ensure that the trustee entity discharged the relevant duty. The Cooper panel was concerned that this application of the section 52 covenants to the directors of trustee entity was ambiguous and unclear.[28] Section 52A was enacted to address this concern.

The Cooper panel also advised that there should be "unambiguous clarity about ... the standard of competence that [directors] should possess and exercise."[29] It is doubtful whether this has been achieved by the Stronger Super reforms, which have laid down a standard that references the degree of care, skill and diligence of a "prudent superannuation entity director". It is generally accepted that this represents a higher standard than the ordinary prudent person or person of business test. However, there is considerable uncertainty at present as to the standard of competence that is required to meet this covenant. It effectively holds all directors to the standard of a professional superannuation director.[30] The federal government has indicated that APRA will issue guidance in relation to this standard at some point in the future.[31] However, ultimately, authoritative guidance can only issue in the form of legislation or from the courts. The requisite standard no longer has regard to a director's particular circumstances by reference to a "reasonable person *in the position of the director*". It appears to be wholly objective, without regard to the skill, experience or qualifications of a director and without distinguishing between executive and non-executive directors.[32] This contrasts with the standard required of company directors under section 180(1) of the Corporations Act.

In addition to the section 52A covenants, directors of corporate superannuation trustees are subject to the "fit and proper" requirements set out in SPS 520 ("Fit and Proper") and the Corporations Act duties applicable to company directors generally.

6.   Prudential Standard SPS 530 – "Investment Governance"

APRA's Prudential Standard SPS 530 sets out further expectations on trustees in relation to investment governance. It provides that a superannuation trustee must have in place an "investment governance framework" that must, at a minimum, include:

- investment objectives for each investment option offered by the fund;

[27] Explanatory Memorandum, Superannuation Legislation Amendment (Trustee Obligations and Prudential Standards) Bill 2012 (Cth) at 1.124.

[28] Australian Government, "Super System Review – Final Report – Part Two" (June 2012) Chapter 2.1.

[29] Ibid.

[30] Chief Justice of New South Wales Thomas Bathurst, "Super powers: Changes make trustee duties unclear" (2013) 51(4) *Law Society Journal* 53.

[31] Explanatory Memorandum, Superannuation Legislation Amendment (Trustee Obligations and Prudential Standards) Bill 2012 (Cth) at 1.133.

[32] Justice Ashley Black, "Understanding the impact of recent cases on directors' duties" (Speech delivered at the 25th Annual Conference of the Superannuation Committee of the Law Council of Australia, 24 February 2012) <http://tinyurl.com/d7pa59z >.

- a methodology for determining investment reporting measures;

- the investment strategy for the whole of the fund and for each investment option as required by section 52(6) of the SIS Act;

- all Board policies relating to investment activities;

- role statements that include the details of each role's responsibilities and reporting structures for all roles related to investment activities;

- structures, policies and processes for investment performance and risk measurement, assessment and reporting; and

- a review process to ensure that the investment governance framework remains effective.

SPS 530 provides that the Board of the trustee entity must, among other things, approve specific and measurable investment objectives for each investment option that it offers and approve an investment strategy for the whole of the fund and each investment option that reflects the trustee's duties to the beneficiaries of the fund.

Other key requirements of SPS 530 are that the trustee must:

- develop and implement an effective due diligence process for the selection of investments;

- determine appropriate measures to monitor the performance of investments on an ongoing basis;

- review the investment objectives and investment strategies on a periodic basis; and

- formulate a liquidity management plan.

SPS 530 came into force on 1 July 2013 and represents regulation of investment governance on a much more detailed level than previously.

7.   Prudential Standard SPS 220 – "Risk Management"

APRA's Prudential Standard SPS 220 sets out certain requirements relating to risk management. A superannuation trustee must have a risk management framework which is the ultimate responsibility of the board of the trustee entity. A risk management framework is:

> the totality of systems, structures, policies, processes and people within an RSE licensee's business operations that identify, assess, manage, mitigate and monitor all internal and external sources of inherent risk that could have a material impact on the RSE licensee's business operations or the interests of beneficiaries (material risks).

SPS 220 specifies various types of risk that the risk management framework must, at a minimum, cover. It must " provide reasonable assurance that each material risk to the RSE licensee's business operations is being prudently and soundly managed, having regard to the size, business mix and complexity of those operations." To this end it must at least include:

- a risk appetite statement;

- a risk management strategy;

- a designated risk management function that meets specified requirements as to resourcing, access to the business and so on;

- all risk management policies, procedures and controls to identify, assess, monitor, report on, mitigate and manage each material risk;

- clearly defined and documented roles, responsibilities and formal reporting structures for the management of material risks throughout the entity's business operations; and

- a review process to ensure that the risk management framework remains effective.

Specific detailed requirements relating to the risk appetite statement and risk management strategy are set out in SPS 220. SPS 220 also specifies detailed requirements relating to a trustee's written strategic business plan.

The board of the trustee entity must annually provide APRA with a declaration on risk management signed by two directors that certifies in relation to numerous matters specified in SPS 220.

A trustee must also notify APRA within ten business days when it becomes aware of a significant breach of, or material deviation from, the risk management framework, or discovers that the risk management framework did not adequately address a material risk.

Prior to 1 July 2013, Division 8 of Part 2A and Division 5 of Part 2B of the SIS Act provided rules relating to the risk management strategy and risk management plan of a superannuation trustee. These divisions have been repealed and replaced with the more detailed and onerous requirements of SPS 220.

8. Investment governance and investment management

Superannuation trustees' power to invest assets under their control is thus constrained by general trust law principles as protected, enhanced and modified by legislation. Trustees are accountable in the exercise of their power to the beneficiaries of superannuation funds and to APRA. The prudential standards made by APRA direct superannuation trustees into practices consistent with their duties and enhance APRA's insight into, and oversight of, investment governance practices.

Overwhelmingly, superannuation trustees outsource some or all of the investment management function to one or more investment managers.[33] In the ordinary course, the relationship between the trustee and the investment manager is governed by an investment management agreement (**IMA**) that requires the investment manager to act as agent for the trustee in the investment of the fund's assets (or a portfolio of the fund's assets). Often, legal title to trust assets is held by a professional custodian who provides custody, settlement and record-keeping services.[34] The custodian holds assets on trust for the superannuation trustee and acts on the direction of the investment manager. The SIS Act prohibits the appointment of a custodian unless the trustee consents in writing.[35]

In this model of investment governance, where investment management and custodianship are outsourced to external service providers, the superannuation trustee typically retains control of the

---

[33] An "investment manager" for the purposes of the SIS Act means a person appointed by a trustee of a fund to invest on behalf of the trustee of the fund.

[34] A "custodian" for the purposes of the SIS Act means a person (other than a trustee of the fund) who, under a contract with a trustee or an investment manager of the fund, performs custodial functions in relation to any of the assets of the fund.

[35] Section 122 of the SIS Act.

investment strategy, strategic asset allocation and rules relating to rebalancing. In many cases the trustee entity would take professional advice as to these matters. Prudential standard SPS 230 sets out specific aspects of investment governance and investment management that must have the direct involvement of the board of the trustee entity. However, within this framework, the investment manager selects individual investments consistently with the mandate and objectives set out in the IMA. The custodian becomes the legal owner of the assets selected by the manager.

Among industry superannuation funds, it is common practice to place a proportion of FUM with an investment manager that is itself set up and owned by one or more industry funds for the purpose of providing services to that sector. However, the majority of investment managers servicing the superannuation industry also offer their services more widely.

Generally, large retail funds form part of a larger wealth management business. In some cases investment governance may be almost entirely handled by an administration entity and the trustee function effectively outsourced to a trustee services provider within the same corporate group. The introduction of SPS 230 limits the ability of corporate groups to keep investment governance separate from trusteeship in this way.

Prior to the Stronger Super reforms, some superannuation funds were governed by trust deeds that required certain functions, such as investment management, to be outsourced to one or more specified service providers. From 1 July 2013, provisions of a trust deed to that effect are void.[36] This effectively ensures that superannuation trustees consider the best interests of their beneficiaries when outsourcing their functions, even within a corporate group.

8.1 Duties of investment managers

The duties of an investment manager will be set out in the relevant IMA. Certain of those duties may be fiduciary in nature simply as a result of the relationship of agency that arises under an IMA.[37] However, there is no general rule under which an investment manager owes fiduciary duties, or any duties, to the beneficiaries of a superannuation fund for which it provides investment management services. The particular terms of an IMA or other particular facts of a case may, of course, give rise to such obligations.[38] This would be an exceptional case.

The duties of a superannuation trustee relating to investment, including general law duties and SIS Act rules and covenants, apply at all times to the trustee. They do not apply to an external investment manager.

The SIS Act does set out certain requirements specifically relating to investment managers and to custodians. It also sets out certain duties of a trustee in entering into an IMA.

An investment manager may only be appointed in writing.[39] An investment manager or a custodian may not be appointed to that role or act in that capacity unless it is a body corporate.[40] A trustee that appoints an investment manager must ensure that the IMA requires the investment manager to provide information to the trustee relating to the making of investments and the return on those

---

[36] Section 58A of the SIS Act.

[37] *Walden Properties Ltd v Beaver Properties Pty Ltd* [1973] 2 NSWLR 815 at 835-836.

[38] *Australian Securities Commission v AS Nominees Limited* (1995) 62 FCR 504.

[39] Section 124 of the SIS Act.

[40] Sections 123(1)(a) and 125 of the SIS Act.

investments, and such information as is necessary to enable the trustee to assess the performance of the investment manager.[41]

An investment manager of a superannuation fund is subject to a number of prudential requirements under the SIS Act, some of which are identical to those applying to trustees. These include:

- a prohibition on loans to members, subject to exceptions;[42]

- a prohibition on acquisition of members assets, subject to exceptions;[43]

- a requirement that investments must be on an arm's length basis, or on arm's length terms;[44]

- a prohibition on contractual provisions that purport to limit an investment manager's liability for negligence;[45] and

- a requirement to provide information to the trustee or to APRA, and to comply with written directions by APRA.[46]

In addition to the above, APRA has made prudential standard SPS 231 which applies to outsourcing arrangements involving material business activities of the trustee. A material business activity is defined in SPS 231 as one that has the potential, if disrupted, to have a significant impact on the trustee's business operations, its ability to manage risks effectively, the interests, or reasonable expectations, of beneficiaries or the financial position of the trustee, or any of its funds. The key requirements of SPS 231 are that the superannuation trustee must:

- have a policy, approved by the board, relating to outsourcing of material business activities;

- have sufficient monitoring processes in place to manage the outsourcing of material business activities;

- have a legally binding agreement in place for all outsourcing of material business activities;

- consult with APRA prior to entering into agreements to outsource material business activities to service providers that conduct their activities outside Australia; and

- notify APRA after entering into agreements to outsource material business activities.

SPS 231 also requires that any outsourcing agreement (including any IMA) deal with the following specified matters:

---

[41] Section 102 of the SIS Act.

[42] Section 65 of the SIS Act.

[43] Section 66 of the SIS Act.

[44] Section 109 of the SIS Act.

[45] Section 116 of the SIS Act.

[46] Sections 102, 255 and 264 of the SIS Act.

- the scope of the arrangement and services to be supplied;

- commencement and end dates;

- review provisions;

- pricing and fee structure;

- service levels and performance requirements;

- the form in which the data is to be kept and clear provisions identifying ownership and control of the data;

- reporting requirements, including content and frequency of reporting;

- audit and monitoring procedures;

- business continuity management;

- confidentiality, privacy and security of information;

- default arrangements and termination provisions;

- dispute resolution arrangements;

- liability and indemnity;

- sub-contracting;

- insurance; and

- to the extent applicable, offshoring arrangements (including through subcontracting).

8.2   *Recent amendments to the section 52 covenants*

As described earlier, the covenants set out in section 52 of the SIS Act have recently been amended, clarified and expanded as part of the Stronger Super reforms. The application of the same (or similar) covenants to individual directors of corporate superannuation trustees has been made clearer (subject to a degree of uncertainty as to the standard of care, skill and diligence now required). Undoubtedly, the legislative changes were intended to affect the investment behaviour of superannuation funds.

There is an argument that some of the duties of superannuation trustees, made express in the section 52 covenants following the Stronger Super reforms, applied to superannuation trustees even prior to those reforms. For example, it has probably never been appropriate for a superannuation trustee to fail to have regard to the availability of accurate valuation information when selecting investments, to ignore the tax consequences of investment decisions or to fail to understand, monitor and manage the fees and costs incurred in the investment of the fund's assets. Explicit reference to these and other matters in the amended section 52 covenants is intended to address perceived shortcomings in investment behaviour by participants in the superannuation industry.[47] It is likely that the amended section 52 covenants (and other Stronger Super reforms) will disincline superannuation trustees

---

[47] See, for example, Australian Government, "Super System Review – Final Report – Part Two" (June 2012) Chapter 3.6.

from, for example, continuing to accept the same degree of opacity in their investment portfolios or making investments that are not capable of independent valuation.

8.3   Engagement with investee companies

There is a widely-held view that proper investment governance requires effective engagement in the corporate governance of companies in which the funds are invested, and that this can have positive effects.[48] This includes, for example, adopting procedures for actively managing shareholder voting rights in the interests of members and the long-term performance of the fund.[49]

The Financial Services Council (**FSC**)[50] has published FSC Standard No.13 ("Voting policy, voting record and disclosure") which sets out compulsory standards for FSC members relating to shareholder voting policy and disclosure. It has also published FSC Guidance Note No.2 ("Corporate Governance: A guide for Fund Managers and Corporations") which includes a number of principles designed to assist investment funds, including superannuation funds, to pursue an active role in monitoring the corporate governance of the companies in which they invest. These documents are aimed at promoting efficient, effective proxy voting and engagement with investee companies.

In practice, there is substantial variation in the level of engagement with investee companies by superannuation funds. Some funds provide detailed information on proxy voting policy and outcomes.[51] Others do not provide any information. Decisions on proxy voting are often outsourced, subject to direction by the trustee if it wishes. There are few systematic data available as to the actual level or effectiveness of engagement by superannuation trustees with investee companies.

9.   Fees and disclosure

The Cooper report identified superannuation industry practices relating to fees that it considered were inconsistent with superannuation trustees' duties to beneficiaries.[52] The Stronger Super reforms reflected the consequent recommendations of the Cooper report. With effect from 1 July 2013, fees for entry into a superannuation fund are banned.[53] Buy-sell spreads, switching fees and exit fees may only be charged on a cost-recovery basis.[54] The cost of advice given to employers (for example, to assist employers in choosing a default fund for superannuation contributions – see section 10 below) may not be attributed to members of the fund.[55]

---

[48] Ross Clare, "Developments in the governance of superannuation funds" (Paper presented at the 17th Annual Colloquium of Superannuation Researchers, Australian School of Business, University of New South Wales, 6-7 July 2009).

[49] Australian Government, "Super System Review – Final Report – Part Two" (June 2012) Chapter 3.6.4.

[50] The FSC is the peak financial services industry body in Australia.

[51] See, for example, the policies and proxy voting registers of industry fund VicSuper available at: <http://www.vicsuper.com.au/www/html/2222-exercising-our-shareholder-rights.asp>.

[52] Australian Government, "Super System Review – Final Report – Part Two" (June 2012) Chapter 1.4.

[53] Section 99B of the SIS Act.

[54] Section 99C of the SIS Act.

[55] Section 99D of the SIS Act.

In addition, it is common practice for superannuation funds to offer "intrafund advice" (which is financial advice given directly by the trustee to members of the fund or prospective members) and to spread the cost of providing this advice across the membership of the fund. The Stronger Super reforms substantially restrict the circumstances in which the cost of this advice may be spread amongst members who may not in fact benefit from its provision.[56]

9.1   Product dashboards and other disclosure

A major element of the Stronger Super reforms has the objective of improving disclosure to members of relevant information regarding superannuation products, and increasing systemic transparency relating to investments.

From 1 July 2014,[57] superannuation trustees must maintain a publicly accessible "product dashboard" on their websites in respect of each investment option that they offer. The product dashboard is intended to provide standardised disclosure of relevant information to foster member understanding and enable comparison of products. The required information will include:

(a)   the investment return target for the investment option;

(b)   the number of times the current target has been achieved for the investment option:

   (i)   in the last 10 financial years; or

   (ii)   if the investment option has been offered for a period of less than 10 financial years—in each of the financial years in which the investment option has been offered;

(c)   the level of investment risk that applies to the investment option;

(d)   a statement about the liquidity of members' investments in the investment option;

(e)   the average amount of fees and other costs in relation to the investment option during the last quarter, expressed as a percentage of the assets of the fund attributable to the investments in that option.[58]

Regulations will prescribe further detail relating to disclosure on product dashboards.

In addition, from 2014 superannuation trustees will be required to maintain the following publicly accessible information on their websites:

(a)   information sufficient to identify each of the financial products or other property in which assets, or assets derived from assets, of the fund are invested; and

(b)   the value of the assets, or assets derived from assets, of the fund which are invested in those financial products or other property.[59]

---

[56] Section 99F of the SIS Act.

[57] For MySuper products (see section 10 below), the dashboard requirement commences on 1 July 2013.

[58] Section 1017BA of the Corporations Act.

This information must be updated within 90 days of each biannual "reporting day". The first reporting day will be 30 June 2014.

To enable this disclosure, provisions were inserted into the Corporations Act requiring a person who uses superannuation assets to acquire a financial product (for example, an interest in a management investment scheme) to notify the person receiving the assets (that is, in the example, the responsible entity of the managed investment scheme) that the assets are superannuation assets. A person notified in this way must report information directly to the trustee of the relevant superannuation fund, sufficient to enable the required biannual disclosure.[60]

In addition to these requirements, reporting standards made by APRA under the *Financial Services (Collection of Data) Act 2001* have been re-drafted to require superannuation funds to report far more detailed information to APRA than was previously the case. Contracts for the investment of superannuation assets are deemed to include provisions requiring:

(a)   the trustee or custodian to notify the other party to the contract that the assets are superannuation assets; and

(b)   the other party to provide the trustee or custodian with information required for compliance with the reporting standards.

10.   MySuper

An employer making superannuation contributions on behalf of an employee, under the SGC regime, must make the contributions to the superannuation fund nominated by the employee. If the employee makes no nomination, the employer must make the contribution to the "default fund" that the employer has selected for that purpose.

Most superannuation funds offer their members a choice of investment options. These options generally embody a variety of investment strategies (typically with labels such as "balanced", capital stable", "high growth", and so on) or target a particular type of asset ("bonds", "Australian shares", "property", etc.). Members who do not make a choice are placed in one or other option by default. In this way, superannuation funds generally offer a "default" investment option. Approximately 80% of members of superannuation funds are in the default investment option (whether by choice or by default).[61]

In Stronger Super changes phasing in from 1 July 2013 to 1 July 2017, the default investment option of a superannuation fund must be a MySuper product. A superannuation fund must not accept contributions as an employer's "default fund" unless it offers a MySuper product. The characteristics of a MySuper product are defined by legislation. It is intended that MySuper products will be simple products with a single, diversified investment strategy bundled with a basic group life insurance policy. Part 2C of the SIS Act sets out rules relating to the fees that may be charged in respect of a MySuper product, including restrictions on performance-based investment management fees. Commissions may not be paid from a MySuper product.[62]

---

[59] Section 1017BB of the Corporations Act.

[60] Sections 1017BC-1017BE of the Corporations Act.

[61] Australian Government, "Super System Review – Final Report – Part Two" (June 2012) Chapter 1.2.

[62] Section 29SAC of the SIS Act.

Superannuation funds may only offer a MySuper product if specifically licensed by APRA to do so.[63]

Section 29VN of the SIS Act sets out additional obligations of a trustee in relation to a MySuper product. The trustee must:

(a) promote the financial interests of the beneficiaries of the fund who hold the MySuper product, in particular returns to those beneficiaries (after the deduction of fees, costs and taxes); and

(b) determine on an annual basis whether the beneficiaries of the fund who hold the MySuper product are disadvantaged, in comparison to the beneficiaries of other funds who hold a MySuper product within those other funds, because the financial interests of the beneficiaries of the fund who hold the MySuper product are affected:

   (i) because the number of beneficiaries of the fund who hold the MySuper product is insufficient; or

   (ii) because the number of beneficiaries of the fund is insufficient; or

   (iii) where the assets of the fund that are attributed to the MySuper product are, or are to be, pooled with other assets of the fund or assets of another entity or other entities—because that pool of assets is insufficient; or

   (iv) in a case to which subparagraph (iii) does not apply—because the assets of the fund that are attributed to the MySuper product are insufficient; and

(c) include in the investment strategy for the MySuper product the details of the trustee's determination of the matters mentioned in paragraph (b); and

(d) include in the investment strategy for the MySuper product, and update each year:

   (i) the investment return target over a period of 10 years for the assets of the fund that are attributed to the MySuper product; and

   (ii) the level of risk appropriate to the investment of those assets.

These obligations cannot be overridden by the rules of the fund.[64] Individual directors of a corporate trustee must exercise the degree of care, skill and diligence of a professional corporate superannuation trustee director to ensure the trustee discharges the section 29VN obligations.[65]

These provisions came into effect on 1 July 2013. Their interpretation is a matter of ongoing discussion in Australia. In particular, it is not clear whether these requirements oblige superannuation trustees to achieve certain investment outcomes in respect of the MySuper offering,

---

[63] Sections 29T and 29W of the SIS Act.

[64] Section 29VQ of the SIS Act.

[65] Section 29VO of the SIS Act.

or whether these obligations fit within the traditional focus of trustee duties on the process of trustee decision-making.

11.   Accumulation and retirement phases

A key issue for members defined contribution superannuation funds, and thus for the trustees of those funds, is the distinction between accumulation and retirement phases, and the appropriate investment strategy for each. Australians have a wide variety of options available to them for the manner in which to receive accumulated retirement benefits, and a wide variety of products are available.

As the large majority of members in the accumulation phase are in a default investment option, there is a strong argument that trustees should develop appropriate default retirement products that are tailored to the needs of retirees who are no longer accumulating assets in their superannuation fund. As Australia's accumulation-based superannuation industry is relatively young, this has not yet occurred. Generally, Australian superannuation funds do not offer an appropriate default fund for their retired members. This can be seen as potentially a failure by superannuation funds to discharge their duties to their members with the requisite standard of care.[66] It is likely that a MySuper default retirement product will be mandated at some time in the future.

---

[66] Jane Paskin and Sonia Lopes, "A ticking bomb?", *Superfunds*, December 2012.

APPENDIX D
LIST OF CONSULTEES

We are grateful to the following consultees who have provided us with their thoughts and materials for us to consider in drafting this Paper.

SHORT PAPER RESPONSES

CFA UK

EIRIS

Network for Sustainable Financial Markets

Philip Goldenberg

ShareAction

The Generation Foundation

UNISON

Vigeo

STAKEHOLDERS WE HAVE SPOKEN TO

Andy Duncan

Asset Management and Investors Council, International Capital Market Association

Association of British Insurers

Association of Corporate Trustees

Association of Pension Lawyers

Association of Private Client Investment Managers and Stockbrokers

Aviva

BNP Paribas

CFA Society of the UK

Christopher Stears, PhD candidate (IALS)

Church of England Ethical Investment Advisory Group

City of London Law Society

Financial Conduct Authority

Financial Reporting Council

Freshfields Bruckhaus Deringer

GMI Ratings

Investment Management Association

John Crosthwait

Julia Black, London School of Economics

Mark Goyder, Tomorrow's Company

National Association of Pension Funds

National Employment Savings Trust

Office of Fair Trading

Paul Watchman

Pensions & Investment Research Consultants (PIRC)

Philip Goldenberg

Pinsent Masons

Robert Stein, Vintage Asset Management Ltd

Roger McCormick, London School of Economics

ShareAction

Social Enterprise UK

Spence Johnson

The Pensions Trust

The Prince's Accounting for Sustainability Project

The UK Sustainable Investment and Finance Association

Tomorrow's Company

Trades Union Congress

Universities Superannuation Scheme Investment Managers

Vigeo

SCOTLAND

The Scottish Law Commission spoke to the following.

Alan Barr and Andrew Dalgleish, Brodies LLP

David Bartos, Faculty of Advocates

David Cabrelli, University of Edinburgh

Iain MacNeil, University of Glasgow

John MacLeod, University of Glasgow

Laura Macgregor, University of Edinburgh

Norman Dowie, Standard Life and Law Society of Scotland Pensions Law Committee

Parker Hood, University of Edinburgh

Patrick Ford, University of Dundee

Ross Anderson, University of Glasgow and Ampersand Advocates

Simon Mackintosh, Turcan Connell LLP

ADVISORY COMMITTEE

We are grateful to our advisory committee, which consisted of the following.

Alastair Hudson, University of Southampton

Anna Tilba, Newcastle University Business School

Deborah Sabalot, London School of Economics

Hector MacQueen, Scottish Law Commission

Vanessa Knapp

We are also grateful to BIS and DWP for their assistance.